Taylor, Ronald B.

HV
741
.T33

The kid business,
how it exploits the
children it should
help

DATE DUE

| | | | |
|---|---|---|---|
| MAY 1 9 1986 | | | |
| JUL 3 0 1987 | | | |
| FEB 2 2 1989 | | | |
| NOV 0 2 1989 | | | |
| FEB 1 2 1990 | | | |
| MAR 0 5 1990 | | | |
| MAY 2 9 '91 | | | |
| OCT 27 '92 | | | |
| DEC 0 5 '92 | | | |
| MAY 1 3 1993 | | | |
| MAY 1 1 1994 | | | |
| MAR 0 6 1996 | | | |

# The Kid Business

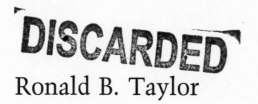

Ronald B. Taylor

# The Kid Business

---

*How It Exploits the*
*Children It Should Help*

Houghton Mifflin Company
Boston 1981

*Library of Congress Cataloging in Publication Data*

Taylor, Ronald B.
The kid business: how it exploits the
children it should help.
Includes index.
1. Child welfare — United States.  2. Children — Institutional
care — United States.  3. Foster home care — United States.
4. Juvenile justice, Administration of.  5. Children — Legal
status, laws, etc. — United States.  6. Kate School.  I. Title.
HV741.T33    362.7′95′0973    81-6292
ISBN 0-395-30515-2    AACR2

Printed in the United States of America

P 10 9 8 7 6 5 4 3 2 1

This book is dedicated to the late
CAREY MCWILLIAMS
whose work as a writer inspired me,
whose skill as an editor
helped me immeasurably

# Acknowledgments

A BOOK about a subject as complex as this can never be the work of one person. Over the six years that I have been at work on *The Kid Business*, I have had the help of so many people that the task of acknowledging their contributions itself becomes complex. In the beginning I knew very little and had to learn so very much. Around every controversial subject like this, there exists a loosely knit network of advocates who work for change, sometimes from within the system, sometimes from without. I found that they shared my sense of outrage and were most willing to share, as well, their knowledge and to pass me along to others who might help expand my store of information.

Without the help of Rochelle Beck, of the Children's Defense Fund, and Valerie Vanaman, of the Los Angeles Legal Aid Society, the book would have never taken shape. They helped me develop a sense of direction through the national house of mirrors we call child care and welfare. Other attorneys, like Bill Rittenberg in New Orleans and California Deputy Attorney General Elisabeth Brandt, worked patiently to help me understand the legal positions and maneuverings in the specific cases they were handling so that I could gain a much better understanding of the larger picture I was trying to piece together. Legal-services lawyers and newspaper reporters across the country told me of many of the individual case studies I followed.

There are three friends to whom I want to give special thanks, Deane Wylie and Harry Bernstein, of the *Los Angeles Times*, who read and reread various versions of this book and who made suggestions and comments, and Lorrie Foster, a person whose sense of outrage and civic responsibility introduced me to this subject. If she had not persisted in her efforts to bring the excesses of the Kate School to an end, I might have passed by the issue, unaware that this tiny tip of the iceberg was part of the larger national scandal.

I want to thank Carl Brandt not only for representing me, but for helping me define the subject, and my editors, Ruth Hapgood and Deborah Kops, who gently suggested just one more rewrite. And, finally, a special acknowledgment to those people within the governmental structures who talked to me, who showed me how the system works and fails, even though it was risky for them to be seen talking to a reporter. They described the details of their jobs, made documents and files available, providing me with information that I could never have gotten otherwise, and they did it because they want the system changed; they want to help children.

# Contents

# Introduction

CHILDREN who are removed from their natural homes are in jeopardy. No matter what the cause of the dislocation, no matter how reasoned the removal processes are, these children are as likely to be harmed by the public agencies set in place to act in their best interests as they are to be helped. Foster care in the United States is seriously flawed; juvenile justice fosters criminal conduct; children who are physically or mentally handicapped or emotionally disturbed are often neglected or mistreated by the various systems established to care for them.

These discomforting thoughts are forced on us periodically by media reports of scandals in public institutions or abuses in foster care or by the account of a juvenile's violent criminal history. We get an uneasy sense that something is wrong — basically, fundamentally wrong. But what? The chore of sorting out the facts, of evaluating the political rhetoric and the quarrelsome debates between social scientists and bureaucrats, is a confusing, frustrating task.

In theory, this country is committed to assisting and supporting the family structure, because we recognize that

children are better off in a home of their own. We have
created the legal structures, provided the public funds, and
assigned the appropriate experts to carry out this commitment quietly, privately. The national business of caring
for homeless children, juvenile delinquents, the retarded,
disturbed and handicapped youngsters, has been closed to
public view, the various systems made obscure to protect
"the best interests" of the children. We have naïvely assumed that our hired experts are all understanding and
compassionate and have the wisdom to act as surrogate
parents. No methods were installed to allow for a public
examination of the various foster-care, juvenile justice, or
child-welfare systems; no way was created to hold these
experts accountable.

This special secretiveness has not worked in the best
interests of the children so much as it has hidden the
ineptness of government acting as parent. Wherever children's rights attorneys have filed class-action suits exposing serious, frequently brutal conditions in kid prisons or
mental hospitals, whenever the media have reported abuse
or mistreatment or financial scandals somewhere within
the various systems, there has been a public outcry. Committees have been formed to investigate, hearings have
been called, and the issues have generally been smothered
in argument and accusation. In this haphazard process of
noisy exposure and little remedy, it has been the journalists
and the legal-aid lawyers who, by default, have become
the public watchdogs.

This book had its beginnings in such a process. *The Kid
Business* is the outgrowth of a newspaper story I wrote in
1975, exposing the Kate School, a private residential facility that used corporal punishment as a therapeutic tool
in the treatment of emotionally disturbed children. The
school employed no psychiatrists or psychologists to di-
agnose, prescribe, and supervise the slapping, hitting,
pinching "therapy" administered by uncredentialed teach-

ers and paraprofessional aids. California law clearly prohibits the use of corporal punishment. Yet the state records revealed that state licensing agents knew corporal punishment was being used in the Kate School. Even so, the state continued annually to relicense the school to care for and treat as many as forty-eight emotionally disturbed children. Equally distressing was the fact that social workers from a half-dozen different county and state agencies continued to place children in the school, at a public cost of $1271 a month for each child.

Most of these children were public wards of the juvenile courts in their "home" counties. Some were abandoned or abused children who were angry and frightened, and they acted out in strange, socially unacceptable ways. Some were autistic or schizophrenic. They had once lived at home, and their parents still wanted and loved them; but, because of the way the laws are written, the parents of these children had to abandon them legally to the jurisdiction of the juvenile court in order to qualify for public funds to pay for care and treatment. Under the eighteenth-century legal theory of *parens patriae,* juvenile court judges had stepped into the lives of these children to act as their legal protectors. However, the judges of these courts, when questioned, refused to discuss their reasons for ordering children to be placed in the Kate School. The social workers who had recommended the placements and then supervised the children's care and treatment in the Kate School were defensive and tried to argue that because the state had licensed the facility, it had also approved the methods of treatment.

These reactions piqued my curiosity. At the outset, I had intended to look only at the school's operations and report my findings in a single story, but it soon became obvious that the real story was not in this one school, but in the system that allowed it — and too many others — to exist. There were horror stories wherever I looked, in

San Francisco and Los Angeles and San Diego. And what was so sad was that in every facility I found children who were simply lost — abandoned and cast adrift in a foster-care system that was indifferent at best, brutal at worst. These children were bounced through foster homes, placed in and taken out of group homes, private and public institutions, in the most arbitrary, capricious ways; I had stumbled into a situation so bizarre that it was overwhelming. At times I could make no sense of what I was seeing. It was as though I had followed Alice through the looking-glass into the backward-living world and was lost in the dark forest inhabited by the Jabberwock:

> Beware the Jabberwock, my son!
> The jaws that bite, the claws that catch!
> Beware the Jubjub bird, and shun
> The frumious Bandersnatch!

In the bureaucratic house of mirrors I found deaf children who were being slapped about the head because they couldn't hear and obey orders; helpless, retarded children who were placed in "homes" for seriously disturbed, aggressive delinquents just out of kid prisons; normal, healthy youngsters who were placed in private institutions for the retarded, where they were drugged, beaten, and forced into manual labor; homeless children who were locked away in jail cells or committed to psychiatric hospital wards because there was nowhere else to put them. All this was done as a matter of public policy, but I could find no accountability in any agency or institution.

Clearly, such things should not be happening. Somewhere, somehow, reason and logic had to be set to work if change was to occur. But when I went to officials of the court, the juvenile justice system, and the various welfare agencies to ask about such problems, most of the technocrats talked about underfunded budgets and overworked staffs and impossible tangles of red tape; they bluffed and argued their way around the questions, rationalizing and explaining, all the while sounding like Tweedledum and Tweedledee: "If it was so, it might be; and if it were so, it would be; but as it isn't, it ain't. That's logic."

I had wandered into a national house of mirrors. Nothing was as it should be or should have been. Thousands of people were rushing about, this way and that, working hard, trying to keep up. But keep up with what? There were no meaningful answers. The place had no design, no sense of unity or purpose. The task of trying to make some sense out of all this and then writing about it in a comprehensible fashion would, I realized, require more than a newspaper exposé or two. I needed a larger format. I left my job as a reporter for the *Fresno Bee* newspaper and, with financial assistance from the Field Foundation, the Youth Project, the Legal Aid Corporation Research Institute, the Fund for Investigative Journalism, and *The Nation* magazine, I followed leads into Chicago, Washington, D.C., and Boston. The trail led south through Florida and New Orleans and beyond, to the Texas kid prisons. I found that the house of mirrors was not a single, cohesive structure, but a collection of constructions, an accumulation of new and old and make-do, none of it quite complete, all of it outdated.

The attitudes of the people working in the house of mirrors were equally puzzling. Some were kind and energetic and had a clear sense of direction. Others were certain they knew the right way out, and when they bumped into their own reflections they became angry and sour-tempered. Supervisors and department heads in this backward-living world were often parsimonious and punitive. They seemed to relish exercising these two legacies of the eighteenth century, Christian charity and English law, brought forward into twentieth-century absurdity.

Change has been terribly slow. For decades, a small number of civil rights attorneys have periodically tried, with limited success, to convince the U.S. Supreme Court that it should grant children the same constitutional rights

that are guaranteed to adults. These court actions brought
on behalf of children's rights have partially lifted the cover
of secrecy, giving the public a glimpse of the problems to
be found within the several arcane systems governing children's lives. By using the public records of these state and
federal court actions, I began to separate out the various
issues and arguments. Early on, however, I discovered
that there was a serious obstacle to my understanding what
I was seeing. The obstacle was *my* point of view. I had
been focusing on individual cases, selecting the case of a
child here, another there, following each case through the
bureaucratic tangles of the bizarre system. I thought of the
system as a single intricate, confusing, frustrating entity.
(We love children, and, whatever their needs, we will care
for and help them. The idea seemed so simple, yet the
system seemed so complex. Why? The question was per-
plexing.) Then I began to realize there was no single system, and, more important, that there were no bridges link-
ing the various systems into a coordinated whole. Each
had its own peculiar regulations and policies; each had its
own qualifications for screening out the undeserving.

Over the years, Congress had created major programs
for (1) foster care, (2) juvenile justice, (3) the developmentally disabled, and (4) special education for the handicapped. Each of the four major areas — set apart by its
individual attendant laws, regulations, bureaus, and budgets — had cracks and gaps in its legal floorboards. As
various advocacy groups began pointing out that children
were falling through the gaps, dozens of new laws and
programs were patched together in an unrelated series of
Rube Goldberg legal constructions. Once you see that the
house of mirrors is not one big structure, but is, rather,
a collection of these Rube Goldberg constructions tacked
on to four basic structures, then it becomes obvious that
the problems are fundamental.

No bureau or agency is set up administratively to take

care of a black child who has been orphaned, has cerebral palsy, is emotionally disturbed, aggressive, and possibly mentally retarded. While this one boy's case may sound extreme, no child comes into foster care or any other of the programs with a single problem. Just the trauma of being orphaned or abandoned or abused creates special needs that much of the time go unmet. Even in the simplest cases of out-of-home placement, the child "at risk" is more apt to be harmed than helped by the processes of child care in many parts of the country. There really are no designs, no overall national policies or guidelines to bring the various parts into a concerted effort to shore up the disintegrating family or find a surrogate home for the orphan.

This is not to say that every aspect of the conglomeration works to the disadvantage of children. There are bright spots. Individuals within each of the systems work hard to help children and protect their best interests. There are large, well-run programs like Boys' Republic in California and the one put together by the Sisters of the Good Shepherd in Brooklyn's Park Slope neighborhood, a unique system that combines the attributes of an old-fashioned settlement house and those of a neighborhood service center. The Park Slope program provides the missing jurisdictional bridges needed to get the kinds of help to keep families together and to care for individual children, no matter what their problems.

But, for me, these bright spots only emphasized the basic problems in this country, and made the possibilities for change seem all the more difficult. It wasn't until I went to Sweden that I could really see that change is possible. The Swedes, living in a technologically advanced society, operating in a capitalistic economy not unlike our own, have made tremendous changes in their approach to child care and welfare. A half-century ago the Swedish government used a patched-together, institutionalized system quite like ours. Today — largely because the people have demanded that the government be responsive to children and family needs — the Swedish government is guided by a national will, a policy that makes it clear people are important. Handicapped children are considered a normal part of Swedish society, and they are accepted *in* that society, not placed out of it. The family structure is protected and sustained, children are treated as individual, important human beings. Even the most handicapped, the most troubled, and the most troublesome children are kept in the nurturing warmth of the general society. They are not cast out into a separate, subsidized existence, as they are in the United States. I use the Swedish example in this book not as a blueprint, but as a demonstration. Change is possible. Radical change is needed. But meaningful, radical change can come only from the people, can come only if we all recognize that government is the instrument of our collective will and we act on that recognition.

# The Kid Business

# 1

## Foster Care

A SMALL PLAQUE above the locked double doors identified the hospital wing: Ward 3-B. Through the reinforced glass windows I could see an old woman in a knee-length hospital gown shuffling down the long, pale green hallway. She turned at the far end and started back, her slippers slap-slapping a cadence as she patrolled. A spindly blond boy in jail-house coveralls brushed past the old woman, moving purposefully back and forth across the hall, trying each locked door, peering through the tiny glass windows into each darkened room.

An orderly stood guard in the hall, his back to me, his arms folded across his chest. He was listening indifferently to a hulking twenty-year-old who was so drugged with tranquilizers that his speech was slurred. Halfway down the hall, a middle-aged man in hospital pajamas leaned against a wall, then slowly slid into a sitting position, knees drawn up tight within the grasp of his arms. At the far end of the hall, an open doorway provided a limited view of the ward recreation room and a shriveled, ugly little man in a wheelchair who pushed himself slowly around the pool table and cautiously through the doorway into the hall, looking furtively back over his shoulder. Once out in the hall, he pushed the wheels harder, grimly, quickly, determined to make his escape. As in a scene from *One Flew Over the Cuckoo's Nest,* a male Nurse Ratchet shouted and ran down the hall in pursuit. The orderly guarding the front doors moved in to help. He grabbed the wheelchair, turned it around, and gave it a push back toward the nurse.

This was Ward 3-B, Kern County General Hospital in Bakersfield, California, a twenty-four-bed crisis center, a locked facility designed for the emergency care and observation of violently disturbed persons. The date was November 30, 1978, court day. Kern County Superior Court Judge John Nairn was scheduled to come into the hospital at 1:00 P.M. to hold sanity hearings in a small public room just outside the ward. By law, no one could be held here for more than seventy-two hours, during which time psychiatric evaluation and placement decisions were to be made. In fact, as many as thirty-five or forty men, women, and children were crowded into Ward 3-B at any one time, having been brought in by police, by relatives, by the staffs of other institutions. Some people spent weeks and months locked up here because there was no other place for them.

At the far end of the hallway, on an old-fashioned oak bench with a curved back and armrests, sat a lonely girl, a pretty, freckle-faced little redhead with pale blue eyes. In another time and place, she might have been waiting to try out for the lead in the musical *Annie.* Wearing bright yellow slacks and a red print blouse, freshly laundered, Mary sat impatiently on the bench, hugging a black and white stuffed Snoopy dog, swinging her legs nervously, smiling brightly, eagerly, as staff people moved past her in the crowded hallway. She wanted to be friendly. No one paid attention.

In addition to this being the day Judge Nairn would decide whether or not she was to be committed to a state hospital, November 30, 1978, was also Mary's fifteenth birthday. But there was no one to sing "Happy Birthday" or wish her well. She had no family, no place where she belonged. She had been brought into Ward 3-B on September 22. One month later — a month during which she had received no education, no treatment, nothing more than a ninety-minute evaluation by a staff psychiatrist — Mary had been declared "gravely disabled" by the Kern County conservator, who petitioned Judge Nairn to have her placed in Napa State Hospital. Without seeing Mary, the judge signed an emergency placement order and, on October 23, she was transported four hundred miles north to the state hospital and placed in a unit for psychotic children. As was established later, Mary was not gravely disabled, nor was she psychotic. She certainly was not a danger to others or to herself, as the law required for such a commitment.

Mary had been a ward of the juvenile court for several years. She did have a temper, and at times she acted in ways that showed she had emotional problems, but she was not crazy. What had happened to Mary in the past and what was happening to her between 1978 and 1980 seemed bizarre, but I was to learn that her case was not unusual, not in Kern County, not in California, nor in any other state. Her case and the cases of other children reported in this book were selected because they are representative. In most of these examples I have changed the children's names, but the details of their lives come from official records, court documents, interviews, and from personal observations. Mary's case stands out in my mind because twice I ran across the thread of her life quite by chance as I pursued this work, and each time I was struck by the fact that she was about the same age as my own daughter and that, but for circumstances beyond Mary's control, she could have been going through the same happy-painful experiences of a normal teen-ager growing up in a family, learning to love and be loved. But the circumstances of her life did not allow that, and the foster-care system of this nation precluded its happening.

Mary had been abandoned by her parents when she was ten. Her father was an alcoholic; her mother refused to care for her. Kern County Welfare Department social workers took the girl into juvenile court in 1974 and had her judged a dependent child. She was placed with one foster family, then another and another; sometimes she was replaced because she was troublesome; sometimes because bureaucratic circumstances made it more convenient to have her living elsewhere. With each move, Mary grew more hyperactive: she was alternately withdrawn, then wildly aggressive. As her mood swings widened, her social worker and a counselor from a child-guidance clinic decided she would be better off in a residential-care facility that could handle emotionally disturbed children.

Working by telephone, the social worker tried several private, residential treatment centers, finally locating one that would take her. It was called the Kate School, and was located near Fresno, a hundred miles to the north. The placement lasted nineteen months. When the Kate School's painful Confrontation Therapy approach to behavior modification became so controversial that the state threatened to revoke the school's licenses, Mary was moved back into a foster home. (The Kate School and the licensing controversy are explored in detail in Chapter Seven.) By this time, Mary's disturbing behavior patterns were firmly established: one minute she was a laughing, touching little girl who wanted to hug and be hugged; the next, she was a screaming, hitting, frightened child who fought off the feelings of rejection and hurt through wild tantrums.

The foster mother who had taken Mary after she had been removed from the Kate School recalled:

> I'd never handled a child like that before. She seemed to have three distinct personalities; the angry one, we called Mariah.

She would throw herself on the floor and bite the flesh on her own arms, or cover her head and scream, "Don't hurt me." The first time I just held her close and had one of the boys call the social worker. I didn't know what else to do. She kept screaming "Don't hurt me," but she calmed down, and the social worker said I'd done the right thing. I had her for a year, and she was a challenge, but she really improved and was in school.

At the time, this remarkable woman had five other troubled foster children in her home, plus two children of her own. Kern County provided little more than the monthly $160 foster-care check for each child; there was no training, no respite care if she wanted to escape for a few days. The county mental health program did offer child-guidance clinicians to counsel individual children. After a year in the foster home, Mary's social worker decided that, as she moved into puberty and reached menarche, she would be under the kind of stress that required twenty-four-hour residential care and treatment. Mary was placed in the Devereux School, in Santa Barbara, where she received understanding care and treatment. Her foster mother brought her "home" on weekends or holidays. Devereux charged $1291 a month. Because she was a dependent of the court, federal Social Security funds paid half the cost, state funds paid $120 a month, and the county picked up the remaining $526.

During the next year and a half, the girl found some sense of herself and began to work through her problems, with the help of the school's skilled counselors. One of her counselors explained that it took Mary six months to adjust to the school. As she settled down and accepted his friendship and became comfortable in the cottage environment, her schoolwork began to improve, the wild mood swings and angry depressions became fewer. But just as she was making good progress, just as her world was becoming a comfortable place to be in, it disintegrated again.

The problem this time was that the California taxpayers

were in revolt. They were eagerly following Howard Jarvis, a fat old walrus in a baggy suit, as he piped his solipsistic tune: government was a bloated evil force; bureaucrats were corrupt dunderheads who confiscated the rewards of free enterprise and squandered tax dollars; cut off the money supply and the bloated evil would die, the dunderheads would be forced to seek honest work. That would leave more profit in the pockets of honest, hard-working capitalists, and it would be good for the economy. The music piped by the gruff, jowly old curmudgeon was heady stuff to a people turning in on themselves, to people focusing only on the reality of their own lives. Californians were already deep into the process of shedding any sense of community and concomitant sense of social responsibility, and they welcomed Jarvis. Proposition 13 was passed by a wide margin in June of 1978, cutting in half the property taxes that financed local schools, hospitals, police and fire services, and most of the welfare costs.

The message to politicians and bureaucrats was clear. Local governments, caught without funds and fearful of imposing new kinds of taxes, turned to the state for help. The combination of an expanding economy and relatively high state income taxes had created a multibillion-dollar surplus in the state general fund. After much wrangling, the state legislature passed a "bail-out" law that substituted much of this surplus for the lost property-tax revenues in a Band-Aid operation that pleased no one. In this environment of parsimony, Governor Jerry Brown was quick to sense the public mood. He ordered a freeze on all governmental costs. No increases were to be allowed anywhere, including those contracts made by the counties with private care facilities, like Devereux. No matter that the state's share of the $1291 was only $120 a month, or that existing state welfare regulations had put the $120 ceiling on such expenditures long before: no increased use of state funds was possible.

Devereux, caught in the inflationary spiral, disregarded the state-ordered freeze and raised its monthly rates to $1800. If Kern County had elected to pay its proportionate $254.50 share of the increase, the federal government would have paid the other half. But the county welfare director, O. C. Sills, said the regulations were clear: the county had no choice but to pull Mary out of Devereux and place her elsewhere. Mary's former foster home was unavailable (her foster mother was pregnant), so another foster home was tried. She "failed" there and was placed in a private, psychiatric hospital for emotionally disturbed patients. She was there only five days. When she "acted out" in an aggressive way, the facility sent her back to the Welfare Department. Her social worker placed her in "shelter care" while he located another foster home. Once again Mary failed in foster care. In desperation, her social worker put her in the county general hospital, in Ward 3-B. For the next thirty days the search went on for an alternative placement, and, failing there, the decision was made to transfer Mary's case from the juvenile court to the superior court, thereby legally clearing the way for her placement in the Napa State Hospital, at a cost of $3158 a month.

The incongruity was astounding. Because of the taxpayers' revolt, it was going to cost an extra $1358 a month for Mary's care and treatment. That's $16,296 a year, and the figure can be multiplied hundreds of times, because the effects of Proposition 13 in other California counties were similar. In Alameda County, across the bay from San Francisco, the county board of supervisors closed two camps for juvenile delinquents. And, though most of the youngsters were placed locally in group homes or foster care, a dozen were transferred to Napa State Hospital. These were youngsters who were judged delinquent, but not emotionally disturbed or psychotic. They did not belong in a state hospital. But officials argued that they had no other choices. In Napa and other state hospitals, officials reported the children and adolescent units filled up, and there were waiting lists. The California Youth Authority's kid prisons were overcrowded and CYA administrators announced they were going to release hundreds of youthful inmates early to make room for the increasing numbers of tougher, more dangerous delinquents being sent to CYA by the juvenile courts in almost every county of the state. Through 1979 the bail-out funds provided by the state forestalled some of the impacts of Proposition 13 on local governments. However, by 1981 the state no longer had large cash reserves to share. With no way to replace lost tax revenues, local governments began to scramble for ways to meet their fiscal problems. Educational and therapeutic services were cut, some facilities were closed, and more youngsters were crowded into those public and private institutions that continued to operate.

When Governor Brown ordered a funding freeze in 1978, Kern County had acted more quickly than most. Mary had been placed in Napa on an "emergency" order by Judge Nairn. She had had no hearing; no one was there legally to protect her best interests. The abrupt way the county had taken her out of Devereux had been unsettling to the counselors in the school. They tried to maintain contact with her, and when she was placed in Napa, they visited her when they could. Through one of these staff people, Mary smuggled a note out of Napa, asking that someone find her an attorney who could help her. The note passed through Los Angeles Legal Aid and ended up with the state public defender, in Sacramento. Laurence S. Smith, a deputy state public defender, was brought into the case.

Smith said:

> Mary is really a classic case. She has never done anything wrong. She doesn't have a parent, so the county has stepped in and declared her a dependent of the juvenile court, but

unfortunately the county and state make lousy parents. They are too concerned about the taxpayers' pocketbook and not the welfare of the children. Mary has been through a series of placements that have not been terribly good for her. When they finally found a place that was helpful . . . they yanked her out of it, for whatever reason, and they put her in a bunch of other inferior places and she acted badly and was rejected, so they took her off and put her in a state mental institution . . . No one could seriously maintain she was gravely disabled, or seriously psychotic, but they try to dump kids one place and if that doesn't work, they try to dump them some place else and hope things work out.

In Kern County, in November of 1978, John Nairn was sitting both as the juvenile court judge and as the judge of the superior court, hearing mental health conservatorships. This placed him on both sides of any jurisdictional argument. Smith filed a motion in superior court, asking for a contested conservatorship hearing. At first, Judge Nairn was not going to allow Smith to represent Mary. In an astounding confrontation in the corridors of the county hospital, Judge Nairn shouted at Smith, telling him he had no legal standing in the case "unless I appoint you." The judge obviously considered Smith an outsider, a lawyer from the state capital sent down by the public defender's office to meddle in local affairs. When Smith tried to argue, the overwrought Nairn described Mary as a "borderline mentally retarded" youngster who was also "schizophrenic" and therefore unable to choose her own attorney. It was the court's duty to protect her interests.

Smith, taken aback by the outburst, told the judge he had already established a client-attorney relationship with Mary during two interviews, one at the state hospital and the other on Ward 3-B that morning. The judge, noticing that I and other reporters were watching and taking notes, turned and went back into the hearing room. A short while later, he convened the hearing. This time a much calmer

Judge Nairn listened to Smith's formal arguments demonstrating the attorney-client relationship and, after brief consideration, recognized Smith as the young girl's attorney.

Bureaucrats, lawyers, and doctors crowded into the tiny hearing room; seated in rows of chairs, they flanked and surrounded Mary. She sat there clutching her stuffed Snoopy dog, looking nervously this way and that, smiling at a social worker she recognized, looking back at the judge, then at her attorney, bewildered. A nervous young lawyer for the county acted as prosecutor, calling county psychiatrists, conservators, social workers, and welfare experts to the stand, leading them through the process of proving Mary was gravely disabled and unable to care for herself. They orally poked and prodded her, muttering terms like "emotionally disturbed" and "mentally retarded"; they expressed the fear that she was so starved for affection that "someone" might take advantage of her sexually, because she constantly was running up and hugging and touching people, even strangers.

The county's conservator, a dour-looking man, had earlier explained to me in an interview that Mary was something of a misfit: "She's got to change. She disrupts the whole ward . . . they [ward attendants] had to tell her to sit down and stay on that bench . . . The other patients were about ready to assault her . . . And her language. A longshoreman would be ashamed of the words that girl uses."

The deputy conservator testified that, though Mary could feed and dress herself, she was considered gravely disabled because she fantasized a lot, telling people she had a baby, or calling nurses or staff "mommy," and otherwise acting inappropriately. In the end, Judge Nairn decided that Mary was, in fact, gravely disabled, unable to care for herself, and needed to be put away in Napa State Hospital.

Smith appealed the decision and demanded the issue be resolved by a jury trial. Several weeks later, a Kern County jury heard the evidence. One of the witnesses was the one foster "mom" who had really cared for Mary and who had kept in touch with the girl, even though she had been unable to take her back into her home. Originally, this woman had been reluctant to testify because, she said, she feared the county welfare administrators might not like it and she had other foster children to think about also. She came to the trial only because she was interested in the girl. "I couldn't believe it. They [county officials] were saying things about her that were simply not true and it made me angry. I really didn't know if I should testify. I didn't want to go against those officials [including welfare workers who placed children in her home and controlled those placements], but what I was hearing just wasn't right."

With the help of witnesses like the foster mother who knew and liked Mary, Smith convinced the jury that the girl should not be locked away in a state hospital mental ward. The conservatorship was dismissed. Judge Nairn remanded the case back to the juvenile court, which, in turn, handed it back to the Welfare Department, and Mary was once more placed back with her foster mom. The county agreed to pay $300 a month for her care, rather than the normal $160-a-month foster-care rate. Once back in a home where she felt comfortable, and enrolled in a regular classroom, in a regular school, Mary began to progress again. She graduated from the eighth grade, started high school, and was once more beginning to live some kind of normal life.

Mary's case was not the first sad story I had encountered, nor was what happened to her the worst example of our society's abusive attitude toward children who are not "normal." But Mary's case was particularly illustrative because it gave a full measure of our collective insanity. In a short five years, an abandoned ten-year-old girl who needed love and a secure place to grow up had been turned into a seriously disturbed teen-ager who had no home, no person to love and accept her. Public agencies quarreled not about how best to care for her or provide for her needs, but about who should have to take care of her and, more significantly, who should have to pay for her care and treatment. In the legal in-fighting, Mary's attorney attempted to force the juvenile court to seek funds from the Kern County Mental Health Department to provide the kinds of therapy she needed, as an adjunct to her placement. Both the juvenile court judge and the mental health director refused the request. Smith appealed. Admittedly, he was stretching the law as he tried to get help for his client. The Fifth District Court of Appeals turned Smith down, on technical grounds, but in doing so the appeals court judge made a pointed observation: in all of the proceedings from 1974 through 1979, no one had been present in juvenile court or in Welfare Department meetings to represent Mary's interests, as opposed to the interests of the county. The judge pointed out this was not only "unfair" to Mary, but that "the present record reflects that a change in placement was made solely because of cost and not because of better care and treatment for the minor."

That was not the way the foster-care system was supposed to work. In theory, foster care was designed to help children. Federal and state laws that fund foster care clearly emphasize that the goals of the programs are family-oriented. If a family has problems or is disintegrating, as was the case with Mary's family, the first efforts are supposed to be toward keeping the family together by providing the kinds of help both the parents and the child need to stay together. If keeping the child in his or her own home is not possible, if a child like Mary is abandoned or in danger, she is to be given shelter with a protective, caring surrogate family. But such placements are supposed to be temporary, interim periods that provide the social workers time to help rebuild the family unit. If the child cannot be reunited with his or her parents, the caseworker is then supposed to find the youngster a permanent adoptive home. The goal is permanence.

The term *foster care,* as its use has developed, is both generic and specific. In the generic sense, it includes all out-of-home placement of children, no matter what the cause or reason. In the specific sense, the words *foster care* denote a surrogate family *foster home.* A foster home is just that — a family home, with a mother and a father and brothers and sisters. A foster home is not a treatment center. Theoretically, foster parents can get specialized help in caring for foster children who are emotionally disturbed or handicapped in some way; but if the child is seriously disturbed or his or her physical or emotional needs can't be met in a family environment, foster care provides group homes and small, privately operated community-based institutions. These foster-care facilities are staffed and equipped to meet the children's needs, or they should be. As foster children's special needs are met, as problems are corrected and rehabilitation is effected, the children are supposed to be returned to a family setting. Again, the goal is supposed to be permanence within a family.

The foster-care system is used by the juvenile courts to place children who are orphaned or abandoned or neglected. Like Mary, these are the *dependent* children, and their cases are handled administratively by the county or city welfare departments. The juvenile courts also place *predelinquent* children who are in need of supervision and who have been made *wards* of the court. These youngsters are usually handled administratively by the county probation office. The Probation Department and the court may also place juvenile *delinquents* in foster care. And welfare and probation departments, acting independently of the courts, also place youngsters in foster care, as do some state agencies.

It has been variously estimated that from five hundred

thousand to seven hundred thousand children were in foster care in the United States by 1980, and that the yearly cost of such out-of-home placement ran as high as $1.5 billion. Those are only gross estimates. There are no accurate figures. No government agency has kept an accurate count or accounting of foster care. Statistically, the 1980 census reveals, indirectly, that the numbers of children "at risk" in single-parent families is growing as inflation and unemployment increase. The stresses on the poor families, on the black and Hispanic families in the ghettos and barrios of this nation, are splitting the nuclear family. The numbers of single women raising children is on the increase, dramatically. Most are divorced, but fully 15 percent have never married. All of these factors are putting more pressures on those children at risk of losing whatever home they have known. Yet, clearly, the foster-care system, as it was working through the 1970s and into the 1980s, was not capable of caring for these children, much less helping to keep their families together.

Why? Finding the answer is extremely difficult. There is no uniform system of foster care to be found when you look closely. No two states, no two counties or cities, operate in quite the same way. There has been a general and historic reluctance on the part of the federal government to lead. Rather than rule by national policy and administrative direction, the Congress and the various administrations have used the carrot approach, dangling monetary incentives in front of the states in an attempt to lure them into expanded foster-care services. The states have tended to impose their own, generally more conservative, views, and then to act as a conduit for funding, passing state regulations along with the federal and state dollars. To qualify for these federal and state dollars in any individual case, a county or a city has to take the child into juvenile court. Children like Mary are made *dependents* or *wards* and are placed under the protection of the court. The court, acting under the legal theory of *parens patriae,* considers the needs of the child, issues orders, and supervises the actions of the various bureaucracies to ensure that the best interests of the child are served. In fact, the officers of the court — judges, social workers, probation officers, attorneys for the prosecution and the defense — are all individuals acting virtually on their own. Historically, the juvenile court proceedings have been closed to public view, and the judge's decisions were beyond review. Even if the judges in most juvenile courts are absolutely qualified to act in each child's best interest, there isn't time. In practice, the courts are simply too busy, their calendars too crowded, to deliberate with care on the case of every child. The courts work on a machinelike basis, with the judge's decisions routinely based on the casework and recommendations of a social worker or a probation officer who may have as many as fifty or sixty troubled youngsters in his or her file. The individual recommendations are drafted briefly, simply, quickly; the judgments are rendered in minutes. There is little time for the consideration of complicated circumstances. By law, the courts are supposed to review each juvenile's case once a year. A study in Alameda County, on the eastern shore of San Francisco Bay, revealed that in 177 cases involving the lives of 321 children, the judges spent *less than two minutes on each annual review.*

There is no time for rehabilitating families or stabilizing the life of a child. In Mary's file, a social worker had noted, "This is the case of three minors who were dependents of the court as the mother did not care for them and the father was unable to do so due to a drinking problem." There is little in the case files or court records to suggest that the Welfare Department did much to try to rectify the home situation or to help Mary's mother or father assume their roles as parents. Mary, her brother, and her sister were placed in separate foster homes. At the time, it was noted that Mary was emotionally disturbed and that she had been referred to a child-guidance counselor. However, there are no indications in the records to show that a comprehensive effort was made to help this child sort out her life in a permanent, nurturing family environment. Rather, she was placed in one foster home after another, then dropped into institutional care in a process that was mechanical and that fitted the child to whatever was available on that particular county's lists of foster-care facilities.

But foster care was intended to meet the needs of children, not to suit the political, fiscal, and bureaucratic demands of a county welfare system and an overworked, underqualified juvenile court system. Mary's case is illustrative of the national problems because it runs the gamut of the foster-care spectrum. And hers is not an isolated case. There are some givens, some generalized problems, that her case demonstrates. The way the system works, when a child like Mary "fails" in foster care, she is moved away from the family structure and toward increasingly severe institutional care. Children are placed in group homes and small, private institutions that, in theory, are staffed to meet and treat their needs, that provide them with the kinds of emotional and physical therapy needed to help them fit into permanent placement in a family setting. But the system doesn't work that way, not in the nation, not in California. In 1974, at the time Mary was made a dependent of the court, there were 55,820 children in some kind of foster care in California. An audit conducted for the state legislature revealed that the $267 million foster-care programs were failing in their primary mission. Far too many children, once caught up in foster care, were not getting out of foster care. Youngsters were being misplaced and mistreated. There were an estimated eight thousand children under the age of six who would never be reunited with their families, yet the foster-care system had done little or nothing to place them in permanent adoptive homes. Judges were reluctant to sever a parent's rights of custody, even in the most severe cases.

Yet that wasn't the only problem. In Los Angeles County, where reports show that there are ninety-five hundred children in foster care, Stephanie Klopfleisch, director of foster-care services for the Department of Public Social Services (DPSS), explained, "The funding in California and this country does not support services to children in their homes. If a child really has a severe emotional problem in our country, we can get better services for him in foster care 'in-service' rather than in his own home."

The result of this built-in anti-family bias too often gets carried to extremes. In San Bernardino County, east of Los Angeles, a welfare caseworker and the juvenile court decided that a five-year-old girl belonged in foster care *only* because both of her parents were deaf and mute. The girl could hear and she could speak. She had grown up communicating with her parents in a kind of sign language that had evolved within the family. Because of their disabilities, the parents received $898 a month in various forms of federal, state, and county welfare benefits. They lived in a modest, well-kept three-bedroom home. This was a loving, caring home, though there were problems caused by the parents' physical disabilities.

Because they were on welfare, their lives were *supervised* by the San Bernardino County Department of Public Social Services. A social worker reported: "Our brief evaluation of [the child's] functioning shows her to be far behind in verbal skills and interpersonal relationships. She has been somewhat isolated with little opportunity to interact with other children." There were no allegations of abuse or neglect, yet the case was brought into juvenile court on grounds of "Dependency: Inadequate Parental Care and Control." The specific legalese: ". . . said minor . . . has no parent or guardian willing to exercise, capable of exercising or actually exercising proper care and supervision."

In the report to the court, "Legal Background and Previous Agency Involvement," the social worker indicated that the girl was being "detained" in the prospective foster home, pending action by the court. The child had already been moved, and the social worker was asking the court to approve the action. On February 10, 1977, the San Bernardino County Juvenile Court made the five-year-old girl a dependent of the court, and she was placed in the foster home, as recommended. The child's parents were in court, but because they could not hear, they were bewildered. They didn't understand what was happening. No one represented their interests.

As the months of separation went by, the parents began to realize they had lost their daughter. They sought the help of an attorney and were referred to Allen King, of the Southern California Center for Law and the Deaf, a federally funded legal-aid group based in Los Angeles. On February 24, 1978, a year after the girl had been taken from her home, King filed a habeas corpus suit in San Bernardino County Superior Court seeking the return of the child. The documents filed to support the suit included the welfare reports and recommendation as exhibits, thus peeling back the veil of secrecy that had previously shrouded the juvenile court action. If the case had been pursued in the superior court, King could have brought the county Welfare Department and the juvenile court officials into an open forum to question why efforts had not been made to keep the family together, as the law required. A compromise was worked out. The girl was returned home, and the county Welfare Department was ordered to provide the entire family with the kinds of social and educational services needed to help the girl and her parents. The suit was dropped.

This San Bernardino County case demonstrated just how autocratic individual bureaucracies can become when there is no public accountability. As the system has evolved in California, the county welfare and probation departments have become the primary agents of foster care, and juvenile

court actions have become little more than a formality.
The state acts only as the expediter of monies, receiving
and parceling out federal funds, collecting general taxes
and distributing proportionate shares to the counties,
matching some portion of the federal largess through complicated formulas, adding dollars to state programs designed to fill needs unmet by federal laws. In California
there are fourteen separate state agencies administering
160 different foster-care services and programs, each with
its own set of qualifying regulations. Some of these services
are mandated; some are discretionary. The relationship of
the federal government to the states is comparable to the
state's relationship to the fifty-eight counties in California.
The counties pick and choose to suit their political and
economic needs, striking an uneasy balance between serving the interests of needy children and the local political
climate. The result is, in the words of the state's auditor
general, a "diffusion of authority [that] precludes the effective supervision and coordination of programs with local
agencies and prevents the assignment of responsibility for
either program failure or success at the state level . . ."
The auditor general's report to the legislature noted that
the result of this "fragmented administrative authority"
and of the state's failure to provide statewide supervision
was a system that varied widely from county to county in
its effectiveness. The counties were on their own. They
could do pretty much what they wanted.

In rural California, welfare is traditionally used as a form
of unemployment insurance for agriculture, not as a public
effort to assist families. Foster care has never had a high
priority, and the task of finding foster homes and placing
foster children often falls to one or two workers. Group
homes and small, private institutions — usually with bu-
colic-sounding names — are frequently located in these
rural counties. However, local Welfare and Probation Department workers seldom have a chance to place children

in these local foster-care facilities because the monthly
rates are too high and these residential treatment "schools"
and "ranches" are most often filled with children from
cities like San Diego or San Francisco. In metropolitan
Los Angeles County, three big agencies run foster care,
the Department of Public Social Services, the Probation
Department, and the Department of Adoptions. Together,
these departments employ twenty-eight hundred people in
a highly structured set of bureaus and agencies, each operating independently of the other. These agencies place
and supervise the cases of ninety-five hundred children in
foster care. The DPSS licenses the four thousand foster
homes used by the three departments, and the County
Administrative Office contracts with another five hundred
private, for-profit and nonprofit group homes and institutions licensed by the state. The number of these foster-
care facilities falls far short of need, the competition for
beds is keen, and, as a result, kids are shipped all over
the state to wherever there's an empty bed. The total cost
of out-of-home care in the county: $118 million.

Individual social workers in Los Angeles County carry
as many as fifty-five or sixty children in their case loads;
one third of these youngsters are apt to be emotionally
handicapped, older, aggressive, and hard to place. The
workers have little time to guide and counsel children and
parents, little time to find the kinds of help that would keep
the family together. Once the child is placed in foster care,
there is no time for work with the youngster, unless there
is an emergency. Daily, these caseworkers must deal with
angry parents, lawyers, judges, with tangles of paperwork
and regulations and the never-ending shuffle of reports.
Their routine has to be crisis-oriented and the impact, day
after day, of working with disintegrating families and with
the compounding bureaucratic structures creates a high
burn-out rate among social workers and probation officers.
If they stay, they build defensive mechanisms around themselves to protect their sanity. Large numbers simply quit

and find work elsewhere. Turnover is high. The result is inconsistency.

In New York City, the system is structurally different, in that the government, over a long period of time, has allowed foster care to develop around eighty-nine private corporations called "voluntary agencies." These corporations — many of them old-line subsidiaries of established Catholic, Protestant, and Jewish charities — develop their own placement services, complete with caseworkers; they subcontract with surrogate families for foster care, develop group homes and specialized institutions, all under purchase-of-service contracts with the city. These voluntary agencies handle 80 percent of the twenty-nine thousand children in foster care, at an annual cost of about $300 million. The city supervises the work of these voluntary agencies and is primarily responsible for the casework and placement of the other 20 percent of the children in foster care. Most of the children in foster care in the city are black (52 percent) or Puerto Rican (26 percent) and are from low-income neighborhoods, where unemployment is high and survival never guaranteed.

David Fanshel and Eugene B. Shinn, over a decade ago, studied hundreds of New York City foster-care cases and wrote: "We are impressed with the number of apparently irrational elements in the system . . . We view the delivery of foster care services as being less than optimally organized and almost impossible to manage soundly." The two social scientists reported finding bureaucratic ignorance, inexperience, and poorly trained social workers who labored in disorganized and poorly administered bureaus and agencies that had a bias toward funding on a per diem basis rather than providing family rehabilitation services. Because of the way the federal laws were written, it was easier to fund the out-of-home placement of a child than it was to provide the family-support services that could keep that youngster in his or her own home.

Clearly, the system wasn't working as intended. Eight

years later a 1978 New York City comptroller's investigation found that children once placed in foster care were
most likely to remain in the foster-care system until they
reached maturity. But more disturbing, the comptroller
reported that 87 percent of the foster children studied
"entered care with no serious emotional or behavioral
problems. After spending years in foster care, however,
19.9 percent displayed significantly increased social/emo-
tional handicaps manifested by such symptoms as severe
anxiety, chronic enuresis, chronic hyperactivity or recur-
ring nightmares. For these children, adjustment to yet another foster home is often impossible and institutionalization becomes inevitable. In effect, they are graduated
from foster care into institutional care . . ."

From California to New York the patterns are the same.
Once children like Mary are taken into the foster-care system, they are not likely to escape. Because of the anti-
family bias built into the laws and regulations, because of
the shortage of appropriate placement facilities, because
of our public attitudes toward children who are different,
who are not considered normal, because of all of these
things and more, the children who are placed in foster care
are placed in jeopardy. Once there, the compounding trau-
mas of their lives suck them deeper and deeper into the
house of mirrors.

The awful irony of all this frequently can be found in
the exaggerated mirror distortions of the way things are
supposed to be. For example, in New York City social
workers were misplacing children who had already been
misplaced, according to the comptroller's report. A child
who should have gone into a surrogate family foster home
ended up in a big, general institution as a result of one
such mistake. A supervisor in one office had recommended,
mistakenly, that the youngster be placed in a group home,
rather than in a foster home. However, the placement
worker in another office ignored the incorrect recommen-

dation and put the child in an institution, replacing the incorrect recommendations with an inappropriate placement. The example was not the exception, but the rule, according to the comptroller's report. The foster-care system was working in reverse of its stated goals. Children were being pulled deeper into the system rather than being returned to their own homes or placed in a permanent adoptive family. The city comptroller reported eleven thousand of the twenty-nine thousand children who had been in placement in the foster-care system six years or more could have and should have been discharged earlier, either into their parents' rehabilitated homes or into adoptive care, at a net saving to the taxpayers of $205 million.

And New York City stood only as an outsized example of a national problem as the 1970s came to an end. After two years of study, the National Commission on Children in Need of Parents reported: "Clearly, foster care, designed as a means to an end, becomes an end itself, a no-exit fate for hundreds of thousands of luckless, innocent children. Permanence, the bedrock of a healthy childhood, is forfeited and replaced by an existence of rootless insecurity."

The problem is presented in a dramatic way by a young mother who had been an abused child, a foster child who had grown into a child-abusing parent. Her odyssey through the foster-care system began when she was a lonely child desperately seeking love; she became a hardened, difficult-to-handle adolescent, a chronic runaway who spent many of her teen years in juvenile halls, *doing* two weeks here, three weeks there, most of it locked away in solitary. Before she was eighteen, she had dozens of tattoos on her body, a record of boredom, frustration, and weakening sanity. She once told a reporter that most of the tattoos were self-inflicted — tediously, painfully inked into the skin with a pin as she whiled away the hours in lockup. The juvenile courts, acting in her "best interests" always, had placed her in one foster home after another, locking her away in group homes and in kid jails. At times, the system abused her; at times, it simply ignored her. She survived, and when the system cast her out because she reached her eighteenth birthday, she had children of her own and became an abusing parent. Then, in desperation, she reached out for help, contacting other child-abusing parents, people like herself who needed and found help and strength in Parents Anonymous. Looking back on her own childhood, remembering the shared experiences of others in foster care, this woman summed it all up: *"It's a piss-poor way for society to handle children."*

The problems of foster care are national in scope; there are no geographic boundaries confining the problem to one area or another. However, the problems within this piss-poor system remain largely hidden from public view, festering and growing, until, like a boil, they become ugly and red and finally break open. Such was the case in New Orleans in the late 1970s. Foster care in Louisiana, like that in New York, is heavily dependent on purchase-of-service agreements with private providers. Most of the state's two thousand foster-family homes were being operated through licensed home-finding agencies. The state had five thousand children in foster care, most of them in New Orleans. Where New York City was paying $13.50 a day for foster care, Louisiana was paying New Orleans foster parents $4.00 to $5.00 a day, depending on the age of the child. Normally, a foster-care home anywhere in the United States takes care of no more than four or five children, because the goal is to maintain a family atmosphere. But in New Orleans, foster-home operators were taking in as many as twelve and fifteen children. One woman had seventeen youngsters crowded into an old house and was receiving $1800 a month, including the bonuses she got for always keeping her door open to any placement-agency's needs.

New Orleans police and Harry Connick, the Orleans

Parish district attorney, received so many complaints about foster child abuse and neglect that they began a full-scale investigation and turned up a scandal that was still reverberating through the Louisiana Department of Health and Human Resources years later. New Orleans police detectives reported:

> Foster care workers completely ignored the recommendations of the home-finding unit, which usually resulted in . . . overcrowding homes . . . placing physically or mentally handicapped children in a home when it was specifically recommended by home-finding not to place this type of child there . . . several complaints were received relative to physical and sexual abuse. These homes were allowed to remain open with no radical changes in their supervision . . . In [one named] foster home an accusation was made by a foster child that she was raped by the foster father and his son-in-law. The complaint was never properly investigated, the police department was never notified, and the child was never examined by a doctor . . . Officers discovered that several homes were overcrowded due to an emergency, temporary placement [that] . . . resulted in a long erm placement with no follow-up on the worker's part . . . the worker would actually avoid the foster parents after making an emergency placement, hoping that no problem had arisen . . . foster children who were legally available for adoption . . . remained in foster care even when the foster parents expressed a sincere desire to adopt them.

Welfare case files were reprinted in the officers' report. These included social workers' year-by-year comments and evaluations, which clearly demonstrated patterns of bureaucratic mismanagement and neglect during the previous decade. Excerpts from just one foster home case file reveal the pattern:

"Foster mother refused to buy milk for foster children, stating it was too expensive" (May 1969).

"Decided the home should not be considered for additional children" (March 1971).

"Definite financial motive" (October 1971).

"Limited intellectual and cultural stimulation. Negligent in getting medical attention for children" (February 1972).

"Foster mother is caring for [named child], infant of former foster child in her household" (July 1972). This entry was stunning. Despite its long history of parsimony and neglect, social workers kept placing children in this facility until finally they placed the infant daughter of a former foster child, in effect making the foster mother a foster grandmother.

Whether in New Orleans or Chicago, foster care is not without its own forms of black humor. Patrick Murphy, a legal-aid attorney, told of a family from Appalachia who had come to Chicago looking for jobs. They settled in Uptown, but could find no work. There was trouble, and the husband was sent to prison. The wife applied for and received Aid to Families of Dependent Children from the Department of Children and Family Services (DCFS). As Murphy talked, a picture of the troubled family emerged: the mother was unable to cope with the children; they were constantly in trouble with school officials and the law. One after another of her children was taken away by the juvenile court and placed in foster care. Then the mother from Appalachia made a discovery: where she had been granted $40 or $50 a month per child by the DCFS, the foster parents were receiving $140 or $150 a month for each of her children. With her own children gone, she had extra beds, so she applied to the DCFS for a foster-home license and was accepted. She was made a foster parent. Murphy explained that the Illinois process for finding foster homes and placing children

> is all very haphazard . . . and once a kid is in foster care, if [officials] don't hear anything, they don't go out and check. So Mrs. [Name] gets a couple of kids; it's a financial boon to her. She's not a good foster mother. She wasn't a good mother. If she had had someone to help her take care of the

kids, to come in and help her, it would have been different. The problem is this. When you go to court and see the kid, maybe he's nine or ten and you hear the tragic story, there's no way to help take care of the kid at home. So someone talks the mother into admitting neglect, or the state takes the kid away if she fights. Then the kid is put into a foster home. The kids are being rejected. These kids, no matter what their parents did to them, always go back to their parents. They don't understand. They feel rejected when they go into foster care. Some of the homes are pretty good, some are pretty bad. Most are just mediocre and the mediocre foster parent will not put up with a kid with problems, so . . . the kid goes through three or four foster homes. Of course he feels abandoned, totally degraded, worthless. So we're stuck. No foster parent wants him, so we send him to all of these other places. For the money we put into group homes and institutions we ought to be able to keep the kid in his own home. There's no question that problems arise [in the family] . . . When the girl runs away, seems to me you don't need to go to court. Why not have a place in the neighborhood where she can stay two or three days, have some services where she and the family can get some help?

Across the country the system is uniformly heartless, more concerned with regulations and structures and dollars than with kids who desperately need help. The local bureaucrats are only reacting to their own problems, in their own different ways. They tell you they didn't invent the system, and they admit they have no control over it, over what happens to them or the child they are supposed to serve. They cannot help families stay together; they cannot provide children with good surrogate family homes, much less find good adoptive homes. The most common problem these officials complain about is the lack of foster homes.

That there is a shortage of foster homes should come as no great surprise, considering the inducements offered by government. Foster parents in the United States are expected to contribute their time, their love, their skills,

their home, and some of their money for the privilege or
the honor or the opportunity to care for children who have
been orphaned or discarded or taken away from their parents. The combined federal, state, and county stipend offered for foster care varies widely from city to city, county
to county, state to state, but wherever you go, it hardly
covers the basic expenses of life, at best. There are few
other compensations or rewards. Virtually no standards
are set for foster parenting; there is precious little training
offered; there are no uniform guides or regulations; no
respite from the daily task of foster parenting; no governmental assistance worthy of the name. Even so, 160,000
couples choose to become foster parents. Why? Their reasons are as numerous as their numbers. Some make very
good foster parents; many are average; some make lousy
parents, having been attracted to the work for their own,
perverse reasons.

Rhonda Kloemken, a Los Angeles foster parent and a
former president of the California Foster Parent Association, passionately defended foster parenting. In an interview, she frequently attacked the county, state, and federal
bureaucracies that failed to give her foster family the kind
of support she feels it needed so that the children could
grow and be helped while "something" was done to reunite
them with their families or to find them adoptive homes.
She said:

> The quality of care is going down. The better foster parents
> are getting out because of the lack of services and the lack
> of assistance when you are in need, the lack of skills on the
> part of the [state and county] staffs, and the fact they don't
> ever have enough people. But the most serious drawbacks are
> the lack of funds. For example, children can only have one
> pair of glasses a year, but I've had to replace glasses for one
> child three times in one month. MediCal would only pay for
> one pair. If a child needs psychological testing or therapy, we
> have just two MediCal stickers a month. That's not enough

When you make the job of foster parents more and more difficult, the only people who will remain in it are people who are apt to be in foster care for the wrong reasons.

According to experts like Mrs. Kloemken and the DPSS's Klopfleisch, the whole make-up of foster care is undergoing major change. Before World War II, most children in foster care were young and relatively stable emotionally; those with more serious problems were institutionalized. Since the 1950s, the kinds of children coming into foster care have been changing, slowly at first, then more rapidly as deinstitutionalizing all forms of child care and treatment advanced. At the same time, the economic and social stresses on the nuclear families were having their disintegrating effect. More and more troubled children were on the streets. By the early 1970s, the children being offered for foster care were older, more difficult to handle. Mrs. Kloemken said:

> By then we were getting really disturbed youngsters. They came to us with learning disabilities, acting out violence, a wide range of problems we had not seen before. This kind of child requires special skills on the part of foster parents and we desperately need much more training, the kind of training that goes beyond basic diaper lectures. We need help in developing the kinds of skills needed to handle and to help these disturbed children. Too often if we can't handle them [under current conditions], probation or welfare says, "We'll put them somewhere else, put them in an institution." And we're saying that many of these institutionalized kids could benefit from placement in a family home if the foster parents were given adequate assistance and training.

Foster parents like Rhonda Kloemken want to help children; they want to stabilize their lives and move them into permanent homes. The Kloemkens have adopted two of their foster children. But not without great difficulty. The primary obstacles are those built into the bureaucratic structures of foster care. It all seems so obvious: large numbers of children are trapped in foster care, yet there is ample evidence to show that many, if not most, of these children can be placed in permanent homes. For example, early in the 1970s the Children's Bureau of the Department of Health, Education, and Welfare funded a demonstration project called Freeing Children for Permanent Placement, which was conducted by the Oregon State Children's Services Division. The Oregon Project focused on 509 children in seventeen of Oregon's thirty-six counties. These children, all under twelve, were chosen because their records showed that they were likely to remain in foster care. Half of the youngsters had been in foster care for three years or more; 40 percent of them had been in three or more foster homes. The federal funds were used to hire fifteen specially trained social workers to augment the work of the regular foster-care staff in each of the counties. The extra social workers were backed up by legal-aid attorneys, auxiliary services for families and foster parents, and by behavior experts who worked on call. The goal of the project was to place the children in their own homes, if possible, and, failing that, to sever parental rights and place the children in adoptive homes. By the end of the third year, 27 percent of the children had been returned to their natural homes and another 46 percent had been adopted.

The Oregon Project evaluators reported: "Our single most important finding was that a sense of permanence was one of the best predictors of a child's well-being."

Of course, such a finding was not a revelation. It was, rather, a rediscovery, and it underscored the fact that the primary problems in foster care seem to result from a lack of focus, a lack of national purpose or policy. The very term *foster care* focuses on children after they have been separated from their families. In the early 1970s, the California Children's Lobby, working with Arlen Gregorio, a state senator, was attempting to change this focus, to redirect foster care through a new Family Protection Act, which would make some radical changes. The first legislative need was information. Gregorio asked the state auditor general to make a study of foster care. The task took two years. In addition to finding that the state's foster-care services were administratively scattered through fourteen different agencies with a general and quite serious lack of standards and policies, the auditor general reported that the numbers of children coming into foster care had increased 120 percent in a decade, while the numbers of adoptions had dropped by half. More and more children were being kept in foster care because county adoptions workers had neither the time nor the resources to place adoptable children. The state was taking little or no responsibility for such problems and was demanding no accountability. The auditor general's report to the legislature and subsequent hearings called by Senator Gregorio made it obvious that changes were needed.

With the help of the Children's Lobby, Gregorio began to draft legislation built around the premise that children have a right to a permanent home. The first task of any family protection system, according to Sue Brock, the unpaid president of the Children's Lobby, is to take a look at the family structure and see if there is any way to help keep the child or children in the home. "We really ought not be taking children away from their mother just because the stove is broken and the gas has been turned off," Brock said, adding, "If the child is in jeopardy, pull him out until the rehabilitation of the family is working." If the family can't be helped after a specific period of time, say, eighteen months, if services to the family fail, then the child's right to a permanent home supersedes the parental rights of custody. The parental rights must be severed and the child placed through adoption, through long-term subventionary guardianship or, failing all else, through long-term foster care.

Gregorio pushed the bill through the state legislature

during the last months of the Ronald Reagan administration in California. It would have provided $25 million to increase casework and supportive services for families so that, in effect, California could do what the Oregon Project proved could be done. But the bill took the process even further: it provided the preventive services that would help families stay together in the first place. Brock said, "We had a statewide policy in that bill, a law that said children had a right to a permanent home."

The bill passed, but Reagan vetoed it. Senator Gregorio reintroduced the bill, SB-30, in the next session of the legislature, and once more worked it through the various committees, with the help of a growing coalition of child-care and foster-care advocates. During this time, Jerry Brown was elected governor. By 1976, Gregorio had moved his bill through the state senate, and the issue was before the Assembly Ways and Means Committee, where it once more ran into trouble. Governor Brown sent word over that he would not stand for a $25 million budget hike, no matter what the merits of the proposal. Brown marshaled his forces in opposition.

In an interview, Gregorio said, "When it became obvious the bill wasn't going to make it because the money wasn't there, when I was sure the governor was going to veto the bill, I took what I could get." What he got was a greatly scaled-down, two-county demonstration project, not a statewide mandate, not a policy that gave children the right to a permanent home. The Family Protection Act was passed and funded by a $2 million appropriation, for an eighteen-month trial period in two counties. While the demonstrations were considered a success, Gregorio lost his bid for re-election, and there was no great push to expand the program.

The California Children's Lobby — the last vestige of an abortive national effort to organize a children's lobby in each state and in Washington, D.C. — was working on both a state and national level. Liz Berger and Sue Brock, the CCL's two volunteer lobbyists, were working hard for changes in foster care and for new and much needed child day-care programs for working mothers. They considered SB-30 the prototype for national legislation. And, while Senator Gregorio was working his bill through the state legislature, Berger and Brock contacted Democratic Congressman George Miller of California and gave him a copy of the bill. Miller had previously been attracted to the issues through the chance reading of newspaper articles on the problems of children in foster care. He was a member of the House Committee on Education and Labor, and sat on the Select Subcommittee on Education. The congressman asked his staff to do some preliminary checking, and what they reported back prompted Miller to dig deeper. With the cooperation of Congressman John Brademas of Indiana, chairman of the subcommittee, Miller wrote the General Accounting Office in September 1975, asking for a full investigation of the nation's foster-care programs.

Coincidentally, Walter Mondale of Minnesota, then chairman of the Senate Subcommittee on Children and Youth, was beginning to look into adoption issues, black-market baby sales, and the problems of long-term foster care. Joint Senate-House hearings, entitled "Foster Care: Problems and Issues," were scheduled. These hearings clearly established the size and scope of the problem. Congressman Miller introduced his own, comprehensive foster-care bill, which incorporated many of the ideas included in California's SB-30. When Miller's bill got stalled, early on, he made a tactical decision. Abandoning his own bill, he attached many of its provisions to a minor Social Security clean-up bill, HR-7200, then moving through the House Ways and Means Committee. Miller sold his block of amendments on the basis that they would, if adopted, provide the means for saving large amounts of money by keeping children in their own homes, and by finding permanent adoptive homes for those children now in foster care, rather than placing them in the more expensive group homes and institutions.

HR-7200 was given budget authority and began moving through the House. John Lawrence, Miller's administrative assistant, explained, "We were compromising and amending the bill, trying to find out what was workable." During the 1970s, the Congress had authorized the expenditure of $266 million a year in foster-care social-service funds to be used to keep families together and to provide needed back-up services for foster parents, such as respite care. However, each year, Congress appropriated no more than $56 million of that $266 million authorization. And this at a time when it was annually spending $350 million to maintain children in out-of-home foster care. The willingness of federal legislators to fund the placement of children in foster care, and the unwillingness to provide the kinds of services that might have prevented the disintegration of the families of children at-risk, was one measure of a strong anti-family bias that has crept into our patchwork foster-care system. HR-7200 was drafted to reverse that bias, Lawrence explained. The Miller bill would have doubled and tripled the social-service expenditures and shifted the focus of federal foster care toward keeping children in their own homes. The bill called for more family "case planning" and more stringent criteria on the out-of-home placement of children. Once a child was taken from his or her own home, the bill required frequent, individual case reviews and dispositional hearings to make sure children were no longer lost in foster care.

HR-7200 appeared to have the kinds of remedies needed to bring about real change, but the Congress failed to pass the bill. The legislative history of the bill is interesting because it gives some insight into the political processes that surround such social issues and it provides some measure of our national sense of priorities. As Jimmy Carter moved into the White House, HR-7200 was moving through the House. Because Vice President Mondale had been such an ardent champion of child-welfare reforms when he was in the Senate, Miller had hoped for strong support from the new administration. It was not forthcoming. Only after the House passed the bill by a vote of 355 to 64 did the cautious Carter give his nod of approval, and only then did Senator Alan Cranston, of California, carry a Carter version of the bill into the Senate. However, the bill did not fare well there. Louisiana's Russell Long, then chairman of the Senate Finance Committee, insisted on a "workfare" provision to force welfare mothers to labor for their welfare checks, and then Daniel Patrick Moynihan of New York tacked on a New York City financial bail-out amendment. The entire package had become so unwieldy by the time it passed the Senate that there wasn't time to work out a compromise between the House and Senate versions, and the bill died as the congressional session ended.

The key to understanding why Congress had failed, year after year, to pass such legislation is found in the Long and Moynihan amendments. If Pat Moynihan had had the children's issues in mind, rather than the problems of New York City in general, he would have known that his legislative maneuver could not help the Miller foster-care proposals. For Moynihan, the fiscal problems of Gotham were overriding. Moynihan represented a special-interest group with a typically narrow point of view. The sharp, narrowly focused political power of such special-interest groups exerts inordinate pressures on the political processes. The actions of Long, on the other hand, represent a point of view that has far more serious implications and explain, in large part, why we have failed to create a national children's policy. Long is a conservative, a Southerner, a staunch defender of states' rights; he symbolizes the self-appointed watchdogs of the welfare "give-away" systems, stands for the advocates of the Puritan work ethic, the

believers in God, Country, and the Free Enterprise System:
If the indolent, all-too-fertile, poor women, especially those
of "color," are to be supported, they must be qualified
and they must earn their keep. That is the rhetoric. Strip
it of its ugliness, tear away the mythology that so carefully
cloaks welfare, and you find the vestiges of the Elizabethan
Poor Laws and the primitive socioeconomic systems that
were developed to keep labor poor, subservient, and readily accessible. The key to all of this was *local control*.
Each parish board, each county council knew the problems
locally. They were given the responsibility for managing
the public dole; they were the keepers of the public
morality.

Such primitive systems visited the sins of the parents
on the children and thereby failed to provide the children
of the poor with more than the bare essentials of survival.
The systems have little changed in their basic approach.
In the last quarter of the twentieth century the children of
the poor in the United States have no guaranteed right to
food, shelter, and health care. Children's welfare assistance
is still conditional on the eligibility of their parents. As late
as the mid-1970s one half of the states still were not providing federally subsidized Aid to Families of Dependent
Children if there was an employable man in the house, no
matter what the plight of the children. To qualify his family
for aid, an unemployed father had to desert. Those families
that did qualify for aid in states such as Alabama received
only 60 percent of what the government estimated it cost
them to survive. In Mississippi the welfare system provided
a family of four with only $60 in cash and allowed $153
a month in food stamps. Even though they had qualified
for aid, the poor were not to be trusted with cash. And
nothing should be given to them free if it could be avoided,
not even school lunches. Hungry school children had to
qualify for the federally subsidized "free" school lunch
program and then they were frequently asked to work off

their "debt" by washing dishes or sweeping floors, just as Russell Long wanted their mothers to work for their welfare checks.

That was the climate in which Miller worked through the 1970s to get HR-7200 through the Congress. Even though he failed, the congressman from California did not give up. He told reporters he would try again, and again, if need be.

## 2

# Discarded Children

CHILDREN who are so emotionally disturbed that they act out in socially unacceptable ways, and those who have noticeable physical or mental handicaps, are selectively cast out of normal society. All of the romantic protestations about love of children and the political rhetoric notwithstanding, we in this country do not provide the kind of help families must have to keep such children at home, even though we recognize that is where they have the best chance to survive and grow to their fullest potential as human beings. We separate and segregate children who are different from our national stereotypes. Even the "special classes" provided in the public schools for the retarded, the deaf, or the learning-handicapped are most often located out back behind the gym or bus garage.

The actual effect of the laws, the regulations, the administration of the large number of programs ostensibly designed to help these children is to keep them out of sight and out of the public mind. As we have seen, the foster-care system separates children from their families, and, once separated, the children are pushed and shoved about as they are pulled deeper into the institutionalized system.

Surrogate parents who would adopt these unwanted children are discouraged from doing so by the very laws and regulations that are supposed to promote home-finding procedures.

It may be that the processes of foster care — as opposed to the designs and intentions — are symptoms of our collective schizophrenia. We are caught between some very powerful currents that are pulling in different directions. Once, children who were unsightly and unmanageable were simply locked away in private closets or public institutions. As we became a growing technocracy, we turned more and more to specialists to solve social problems, and we were convinced that the kindest act we could perform for retarded children was to construct special institutions designed and equipped to meet their particular needs. Disturbed children who were aggressive and acted in antisocial ways needed to be reformed, so institutional schools were built to reform them. But too often the various establishments we created and staffed were not effective; rather, they turned out to be big, foreboding structures that were the antitheses of home and family. Worse yet, children were being emotionally and physically maimed in these stark, often cruel environments.

Change was needed, radical change. The social technocrats, sensing the shift in public mood, coined a technocratic word, *deinstitutionalization,* and began to work on a new wisdom that held promise: a child who was removed from his or her home, for whatever reason, should be placed in the "least restrictive" setting consistent with that child's diagnosis and resulting "case plan." Within each community there was to be a network of services that started with surrogate families providing simple foster homes; there were to be specialized foster homes for long-term care and treatment; small group homes that were staffed with paraprofessionals trained for more intensive care and treatment; larger group homes with behavior therapists working with the paraprofessionals; and there were to be small, private nursing homes and psychiatric hospitals to care for and treat the most severely affected children. The state institutions were to be the options of last resort. The goal of the entire system was either to get the children back in their homes, or, if that was not feasible, to place them in permanent surrogate families, through adoption.

At the federal level, the bureaucratic leadership early sensed this change in direction, and every agency that had been involved in any work with children scrambled to put together fundable programs. By the mid-1970s, the various bureaus within the U.S. Department of Health, Education, and Welfare alone had patched together twenty-five or thirty different programs and projects, and HEW was budgeting $10 billion to fund them. Out in the states, the same processes were under way, and California was one step ahead of the pack. The Golden State has always had a reputation for excellence in all forms of social welfare and juvenile justice. From earliest statehood, California had moved progressively to educate and care for the children within its boundaries. The legislature, early on, funded widows' pensions and foster care in private homes; church-operated orphanages were subsidized by state grants; and the state developed a new approach to the problems of juvenile delinquency, through the California Youth Authority. Instead of trying to reform young hoodlums through a harsh kid prison system, the CYA set up diagnostic and treatment facilities that included forestry camps, where youngsters were taught conservation work and fought forest fires, and group homes, where parolees could be eased back into community life. California was spending $3.7 billion on all forms of public education and another $800 million for the care and treatment of children who had been abandoned or neglected or abused and no longer lived at home.

Earlier, California had gained national recognition for putting together a state hospital system that was far and away the best of its kind anywhere in the world. By the late 1950s the pendulum had swung as far as it could in the institutional direction, and it began the swing back. Community-based care became the new goal, and California was once more on the cutting edge. Institutional care was being replaced by smaller, private community-care facilities that operated on purchase-of-service contracts negotiated through the various county agencies, or through the quasi-governmental regional centers that were incorporated as nonprofit agencies to manage individual "client" cases, developing services for the "developmentally disabled" children and adults.

California was showing the way, as it was then perceived. When ABC-TV reporter Geraldo Rivera exposed the horrors of New York State's institutional care of mentally retarded children at Willowbrook, he wanted to show just how a state should care for and treat such children. He reported, "California was immediately recognized as the obvious example . . . The people who run the California system will no longer settle for the large Willowbrook-like institutions." Rivera flew out a film crew to record the model. But what he and his camera crew missed in their brief inspection was the fact that the California system was in chaos. *Deinstitutionalization* was only a twenty-two-letter catchword: the children caught up in the system were strung out between institutions and community care, with never enough resources in either place to meet their needs. Although the state had developed a wondrously big, efficient state hospital system, and though it had switched directions and was closing down wards and whole hospitals, placing children and adults in community care, there were not enough community-care beds, and many of those which were available were of questionable value. As it turned out, California was the harbinger of bad tiding in other states.

The design had sounded good. Nationally, the jobs had been assigned to the technocrats of social well-being;

money was appropriated, lots of it; and there was a sense of accomplishment. But, like Rivera, we had not looked deeply enough into the subject, and what we had created was a perfect environment for virulent weeds that had been in our national child-care garden all along, but had never had the kind of government-dollar fertilizer they needed to flourish. To understand how these weeds grew, it is important to understand the history of the garden. Charity has usually been the province of religion and philanthropy; private groups and organizations traditionally have run orphanages and hospitals and cared for homeless children. The government has taken in those outcasts too grotesque for family or private charity and has had the burden of reforming delinquent youths. The charitable child-care institutions were financed in part by tithes and donations and in ever-larger part by government subsidy. While some of their methods may have occasionally provoked controversy, for the most part these charitable organizations were a welcome part of the system.

But always hanging around the periphery of this charitable business has been a ragtag gathering of ne'er-do-well entrepreneurs, religious and philanthropic zealots, and those few individuals who have combined enterprise and charity to the advantage of their own pockets. They are the weeds in the system — some benign, some noxious. Until recent years they were never much of a problem, because not enough public money was offered to attract large-scale exploitation. However, as the moves toward deinstitutionalization were made, the governmental purse strings were opened and the kid business was begun. The traditional charitable institutions reordered their systems, creating foster-care and group home services and psychiatric hospitals. While the government picked up most of the costs, these programs were still reliant on private donations to some extent. Thus, the roles were reversed, and private charity was now subsidizing government programs.

This role reversal is critical, because it provided cost-conscious bureaucrats an opportunity to fund child-care programs at something below actual cost, and this pay standard was stretched all across community care, applied to both nonprofit and for-profit facilities alike. Each group home or institution negotiated a rate, based on its demonstrated cost of operations. There was little or no allowance for profits; in fact, the regulations governing federal foster care forbade payment to a for-profit facility. However, counties and cities seldom audited the books, required little or no proof of demonstrated cost, and their hurried routines invited fiscal manipulation. The opportunity to cheat was there.

The closing of state hospital wards and entire institutions, combined with the emphasis on placing youngsters in community-care facilities, rather than in state institutions, created a burgeoning demand for more bed space in communities. The traditional private-care facilities were quickly filled. As demand exceeded supply, entrepreneurs purchased old motels and big, run-down homes in older neighborhoods, did a little remodeling, and went into the kid business. Some social workers and probation officers saw opportunities to get into business for themselves. They could purchase a suburban home, staff it with paraprofessionals, and open a group home. The $500 or $600 a month per child, times six children, covered expenses and the house payments, and the rapidly appreciating real estate market made the deal attractive. Real estate speculators saw opportunities and set up lease arrangements and management fee charges that made the kid business lucrative.

The kid business boomed in New York, Florida, Texas, Nebraska, and a dozen other states. In California, from San Diego County to the Oregon border, the county welfare departments and probation offices, regional centers and juvenile courts, were dumping kids into community care at costs ranging up to $2000 a month. The old-line, reputable group homes and institutions were always the first choice on the placement workers' lists. These facilities became extremely selective about whom they accepted. They screened out the youngsters who were difficult to handle, taking only those boys and girls they felt would "succeed" in their programs. Some of these facilities would "take a chance" on a tough kid, but after one or two mistakes, the youngster was out. This left a void that had to be filled. New foster-care services were opened that were reputable and did provide the kind of care needed, but the lure of federal and state dollars, the lack of real regulation, and the constant supply of children created an environment in which the weeds could grow.

The opportunity for making money in the kid business rested entirely on how much could be diverted from the monthly rate paid for the care and treatment of each child. But not all of those coming into the kid business were prompted by profit motives. Some who opened group homes or institutions felt "called," for one reason or another. They usually had their own peculiar ideas of how best to treat emotionally disturbed or retarded children. Often, there was a strong undercurrent of Calvinism in the program content and approach to discipline. Such programs were usually run by rigid, strong-willed men who attracted both a loyal following and controversy. Frequently, these new group homes or institutions were shoestring operations founded on small cash reserves and a reliance on the monthly cash flow from the government. Because of bed shortages in the various systems, few questions were asked by state licensing agencies or by placement workers. If the place looked physically good and the owners and operators seemed like nice, well-motivated people, okay.

In this kind of environment, child abuse flourished. Without adequate program evaluations, without adequate methods for accountability, each of these community-care facilities became a world unto itself. No matter how "good" or how "bad" the approach to child care and treatment was, the system within any one of these programs became institutionalized; these were self-serving programs with no one to criticize technique. Those staff people who did not agree with the operator's theories or methods were fired or quit; those who remained were loyal believers. Some of these community-care programs, perhaps most of them, did care for and treat children in a way that was helpful to the child and to the society as a whole. Many did not. And where most got into trouble was in the use of the therapy technique called *behavior modification*.

When used by skilled, trained professionals who understand this very technical, broad-ranging set of therapeutic tools, behavior modification can be, and often is, very useful in helping children. However, one side of behavior modification is negative and requires the use of a spectrum of negative stimuli, including pain as a "punisher." Any kind of punishment is a powerful stimulant, but *pain in particular is quickly rewarding for the therapist because it brings rapid response*. Too often, the therapist is seduced by this response, and the patient becomes the victim. In this, and in other ways, child abuse has been built into the institutionalization of foster care.

Some measure of these problems was reflected in the 1974 testimony of a U.S. Senate subcommittee staff investigator who had been probing problems with the $500-million-a-year Department of Defense's Civilian Health and Medical Program for the Uniformed Services (CHAMPUS). CHAMPUS had placed several hundred emotionally disturbed children — the dependents of military personnel — in 486 different residential facilities around the country. Senate investigator John Walsh testified:

> Privately owned, commercial "psychiatric hospitals" or "residential psychiatric treatment centers" or institutions with similar names are springing up all over the country. This is because juvenile authorities at a state, county and local level are

finding that it is more convenient for them to subcontract for the care of troubled adolescents to such commercial institutions — frequently in far-removed states — than it is to find a foster home nearby or place the child in a state or county operated institution.

In Florida, one private institution calling itself the Green Valley School advertised in the *Journal of Clinical Psychology* that it was a "dramatic community for teens who 'fail' in ordinary schools." Ironically, this advertisement appeared in a special issue devoted to child abuse. The Green Valley School was one of the focal points of Walsh's investigation for the Senate Permanent Investigations Subcommittee. During the hearings, witnesses testified that Green Valley had a long history of child abuse and questionable treatment practices, and that the operators of the school had had repeated confrontations with state and local officials who objected to the way the children were being treated but had been unable to do anything to prevent what was happening. Witnesses told of children being beaten, of children being chained in leg irons, of children being made to dig their own graves and lie in them, all as forms of punishment and "therapy."

Senator Henry Jackson, subcommittee chairman, said staff investigations revealed that "children appear to have been subjected to some of the basest indignities imaginable . . . we are not finding isolated instances, but a pattern that has been going on for years . . . it appears CHAMPUS management has dumped taxpayers' money into the pockets of people who have perpetrated monstrous abuses."

The CHAMPUS hearings focused attention on the subject, but they didn't really give much more than an indication that there were serious problems within the community-care system. In 1977, the General Accounting Office informed the Congress that a five-state investigation of children in foster-care institutions revealed that "almost half of the institutions visited were either unlicensed or had serious physical deficiencies." These private institutions ranged in size from a twenty-bed facility in an urban Georgia city up to a one-thousand-bed facility in rural Pennsylvania. These institutions were being paid from $311 to $1330 a month per child by a variety of local, state, and federal agencies. Frequently, several bureaucracies, each with its own set of requirements and restrictions, contributed to the funding of a single child, and any one child might have two or three caseworkers, each one filling out the needed forms, shuffling paper, but seldom seeing the child. The GAO investigation of the financial records of these institutions showed that "they often reported inaccurate or unsubstantiated costs to support their rates." In California, New York, and New Jersey, the GAO investigators found unallowable federal payments being made to profit-making, private, community-care homes for children.

A subsequent HEW audit of just two urban California counties revealed that unallowable payments to profit-making group homes and institutions totaled more than $900,000 in fiscal 1976. Several nonprofit corporations operating child-care facilities were found to be *legally* skimming large amounts of government money through leaseback arrangements. Operators not only owned the land and leased it to the nonprofit corporation; they often paid themselves handsome salaries and had the free use of homes, cars, and credit cards. The level of care and treatment in far too many of these group homes was minimal at best, because the money was being skimmed off for personal gain.

By the late 1970s, the situation in California was reaching critical proportions, not only in foster-care–community-care services, but in the state hospitals as well. In these institutions, there were never enough doctors, and those doctors who were employed were too often undertrained, lacking the necessary skills. There were never enough nurses or aides. Parents of children placed in the Camarillo State Hospital's once-excellent program for the autistic complained that the program had so degenerated that their children were in danger. With the help of the National Society for Autistic Children, they forced the California Department of Health to create a task force to study problems at Camarillo. The task force found the sixty children in the two units were receiving nothing more than custodial care. The children went unwashed, were heavily drugged, and only partly clothed. The hospital administrators argued in the press that the hospital's problems were due primarily to staff shortages created by budget cuts. California's model hospital system was clearly coming apart.

It is difficult to convey just how abusive some parts of the systems had become, because there is a self-protective tendency among us all not to believe that the truly shocking event is indicative of some deeper, basic problem. We seem unable to examine the horrible examples and learn more about the systems themselves. It is quicker and less painful to glance at these shocking events in headline form one by one and believe they are aberrations, quirks. But they are not quirks. It is the system itself that is abusive.

Green Valley. Pennhurst. Kate School. Oak Creek Ranch. Napa State Hospital. Stockton State Hospital. Jones' Children's Haven. Forest Haven. The names, the places, the problems blur; public institutions, private care, community care. Here is Willowbrook, located on Staten Island, Geraldo Rivera reporting:

> Wilkins made a turn and opened a heavy metal door with a small glass window that looked like the entrance to a dungeon. It was. I could use words like horrible, wretched, awful, and all of their synonyms a thousand times over, but the description of what I saw would still be too flattering. There were perhaps sixty to seventy severely and profoundly retarded children living in a room that looked like an unfinished basement . . . Wooden benches and hard chairs were scattered

randomly around the room. Plaster was peeling off the dirty, greenish cement walls . . . The residents of the ward bore only a passing resemblance to children I have known. Their heads were swollen. Their bodies were bent and twisted . . . The single attendant was struggling to separate a cluster of children near the center of the ward . . . The kids were either naked or wearing fragments of clothing. Some wore just straitjackets. Several of the toilet bowls had no seats . . . all of the facilities were caked with filth. I watched one kid lower his head into the bowl and drink like a dog . . . The ward was filled with noise, but none of it seemed human.

And there is Willowbrook as viewed by a former ward employee and reported in the Human Ecology Forum, New York State College of Human Ecology, Cornell University:

Willowbrook was called a school, but . . . only a relatively small number of the five thousand residents [in 1970] were receiving anything that might be called schooling . . . What I see most clearly of Willowbrook is not the building I worked in, but the halls of the infirmary ward. They were filled with little wooden carts set on two-spoked wheels. The carts came and went, quietly attended by black men and women dressed in hospital whites. Inside the carts were contorted little creatures, impossible tangles of tiny twisted limbs with open sores where bone and flesh were in contact with the wood. Their great round heads were motionless for the most part, but the eyes, incongruously beautiful, were always looking . . .

We attendants were keepers in a prison . . . Staff and residents were partners in a ritual of reward and punishment that left both sides deeply scarred . . . The trick was to make the residents fear you and hate you just as a recruit hates his drill instructor . . . The residents were not criminals, nor were the attendants inherently evil men. Staff and residents were acting out a pattern of relationship that had been established long before any of us had arrived on the scene . . . Many of us were always tired, overextended. There was a quiet bitterness: the staff weren't getting any breaks, just a couple of stingy paychecks, so there wasn't much left for them to give . . .

The residents, the "kids," knew what the score was: get away with what you could, because that was all you were going to get.

The horrors of Willowbrook were not unique, merely repetitious. Pennhurst State School, founded by the Commonwealth of Pennsylvania in 1908, had a history of overcrowding and understaffing. Its population had reached five thousand in the 1960s; then, in the name of deinstitutionalization, had declined to 1230 by the time U.S. District Court Judge Raymond J. Broderick concluded, in 1977, "All parties to this litigation are in agreement that Pennhurst as an institution is inappropriate and inadequate for the habilitation of the retarded." A thirty-two-day trial had revealed just how inappropriate and inadequate Pennhurst was. Restraints and psychotherapeutic drugs were frequently used because of staff shortages. There often was excrement and urine on ward floors; outbreaks of pinworm and infectious diseases were common; toilet areas had no towels, soap, or toilet paper; injuries to residents by other residents and through self-abuse were common. Patients were raped; patients were beaten. A girl admitted to Pennhurst when she was twelve years old had lost several teeth, suffered a fractured jaw, fractured fingers, a fractured toe, and numerous lacerations, cuts, scratches, and bites in eleven years of confinement. Before her admission, the girl had been able to say simple words like "dadda," "mamma," and "noy-noy," meaning "no." At the time of the trial, she no longer spoke.

In the 1970s, the problems of institutional care were not confined to mental hospitals or institutions for the retarded. Peter Smith, a law professor and director of the Maryland Juvenile Law Clinic, inspected the juvenile detention facilities of the city of Baltimore and found that kids had been locked up for months without a hearing. Smith reported:

There was a tremendous commingling between juveniles and those who had been waived to the adult authority. We found persons whose records had been completely lost. Indeed we found one person, who, according to a jail printout, was there ... he in fact was not there and was supposed to be at the Crowsville State Mental Hospital. But he was not at Crowsville either ... We spent weeks trying to locate him. No one knew where he was.

Juvenile Court Judge Robert I. H. Hammerman ruled that conditions were so bad, they constituted "punishment which is cruel and unusual." And he noted that "punishment of any kind for those merely waiting trial is prohibited." He ordered conditions rectified within sixty days. The city administration dragged its feet; Judge Hammerman ordered the juvenile detention facilities in the jail shut down *immediately*. The city skirted the issue by moving juvenile detention to district precinct stations, using the station house detention cells as substitutions. Kids were held twenty-four hours a day, two to a cell, in filthy conditions. The tiny cells were equipped only with a wash basin, toilet, and a wooden bench. There was no reading material, no mattresses, no blankets or sheets, no toilet paper. At least half the jailed children had committed no crimes, and when their cases finally came before the court, they were released to their parents. Two years had passed since Judge Hammerman had first ordered Baltimore to clean up its juvenile detention facilities. On Tuesday, June 12, 1973, the judge made an unannounced inspection. He ordered that the cells be cleaned, bedding provided, that all meals be served hot, that the youngsters be provided with writing materials, reading matter, toilet articles, and that they be allowed to make phone calls. In his order he wrote: "I would reiterate what I previously mentioned ... that we are dealing with youngsters who in the eyes of the law are presumed innocent. Even if these youngsters ... were convicted of an offense, I would insist that the same standards be present."

The words and the incident were disturbing. Hammerman was obviously a forceful man, a man of some power, who, when angered, could move quickly. Even so, the city's jailers and juvenile justice administrators just as obviously failed to carry out the judge's orders. And the questions nag: How many kids had been locked away in the Baltimore city jail, without hearing, without trial; kids who had run away, who had skipped school and maybe gone joy-riding and who were then thrown in with young thieves and hoodlums, the innocent and the untried mixed with these youngsters who had already been judged and ordered to stand trial as adults? What happened to the innocent? In any jail? In any of the big kid prisons? In Sheridan or Elmira or Whittier or Mountain View?

As I began the task of learning more about the child-care systems and the juvenile justice systems, I was exposed to what seemed like an unending series of horror stories, and, almost unconsciously, I would hold each of them up and measure it against one place, Oak Creek Ranch. Oak Creek Ranch was one of the first case studies I had done after my initial newspaper exposé of the Kate School, and I was really unprepared for what I learned. What happened to children in Oak Creek was truly horrible and became something of a measure. Were there places that were worse?

Oak Creek Ranch was located in the hot, dry hills of Alameda County, east of San Francisco Bay. Licensed by the old Department of Mental Hygiene in early 1964, Oak Creek Ranch was a private, profit-making facility "planned and developed to create an environment where the retarded could live their lives as human beings." The words were from an old brochure in the state Licensing Department files. The four-acre "ranch" was located out in the country and was licensed to take in thirty-seven mentally retarded boys and young adults. It was operated by a husband and wife, who had a retarded child of their own. They charged $560 a month for board and care. Most of the children attended special-education classes in the public schools in the Castro Valley. The children and adolescents were placed in Oak Creek Ranch by several counties and regional centers. The San Francisco Department of Social Services (SFDSS) used the place most, sometimes assigning as many as sixteen San Francisco youngsters to Oak Creek Ranch at any one time. Between 1972 and 1975, their cases were supervised by Bernice Hendryx, an SFDSS social worker who also acted as an unpaid consultant to the owners of Oak Creek Ranch.

There was evidence in the records that two or three, maybe even four, of these San Francisco children were not retarded and should not have been placed in a facility licensed for retarded youngsters. One was a little five-year-old boy named Jacky. Teachers who worked with Jacky in special-education classes reported that they felt the boy was not retarded and had been misplaced. The picture of Jacky that emerges from these reports is of a very troubled young black boy who, according to one teacher, "is very definitely in need of warm affection and love. He would kiss staff on the hands frequently and manipulate staff's arms around his shoulders when he wanted to be hugged or given affection . . . I really feel he deserves the love and personal caring which only a home or foster home can provide."

Hendryx and her SFDSS superiors agreed to order psychological testing, and the school district psychologist reported: "Under the present [1973] institutional placement [Oak Creek Ranch], he receives no attention or training except during the three- or four-hour daily period the school district teachers work with him . . . Little positive contact is made with Jacky twenty out of the twenty-four hours . . . Placement in a more appropriate residential school where Jacky's potential could be realized is highly recommended."

For reasons that are not clear, Hendryx resisted these recommendations. In a letter to the supervisor of special education of the Castro Valley Unified School District, she said she felt there were dangers "inherent in any plan for immediate change for the boy" and advised that "extreme caution is a prerequisite in planning for any change." Jacky was left in Oak Creek Ranch. It was not a nice place to be, as court records and depositions and trial proceedings were later to establish. The children at Oak Creek were physically abused, struck, and spanked; they were strapped to their beds; some were caged for hours in an outdoor, wood-and-wire "time-out" booth; the toilets were kept locked most of the time so that patients could not foul them, and those youngsters — including Jacky — who urinated or defecated in their pants, or relieved themselves in a corner somewhere, were "toilet trained" by having their faces rubbed in their own excrement or by having their dirty underpants sacked over their heads.

Studying the records on these toilet-training episodes and on the use of the outdoor cage focused my attention on the case of another black youngster, Tyrone, who was older and more aggressive. Tyrone had been abandoned by his mother. There was no record of his father in the files of the San Francisco Department of Social Services. The records are sketchy: there is a 1956 birth certificate; some notes, by an intake worker, with an obscure reference to a cerebral palsy clinic; not much more. Tyrone, who is crippled, is labeled retarded, though other experts later would question that label. The youngster had been in and out of a half-dozen foster and group homes; then, in 1967, his SFDSS worker placed him in Oak Creek Ranch. Hendryx took over Tyrone's case — and the cases of fifteen other youngsters in Oak Creek Ranch — in 1972.

By this time, Tyrone was an extremely difficult youngster to handle. Because his body was badly deformed, he could not run, and one of his arms was withered and drawn. But he had one good arm, and he learned to throw and to strike back. In the abusive environment of Oak Creek Ranch, rage became his defense; his weapon was retribution. He learned to be manipulative. Once, in a fit of rage, he hurled his feces-encrusted underpants in the face of an attendant. In retaliation, she rubbed them in his face. The following morning, as punishment, Tyrone's good arm was bound to his waist, his dirty underpants were pulled down over his head, and attendants roughly threw him into the wood-and-wire cage and left him there most of the day. In a statement to authorities, one of the attendants explained, "I wanted the shorts to stay on him so that he would learn a lesson as far as the prior night was concerned. On that occasion he was in the booth about seven hours . . . These actions were to punish him for throwing [the shorts] at the housemother and also for training purposes . . . I liked Tyrone and wanted to do what I could to help him."

It was not the first time he had been caged. A log kept by the staff to record the use of the time-out cage shows Tyrone was caged for hitting staff members, for "messing his pants," for being "bad in school," for "causing trouble in the dining room"; and the duration of his confinement in the cage ranged from fifteen minutes to several hours. These records show that by 1975 his conduct was getting worse, that on successive days in January he had been "bad at school" and was kept locked in the cage all of one afternoon and all of the next day. By early summer, the school owners told Hendryx the boy had become so "assaultive and unmanageable" that they wanted him removed. Hendryx quickly agreed. She moved Tyrone to the nearby Alameda County Hospital and began the search for another placement. Tyrone had spent eight years in Oak Creek Ranch.

He was transferred to the county hospital in July. One month later, Richard Michaels, the Alameda County assistant district attorney — in a move that caught the school, Hendryx, and her SFDSS superiors and state licensing officials by surprise — filed a civil suit against Oak Creek

Ranch, alleging that the school owners and staff abused and mistreated children. Normally, in the scheme of community care, it is the Licensing Division that polices such facilities. And, routinely, social workers like Hendryx keep track of how their individual clients are being cared for and treated. For the district attorney to step in was unusual, but something had to be done. Michaels had received a tip from an employee of Oak Creek Ranch who had worked there a short time and quit because of the way patients were treated. She reported what she had seen to the sheriff, who contacted the district attorney.

Michaels discovered that the public files kept by the state licensing investigators revealed a pattern of complaints and suspicious happenings dating back to 1968, when a distraught mother had telephoned and written letters to the Golden Gate Regional Center — with copies to state licensing — to complain that she had found her eleven-year-old son tied to a bed, hand and foot, and left alone, even though he was terribly ill and running a temperature of 104°. No doctor had seen the boy. The Golden Gate Regional Center — one of twenty-one private, nonprofit corporations funded directly by the state to coordinate services for developmentally disabled people — had placed the boy, had found funding to pay for his care, and was supervising his treatment, in theory. Records show the regional center ordered Oak Creek's operators to provide medical attention, but did little else.

One of the senior GGRC executives told me, "Working with Oak Creek Ranch was not a partnership we liked," but he said the regional centers really had no authority to remove such youngsters just because parents complained. The center had placed a half-dozen youngsters in Oak Creek, he said, adding, "After all, the state Department of Health did license the place, and the state provides most of the money for placing youngsters there."

That was the single most often heard excuse. The State

of California, first through the old Department of Mental Hygiene and later through the Department of Health (DOH), had, year after year, continued to license places like Oak Creek Ranch, despite controversy, without resolving questions of abusive conduct. And the state licensing agents had a standard rejoinder: "If there was something wrong with the place, why did they put the kids in there? Why did they leave them there? Why didn't they call us?"

Complaints were made and investigated and forgotten. In 1972 a boy had drowned in a sandbox during a heavy rainstorm, in an inch or two of water. The boy had wandered out through a door that opened out, but was locked, so he could not get back in. It was a dark, stormy night. He was retarded and physically handicapped. No one heard his desperate attempts to get back in, and, hours later, he was found lying face down in the partly flooded sandbox. An accidental death.

I asked licensing evaluators if they had known about the use of the wood-and-wire time-out cage at Oak Creek, if they realized that school records showed Tyrone and other aggressive kids had routinely been locked up for hours on end. At first the bureaucrats tried to disclaim any knowledge of the cage; then one acknowledged that the department had gotten wind of the incident with Tyrone and the crusty underpants. A license evaluator had warned the school's operators that if they could not control the boy by other means, they should get rid of him. The school operators were also warned that they should never use the cage again, the supervisor told me, explaining, "Our [DOH] policy is to work with a facility, to help bring them into compliance."

Actually, every county or state official entering Oak Creek Ranch could have easily learned how often the cage had been used by inspecting the staff-kept log, in which hundreds of incidents were detailed, including time, date, and offense committed by the caged child. I asked how it was possible for the licensing evaluators to overlook the log, since the cage itself was there, in plain view. The supervisor explained, "That was an oversight. They [the inspectors] didn't check the log; that was an oversight."

Assistant District Attorney Michaels explained to me that he had filed the civil suit, using consumer fraud statutes, because it was the quickest and simplest way to get the case into court. The filing of the suit caused immediate political reactions. The state attorney general, acting on behalf of the Department of Health, began its own investigation, and shortly afterward filed suit to close the facility down. And Ed Sarsfield, then the newly appointed director of the San Francisco Department of Social Services, ordered the twelve San Francisco children then in Oak Creek to be removed. As Michaels was preparing for trial, he discovered that the owners of Oak Creek Ranch had destroyed a large number of documents recording the use of corporal punishment, the withholding of meals as punishment, and the use of both physical restraints and the time-out cage. Michaels had enough evidence to force the school's owners to admit legally, in a signed stipulation, that they had destroyed the records.

The case was heard before Alameda County Superior Court Judge William J. Hayes, early in 1976. As the case was laid out by Michaels, the horrors of Oak Creek Ranch were exposed to public view for the first time. Media accounts of the trial described the corporal punishment and the use of the cage, and expert witnesses testified that the school had no useful programs or activities for the children. One of the key witnesses was Bernice Hendryx, who was called by the defense. Earlier, in interviews with various San Francisco Bay Area newspaper and television reporters, Hendryx had staunchly defended Oak Creek Ranch, telling *San Francisco Examiner* reporter Don Martinez, "I would be guilty of gross dereliction of duty if I kept my kids at a place as described by the district attorney." She described the place as "more of a normal home than an institution." On the stand, directed by friendly defense counsel, Hendryx explained that not only did she have as many as sixteen San Francisco youngsters placed in Oak Creek Ranch, but she was also working as a special consultant to Oak Creek Ranch. With the permission of her superiors in the SFDSS, she acted as a social worker–consultant for Oak Creek Ranch on an unpaid basis. Hendryx testified that she and her immediate supervisor "mutually agreed that if I could help the ranch provide better services, it would benefit the children from San Francisco." In this capacity, and as a caseworker for certain children, she visited Oak Creek Ranch four to six times a month, staying several hours each time, sometimes eating lunch or dinner with the owners. On occasion she spent the night in their house. Her description of Oak Creek Ranch operations was benign; she had seen none of the excesses described in the accusations or the testimony presented by the district attorney. She had seen the wood-and-wire time-out cage used, but only briefly, and she felt it had been used properly.

Under lengthy cross-examination by Michaels, Hendryx revealed, sometimes unknowingly, a great deal about how the placement system itself worked.

MICHAELS: When you came to Oak Creek Ranch did you familiarize yourself with the laws that govern such a facility?

HENDRYX: No.

MICHAELS: Didn't you feel that that would be important to ascertain whether or not Oak Creek Ranch was a proper placement for some of your clients?

HENDRYX: Counselor, that is not my forte. If the State of California licenses a facility to care for mentally retarded people, I assume the state, you know, is right in this.

No mention was made of the several boys who had been

placed in Oak Creek Ranch even though experts believed they were not mentally retarded. As Michaels questioned her, Hendryx generally denied she had seen any of the alleged physical abuse or misconduct. Then he asked questions about how Tyrone had been bound and placed in the time-out cage with his dirty shorts tied over his head. Yes, she said, she had talked to the staff about that and she knew that Tyrone had thrown the dirty shorts in the face of the attendant and that the woman attendant "had become very upset and she had taken the same pair of underpants and after getting her face cleaned, she rubbed them in Tyrone's face." She knew that Tyrone had been caged following the episode, but she did not know any of the details. The episode did disturb her, she said.

Hendryx said she had not been informed of many of the other specific episodes that had been introduced at the trial; for example, she had not been told that the owner of the ranch had rubbed Jacky's face in his own feces. This question-and-answer exchange led into the subject of the five-year-old's placement in a facility for the retarded, and the fact that Hendryx disagreed with both the psychologist and the teacher who had recommended that Jacky be removed from Oak Creek Ranch and placed in a more appropriate facility. Hendryx became argumentative, contending that neither the psychologist nor the teacher knew what he or she was talking about.

At this point, Judge Hayes interrupted the proceedings, and in a most unusual sequence of questions — questions that sometimes took the form of an angry lecture — he cross-examined Hendryx. The San Francisco DPSS had ordered the psychological work-up on the boy, and the ensuing report had indicated that the boy was not retarded and was not receiving the kind of care and attention he needed, yet Hendryx disagreed with the report and the teacher's recommendation. Why? She said it was because the reports and recommendations were based on "assumptions" that she did not agree with. Finally, badgered by the judge, she helplessly explained, "I didn't have another facility to place him in, Your Honor."

The judge ordered her to produce records to show that she had tried to find another place for Jacky and couldn't. He lectured her sternly, and when she asked, "Your Honor, may I interject?" he snapped, "No, you may not!" Then, looking up at Michaels, he said, "Ask some more questions, please." But before Michaels could open his mouth, the judge was back at Hendryx: "You've been defensive all afternoon . . . Didn't you consider it a conflict of interest to be sleeping overnight with the principals who you had to evaluate to your department, accepting their hospitality?"

HENDRYX: No, I didn't.

THE COURT: You didn't?

HENDRYX: No.

As the trial was going on, the Department of Health's licensing computer automatically reissued the Oak Creek Ranch license. An embarrassed supervisor in the Licensing and Certification Division later explained how this was not only possible, but was *logical* in the fiscally conservative atmosphere created by Governor Jerry Brown. Even before Proposition 13 had been conceived, Brown had ordered all budgets cut. It was decided that, rather than have license evaluators check thousands of community-care facilities each year, the division would save time and money if the information could be stored in a computer and licenses be reissued automatically unless complaints had been filed during the previous year. In theory, county welfare departments, probation officers, and the two or three state agencies placing children in facilities like Oak Creek were keeping track of things, so there was no need to add to the confusing numbers of government workers already passing through each place. Some licensing evaluator jobs were eliminated; budgets were cut. Those evaluators who remained had case loads of 150 or more institutions, plus "new apps" to investigate. Since no complaints had been filed against Oak Creek Ranch with the Berkeley regional office of the DOH Licensing and Certification Division, the supervisor explained, the license was automatically renewed: "You don't dig if the license is ten years old; you only dig on a new license."

Judge Hayes ordered Oak Creek Ranch closed, and he fined the owners $57,000. The facility was put out of business by a civil court, not by the state regulatory agencies charged with the responsibility of licensing and quality control, or by the various agencies placing children in the school. The SFDSS executive director, Sarsfield, ordered Hendryx fired, over the protests of her attorney, who argued that she had become a scapegoat. She was a scapegoat. Whatever her faults, proven or unproven, no matter what the allegations, proven or unproven, Hendryx was forced to take the blame that should have rested in equal measure on all the bureaucratic components of the system. The state had continued to license the facility year after year; other county welfare departments and the Golden Gate Regional Center had placements in the facility and had social workers monitoring their cases; and Hendryx was only the agent of the San Francisco Department of Social Services, a social worker whose work was rated highly by her SFDSS supervisors. These supervisors within the SFDSS knew Oak Creek Ranch was a problem facility. One of them told me the department considered it an "end-of-the-line placement" for those young men and boys who were aggressive and had failed in other places. Both SFDSS and GGRC executives told me they had been actively trying to "upgrade" Oak Creek Ranch operations, but they loudly denied they knew the school was using abusive tactics. Then a welfare official said something truly frightening: *"On a scale of one to ten there were some things ten-ish about Oak Creek Ranch, but if you went to all mental retarded facilities as a layman, you would find some of this"*(emphasis added).

Oak Creek Ranch was closed, but that did little for youngsters, like Tyrone, who had grown to manhood there. Soon after Hendryx had taken him out of Oak Creek Ranch and had begun the process of finding another facility that would take this troublesome, troubled young man, his case was transferred from the SFDSS to the Golden Gate Regional Center. The transfer of jurisdiction did little to solve Tyrone's problems. He remained suspicious and aggressive. He would last a day or two in one place, a week in another. Always he ran away, was picked up. The GGRC's staff agreed that Tyrone needed very intensive case management by a trained GGRC social worker. Unfortunately, given the climate created by the order to cut budgets, this was not possible. The DOH funding for regional centers was so limited that the regional center had but one caseworker to handle 235 cases needing institutional care. Tyrone was one of the 235. He was placed in Napa, but refused to stay. He was placed in another state hospital and then another, but, because he was now twenty years old, California law did not allow him to be held against his will.

Each time he escaped or walked away, Tyrone returned to San Francisco and, after a day or two on the streets, would turn himself in to the San Francisco County Hospital psychiatric ward. The crippled young black man was thoroughly institutionalized: he had no concept of home, and, to him, the psychiatric ward in the county's hospital was where he felt most comfortable. Tyrone's caseworker at the GGRC asked the court for help, and a judge appointed a private attorney to help with the case. This lawyer soon became convinced that Tyrone was not retarded, but he said, "If no one takes care of him, he will end up down on Sixth Street [skid row], and I couldn't stand the thought of him down there. He would be victimized; he can't run and he can't fight, not out there, on the street."

Tyrone was put through a conservatorship hearing; he

was found to be gravely disabled and in need of specialized
treatment and care in one of the state's hospitals. The
judge signed the order committing Tyrone to the Stockton
State Hospital. By the time I had begun tracking his case,
Tyrone had been in the state hospital more than a year.
I asked for, and was granted, permission to visit him. The
hospital is huge. It sprawls over acres of manicured lawns
and shaded trees, a campus that was once considered a
model institution. At its peak, Stockton contained nearly
five thousand mental patients. Then progressive reforms
and fiscal conservatism were blended to create a policy of
deinstitutionalization; four thousand men, women, and
children were moved into community care, or simply returned "home," wherever and whatever home might be.
As a result, Stockton was ghostlike. As I walked through
the long corridors of the old, rambling hospital wings, ac-
companied only by the sound of my footsteps echoing, I
had the feeling the place was empty, abandoned. There
were fewer than one thousand "clients" here; all who were
left were the most seriously disturbed, the most severely
handicapped, the most unwanted and unacceptable.

Tyrone was in a special, second-floor ward with twenty-
eight other "high-functioning" adolescent males, some of
whom were "moderately" retarded. This was a locked
"secure" ward for the fourteen- to twenty-four-year-old
aggressive patients who were sometimes violent. A staff
person met me at the locked doors and, after I identified
myself, admitted me. It was near noon, and some of the
patients were milling about the hallway, waiting for lunch
to be set up in the small, prisonlike dining room just off
the corridor. When the staff person and I passed by, two
of the youths came up to us quickly, smiling, asking questions, seeking attention, touching. The staff person was at
ease with them, easily answering their questions, joking
and calling them by name. He spotted Tyrone and called
him over, introducing us. It was an awkward moment: I

had reached out to shake Tyrone's hand and at the same instant I saw that his right arm was withered and badly deformed. If he noticed my embarrassment, it didn't show. He smiled, genuinely pleased to have a visitor. We started down the hall, toward a small office within the unit. Tyrone limped badly, his whole body lurching sideways to compensate for his crooked, short right leg. As we walked, Tyrone asked questions about how a journalist worked and about the book; what it would say. During our interview, it became obvious to me that Tyrone was not retarded mentally, at least not as retarded as the early reports indicated. He was putting thoughts together, slowly working the words through the muscular dysfunctions of his face and mouth, moving his head in little, sideways jerks as he forced words into sentences.

I asked if he remembered Oak Creek Ranch. At the mention of the name, he reared back convulsively: "Oh, my God! Yes." His words were explosive, tumbling over each other; his face twisted as he concentrated on getting the words out faster: "Th-th-they pi-pi-picked on me, treat-ted me like a dog. Di-didn't giii-ve me eee-nough to eat."

Did he remember anything about the place? Yes, he recalled his mother once came to visit, that she had taken him out for a drive on his birthday. Suddenly, without warning, Tyrone switched the subject. He told me that if he were a mother or a father, he would get his son out of Stockton; he would send him to another treatment program. "Thii-is i-i-isn't ah, ah, nice pl-ay-ce."

The change of subject had been so abrupt, I was confused. With great concentration, he tried to explain again that he did not like the Stockton State Hospital or the special ward. I encouraged him to go on, but once more he quickly changed the subject. Later, after I'd said goodbye and had returned to the ward's main office, I met with a psychologist who had been working with Tyrone. I asked if what had happened to the youngster had had any lasting effect. The psychologist looked as if he didn't understand what I was saying. So I asked if he knew about Oak Creek and how Tyrone had been treated. He shook his head. No. I explained how the boy had been tied, how his dirty shorts had been pulled over his head and he had been caged. The psychologist shook his head in disbelief. Nothing like that appeared in the boy's case file, yet obviously such treatment would have a great effect on behavior. It simply wasn't mentioned.

I asked what Tyrone's prognosis was, and the psychologist explained that the youth was emotionally disturbed, manipulative, and that he appeared to be quite a knowledgeable person for someone who had been labeled developmentally disabled. Then he added, "I think there is hope for him. He can change, but it's going to take a lot of individual, one-on-one effort."

The special adolescent unit was designed to take such cases, and as the psychologist talked about the program, it sounded as if, finally, Tyrone was where he could be helped. In the late 1970s the program cost $91 a day, or about $33,000 a year, per patient. That *was* expensive, but after so many years of abandonment and mistreatment, Tyrone was at last getting the individualized, intensive treatment he needed. Right?

No. He was not. Although the program was well designed, it was very short of funds. The unit was so shorthanded, it could provide little more than custodial care and some generalized treatment. Tyrone was not getting individualized care; the Brown era of limited expectations would simply not provide the dollars.

## 3

# Building the House of Mirrors

FROM HIS FIRST BREATH, Oliver was a pauper, born in an almshouse. Before he was a day old, he was an orphan. He was given a name and was transferred by the keepers of the parish poorhouse to a private home that was under contract to the parish to care for twenty or thirty dependent children. This was a group home, operated by one Mrs. Mann, "*a woman of wisdom and experience; she knew what was good for the children and she had a very accurate perception of what was good for herself. So she appropriated the greater part of the weekly stipend to her own use and consigned the rising parochial generation to even a shorter allowance than was originally provided them.*"

Mrs. Mann was in the kid business. By crowding more orphans into her home, by skimping on food and limiting the services, she could increase the profits, but not without some problems: "... *for at the very moment when a child had contrived to exist upon the smallest possible portion of the weakest possible food, it did perversely happen in eight and a half cases out of ten either that it sickened from want and cold or fell into the fire from neglect or got half smothered by accident; in any one of which cases the miserable little being was usually summoned into another world.''*

The words of Charles Dickens, written a century and a half ago, create an uncanny sense of déjà vu, a time warp. The institutions of Dickens' London blur and come into focus again in New Orleans or Boston, Chicago or Los Angeles; children banished to the emotional and economic wastelands of public institutions or consigned to private care for a profit, children abused, neglected, starving; the welfare bureaucracies working with the courts and the entrepreneurs, all in the name of charity and in the best interest of the children, of course.

*"The trustees are very sage, deep, philosophical men; and when they came to turn their attention to the workhouse they found at once what ordinary folks would never have discovered . . . the poor people liked it. It was a regular place of public entertainment for the poorer classes; a tavern where there was nothing to pay; a public breakfast, dinner, tea and supper all the year round; a brick and mortar elysium where it was all play and no work. 'Oh-ho!' said the board, looking very knowing, 'We are the fellows to set this to rights; we'll stop it all in no time!' So they established the rule that all poor people would have the alternative — for they could compel nobody, not they — of being starved by gradual process in the house or by quick one out of it."*

The Christian work ethic was the cornerstone of the society; even the smallest children learned to work. In the group home, toddlers learned to toil as they learned to walk; by the time children were eight or nine, they were back in the workhouse. There the orphans labored in the mill and received but one porringer of gruel, no more. In the well-known dining hall scene, Oliver Twist is selected by lot to confront the establishment: *"Child as he was, he was desperate with hunger and reckless with misery. He rose from the table, and advancing to the master, basin*

*and spoon in hand, somewhat alarmed at his own temerity:
'Please, sir, I want some more.'* "

The words brought the system to a standstill. No one
had previously dared question the orderly processes; routine was destroyed; power was usurped and had to be
quickly restored. Oliver was banished, then flogged daily
as a warning to other upstarts. No hint of rebellion was
to be tolerated; every act of insubordination, no matter
how small, had to be repressed. And each succeeding act
of repression became the foundation upon which the next
was built.

Year by year the process grew and spread, across the
Atlantic, into the colonies, into the West, until finally, in
1970, a state bureaucrat in Texas could seriously explain
under oath why a teen-aged boy had been locked in a tiny
prison cell and tear-gased: "You cannot permit any [child]
to completely refuse to carry out his assignment . . . you
cannot permit mutiny or complete disruption of everything
. . . we will not and cannot tolerate one youngster completely disrupting a large group."

Dissent is not tolerated. Disobedience is punished. Rebellion is suppressed. When kids like Oliver earn a troublemaker's reputation, they are transferred, pushed out,
banished. But the trustees and the parish beadle — pred-
ecessor to the public social worker — had a problem. Oliver
was small, so employers in need of an indentured boy were
not attracted. The trustees finally offered five pounds ster-
ling as a subsidy to any tradesman who would take Oliver
off the public dole and promise to "train him up" in honest
labor and Christian piety. A taker was found, and the lad
was hauled into court to have the process officially approved. The magistrate completely disrupted the process
by showing some compassion. He ordered that Oliver be
taken back to the orphans' quarters in the workhouse and
there be treated decently. The bureaucrats obeyed, but
they were not to be denied. Soon they found a coffin-maker

who needed money to pay off his debts, and Oliver was indentured. As the little boy was led away by Beadle Bumble, he began to cry, and Bumble hushed him, accusing him of being ungrateful.

" 'No, no sir!' sobbed Oliver, clinging to the hand which held the well-known cane. 'No sir, I will be good indeed, indeed I shall sir. I am a very little boy sir, and it is so, so . . .'

" 'So what?' inquired Mr. Bumble in amazement.

" 'So lonely, sir, so very lonely!' cried the child. 'Everybody hates me. Oh, sir, don't, pray don't be cross with me!' The child beat his hand upon his heart and looked in his companion's face with tears of real agony."

Oliver the ingrate, the troublemaker. Pulled deeper and deeper into the nightmare of his own life, Oliver the victim of a brutish system, roughed up by the coppers, thrown in a dungeon, summoned before another magistrate, only to have this curmudgeon convict and sentence him in a wink, despite his innocence, despite the pleas for leniency by the complaining shopkeeper.

Dickens wrote to expose the excesses of the child-care systems of early nineteenth-century England, but some passages from *Oliver Twist* read like descriptions of the child-care systems I was finding in the United States during the last quarter of the twentieth century. During the past 150 years, the basic structure of the house of mirrors had changed but little; the haphazard design had been transported across the Atlantic, virtually intact. Once set in place in the colonies, additions were made to this basic structure, expanding and adapting it to local custom and need. To understand what was happening in the United States it was necessary for me to understand something of the English systems, and this search for some historical perspective led to the very roots of capitalism and the Industrial Revolution.

Traditionally, the churches had cared for the needy, doling out bread, providing shelter and clothing. But these forms of outdoor relief were overwhelmed as the Middle Ages came to an end and the feudal economic system gave way under the pressures of expanding trade. Europe and England were caught up in a series of power struggles as empires were expanded, new trade routes and colonies established. Families who had once been tied to the land either escaped or were pushed off the land and out of the villages that had grown up around the manor or castle. A large, floating lower-class population was created, and social forces pushed it out of the countryside and onto the highways. Peasants, yeomen, artisans, and tradesmen, no longer protected servants of the landlord, had to compete for work that was often seasonal. Economic depressions were common; unemployment was frequently high. People worked when they could, starved when they could find no jobs. Without food or money, the rootless, unemployed mobs rioted. Petty crime and begging were chronic problems.

As a result, governments on the continent and in England began to experiment with forms of public relief. By 1597, Queen Elizabeth and Parliament created the first of the Poor Laws to secularize charity. A poor tax was levied against property values to subsidize public relief. Each parish was authorized to construct an almshouse that would include a place of manufacture, a workhouse. The impoverished were to be gathered into institutional care and set to useful work to help pay for their keep. Each parish was made responsible for the paupers within its boundaries, and by 1662 the poor were required to establish an official residence within a given parish as a condition of receiving welfare. Without such an established residence, there was no relief. These English common laws were broadly cast directives, written to give the local parish bureaucracies as wide discretion as possible. Welfare was a local matter, to be adapted to the needs of local industry. The residency laws were crucial, because they held the workers in place during times of unemployment. From the outset, welfare benefits were designed as a subsidy benefiting entrepreneurs.

England, rich in the resources of her colonial empire, was becoming the dominant world power. But the expanding British economy was stifled by a system of manufacture that depended on small workshops and cottage assembly systems, where the entrepreneur provided individual families with the resources and they labored in their own homes to turn out finished products. The system was profitable but inefficient. With the development of the steam engine came the source of power needed to industrialize. Using invested capital, manufacturers built mills and factories, equipped them with labor-saving machines, and hired unskilled workers to tend them. Worker productivity, in terms of pounds invested, soared. But the system was predicated on the availability of large supplies of cheap labor as needed. If the managers of invested capital could maintain an oversupply of workers, wages could be kept low and profits would be guaranteed. The Poor Laws were used to ensure an available supply of workers; benefits were kept below prevailing wages; and residency laws, requiring unemployed workers to remain in their local parish if they were to receive aid, were enforced. The outdoor relief and the almshouse operations were run by the church administrators, through the local parish hierarchy. The parish collected the poor tax, and the church wardens dispensed the aid and were the overseers of the poor.

There were obvious problems with this marriage of the newly emerging capitalistic system and the Christian church; the exploitation of the work force created social problems that could not be hidden. The system was harsh, especially on children. They were put to work at an early age — in the coal mines, where they were harnessed to ore cars, in the mills and factories. The combination of low wages and periodic unemployment left families destitute. Many never earned enough to survive; malnutrition, sickness, job-related injuries all led to horrible living conditions and early death. It was impossible to deny the misery and deprivation. Seen in the full light of its ugliness, the workings of the Industrial Revolution conflicted with the expressed moral values of Christianity, so artful hypocrisies were fashioned into a welfare mythology. The Protestant Reformation, and the rise of Calvinism and similar sects, provided the rationale for these myths. The virtues of hard work, sobriety, and thrift were extolled. Wealth was the reward of hard work; poverty was the sign of failure. The poor were flawed people, to be pitied and, when they were in dire need, to be made the recipients of Christian charity. To be charitable was to be virtuous. However, caution was required. Pauperism was an infectious disease, recognized by its symptoms: laziness, deceit, intemperance, improvidence, extravagance, and an appetite for the sexual vices. The dole was an infectious agent that led to pauperism. No man, woman, or child could receive something he or she had not worked for without losing some self-respect, without suffering some moral decay. Charity had to be used wisely, judiciously, and with reservation.

Because welfare recipients were public wards, they had to qualify for relief. If, in the process, these recipients were manipulated by the beadles and the bureaucrats to the advantage of industry, it was only to help them better themselves. If they were forced off the public dole and back into the labor market by short rations and hunger, so much the better for both the indolent recipient and for society. Children were caught up in the system, as members of recipient families, as orphans, as hungry, displaced persons. If a child's father was judged a drunk and a pauper, no aid was given the family, on the theory that the pressures of hunger and privation would force the errant father to find work. No matter that he was crippled or sick or alcoholic, or that there was no work available. Children were caught up in the system because child labor was an exploited resource of industry. Children in the mines, textile mills, and factories worked for long hours at extremely low pay. If a child's parent was injured or sickened and died, as was frequently the case, the child's life, the lives of his brothers and sisters, disintegrated into despair and horrible circumstance. The children either roamed the streets or were placed in an almshouse, there to be worked, or they were "bound out" by contract, indentured to work for a family or a tradesman until their majority. In theory, the overseers of the poor and the courts had an obligation to inspect each child's situation to see if he or she was, in fact, being treated well and was being "trained up" in proper fashion. This seldom was the case.

Children were used to supply the labor needs of the expanding New England colonies. As early as 1619, officials of the Virginia Colony were writing officers of their parent company in England asking that one hundred pauper children twelve years or older be shipped out to them. The primary need was for workers, but a façade of Christian charity was laid over this harsh fact. In their letter, the Virginia colonists concluded ". . . the city [of London] deserveth thanks and commendations for redeeming so many poor souls from misery and ruin." The redeemed children were Oliver's predecessors, the children of the streets, cast adrift by poverty and circumstance, exploited by the economic system that could squeeze yet a bit more profit out of their miserable condition.

The street children of London and other European cities were valuable because they could be indentured in the colonies; they were literally snatched off the streets by kidnapers working on commission, loaded on board trading vessels, and hauled to the New World, where they were auctioned off or bound out by contract. The children were chattels; they had no rights, no guarantees, no protections under the law on either side of the Atlantic. An unruly child could be whipped, banished, sold, abandoned, even put to death. Whether or not the one hundred teen-agers abducted to the Virginia Colony were better off for the experience may be open to argument, but certainly the practice of kidnaping children off the streets of London provided no solution for the problems that put the children on the streets in the first place.

Through the colonial processes, the Poor Laws and the welfare systems of England and, to a lesser extent, of Europe were transported here. And from the outset, those laws and systems, once set down, were adapted to meet the peculiar customs and needs of the colonies. In Massachusetts, there was a concern that paupers would raise their children to be paupers. Laws were passed to allow the Overseer of the Poor to inspect poor families to make certain they were not neglecting their children. If the family was found wanting, indolent, or negligent in its Christian duties, the parents could be taken before the magistrate and publicly censured; their children could be taken away and placed elsewhere, in more "suitable" surroundings. Children twelve or older were bound out to be worked. If younger, the local government or parish would place them in subsidized foster care.

Baltimore city officials combined the almshouse and the poor farm on three hundred acres just outside the urban area. The institution contained an infirmary for the sick and the insane, a workhouse, and an asylum for destitute children. New York City's almshouse was a four-story structure that contained a penitentiary, a hospital, a large manufacturing room, and great dormitories, where as many as two thousand men, women, and children lived in crowded misery. In rural areas, two or more counties might combine to build a common almshouse, or local government would contract for institutional care, rather than have to pay the cost of construction and operation. In some areas, private entrepreneurs provided public welfare, for a profit. The results were predictable: the county or city paid less for the care of the indigents, and the paupers ate less and were worked harder. Although attempts were made in some of the larger, more progressive institutions to separate the children, the insane, and the mentally retarded, most almshouse populations were thrown together indiscriminately.

By the early nineteenth century, conditions in such institutions had become notorious. Children were being mistreated, worked hard by unscrupulous operators. The New York State legislature investigated the county almshouses in the 1850s and found that they were poorly built, poorly arranged, poorly warmed, and poorly ventilated. In one county, nearly a third of the paupers had died the previous year due to "inexcusable negligence." In two other counties, the private contractors providing institutional care for paupers were found to have serious conflicts of interest; each contractor was in the employ of the county in question as its Overseer of the Poor. Each was administering his own contract, fixing his own profits, and all the while collecting salary as a public official representing the public interest. The legislative committee reported: "Common domestic animals are usually more humanely provided for . . . the children are poorly fed, poorly clothed and quite untaught . . . the poor idiot is half starved and beaten with rods because he is too dull to do his master's bidding . . ." The committee recommended that all children be removed from the almshouses and that they be placed in private, subsidized orphan asylums.

Reformers like Dorothea L. Dix worked tirelessly to expose the horrors of the almshouses and to bring about change. Finally, in 1854, Congress authorized the granting of several million acres of federal lands to the states for the purpose of subsidizing the construction of "comfortable," inexpensive asylums for the feeble-minded and the insane. But the legislation was not popular. And President

Franklin Pierce vetoed the measure, contending that if the federal government subsidized construction of public institutions for the insane, it would then have to subsidize the "whole field of public beneficence"; thus, the federal government would become the "great almoner" of public welfare. Pierce argued that such was not the proper jurisdiction of the federal government, but was the right and the duty of state and local governments. This states' rights argument dominated the child-welfare system, dominates the system even now.

Slowly, through the last half of the 1800s, the problems of indigent children were being separated from those of adults, state by state, county by county, with no two agencies setting about the task in quite the same way. Foster-care systems were begun, orphanages were constructed, special institutions for the blind, the deaf, and the feeble-minded were developed. The juvenile justice system was separated from the adult courts, and a separate and unique juvenile court was created. All of this progress was seen as the natural evolution of a single legal theory, *parens patriae,* which had been articulated as early as 1772 in the English Court of Chancery. That court, as keeper of the Great Seal, was assumed to have the power to exercise the ancient prerogative of the Crown to care for and protect the property of orphaned heirs. On the death of the lord of a freehold estate, the king could step in and act as the protector of the child's heritage, in effect to act as the child's parent. Over the centuries this theory was stretched to allow government to act as parent in all matters, and by 1828 the Court of Chancery was directly involved in the lives of children, orphaned or not, acting "in their best interest," as interpreted by the judges. The theory was incorporated into the court systems in the colonies, and, following the Revolution, into the legal systems of the United States. But it wasn't until the 1890s, and the creation of the first juvenile courts, that it was carried to its ultimate extremes. The juvenile courts from the start began exercising very broad authority over children's lives in both civil and criminal matters. Acting under *parens patriae*, judges, social workers, and probation officers have taken children from their homes and placed them in foster care or institutions or kid prisons, all without due process, without hearings or trials.

The Industrial Revolution quickly took hold in the United States, and the expanding industrial output created a demand for more and more unskilled workers. Waves of immigrants swept onto the eastern shores, lured by the possibilities of factory jobs or homesteads on the frontiers. The immigrants overwhelmed the job markets, settled into the burgeoning urban slums, and were trapped by poverty. They crowded into tiny one- and two-room flats or derelict hotels. Unable to find work for more than a few days at a time, unable to hold their jobs if they got sick, because others were immediately recruited to take their place, drinking too much, suffering too much, the families endured as best they could. Thousands of children were running in the streets, begging, stealing, shining shoes, selling newspapers — anything to help the family survive or to break away and make it on their own. Children as young as ten and twelve were routinely employed in even the most hazardous jobs. Injury and death were commonplace.

Historically, these indigent families and their children have been the subject of debates in the liberal parlors and legislative cloakrooms: Was it wise and prudent to remove children from such circumstances? Shouldn't they be placed in good Christian homes, where they could receive a sense of morality and be taught the value of work? Was such charity the proper jurisdiction of government, or should it be left to the churches? These issues have never been fully resolved. Within the uneasy mixture of public and private welfare there exists a debate begun with the Elizabethan secularization of charity and the institution of poor taxes. The focus of that debate is whether it is better to use *outdoor relief* to provide assistance to a child or a family in its own home or to place the child, even the entire family, in *institutional care*. Outdoor relief, in the form of cash grants or food, clothing, and subsidized shelter, gives the welfare agency less control over the recipients, but institutional care allows for a more "efficient" gathering of recipients into one facility where they can be aided and reformed at the same time.

No federal policies were developed to help state and local governments resolve these issues. In England and the United States, the matter of how the indigent, the unemployed, the handicapped, and the emotionally disturbed children — and their families — were to be treated was left entirely up to local officials, public and private. Along the eastern seaboard the child-welfare programs were dominated by Catholic and Protestant churches, by synagogues and philanthropic groups. Among the hierarchies of these religious and philanthropic organizations there was a fierce determination not to give up their charitable functions. It was all right for government to subsidize charity, but its functions within the field of welfare should be limited. In cities like New York, the so-called voluntary agencies developed orphanages, foster homes, homes for the retarded and the insane. Each institution was licensed by the state Board of Charities, but the placement of children and the supervising of their care rested with the New York City Department of Charities. By 1914, the city was paying out $5 million a year for out-of-home child care. But with the licensing and placement functions divided between the state and the city, problems developed. In theory, the state set licensing standards and enforced them; in fact, city inspectors reported, "We found that conditions in some of the institutions bearing the certificate of approval of the State Board of Charities were such as to be little less than a scandal and disgrace. Beds were alive with vermin . . .

antiquated methods of punishment prevailed . . . children
were disgracefully overworked and underfed.''

The city began to impose its own set of standards, refusing to place children in a facility that inspectors did not
approve, even though it had been licensed by the state.
This, in turn, imposed more problems. From the very outset the voluntary agencies had never provided enough beds
for all of the children New York City placement workers
had to care for, so the city had to develop its own sup-
plementary foster-care network. By the 1870s, there were
an estimated fourteen thousand children living in private
"lodging houses." These foster homes were subsidized
either through direct cash grants or, more commonly,
through contracts of indenture. A family could take a very
small child with the stipulation that as the child grew, he
or she could be worked. Problems were inevitable. In the
spring of 1874, the *New York Times* exposed the pathetic
story of Mary Ellen.

Mary Ellen had been placed with foster parents by the
Department of Charities when she was eighteen months
old. Records showed that, even though she was only an
infant, her placement had been made by a contract of indenture that bound her to the service of the foster parents
until she was eighteen years old. Mary Ellen was regularly
beaten and abused; she slept on a small rug on the floor.
When the girl was eight, a neighbor reported the child's
mistreatment to authorities. Charges of felonious assault
were lodged against the foster mother. During the trial it
was revealed that the Department of Charities had several
hundred children similarly placed, but the department social workers never checked to see how the children were
faring. By the terms of the indenture contract, all that the
foster parents were required to do was report twice a year
on the child's condition and progress. Other than demanding these brief, self-serving reports, the government
took no further interest in the child.

The exposé brought a flurry of reform, but neither the exposé nor the reforms did much to resolve the long-standing problems within the child-care systems. The separation of licensing and placement functions, the selectivity of the voluntary agencies, the lack of supervision and accountability in city-operated foster-care programs, were all symptoms of the basic flaws in the fundamental structure and subsequent patchwork additions. And these weren't the only flaws; there was another: no one wanted to take in the street children, like Oliver Twist. The voluntary agencies and city foster homes shut their doors to delinquents, to mentally retarded or emotionally disturbed children, who had to be cared for in city- or state-built institutions. New York even built a special orphanage for black children. These institutions had been designed for the care of children who had special needs, but they were never fully financed or staffed, and often were little better than ugly warehouses.

In cities and counties across the country, the mixture of private, voluntary agencies, city- or county-run foster care, and government-operated institutions was different only in degree; the basic problems were the same. The systems, operating more or less independently of each other, were frequently at odds. The competition for funding and the inconsistencies in the regulations and procedures created an abrasive system that ground up children. Reforms were attempted. In 1880, the Massachusetts legislature established a $2.00 per day board and care subsidy for foster care that would allow social workers to take children out of such institutions and place them in foster homes. This was one of the earliest recorded attempts to "deinstitutionalize" the care of children in need.

The period between 1870 and 1925 was one of the darkest in the turbulent history of child care and welfare because of the rapacious expansion of industrial output, the unchecked growth of a virulent form of capitalism that used

people in the most exploitative ways. By 1900 there were
1.7 million children between the ages of ten and fifteen
years at work on the farms, in the mines, factories, and
mills. Progressives and muckraking journalists were exposing the awful working conditions in the factories and
the living conditions in the slums. The reformers called for
a six-day work week, an eight-hour day, minimum wages,
workmen's compensation and health insurance programs,
the abolition of child labor, and unemployment insurance
programs.

Through the first decade of the twentieth century, a
movement was started to provide more direct outdoor relief, including widows' pensions, in an effort to keep families together. Such programs were strenuously resisted by
conservatives, by politicians, by theologians, and by the
administrators of established charities, who argued that
such liberalization of the welfare laws would weaken the
moral fiber of the nation and reduce recipients to the status
of permanent paupers. The wisdom of those opposing
mothers' pensions held that it was better to remove a child
from a destitute home than to provide unearned income.
In 1913, a New York State legislative investigation revealed
that there were 3716 children in foster-care institutions of
various kinds simply because their mothers could not afford
to keep them at home. Such facts were used to help pass
the New York State Child Welfare Act of 1915, thus clearing the way for counties to implement mothers' pensions.
By 1925, a total of forty states had adopted or were adopt-
ing similar laws.

When it was obvious they were losing the battle, the
conservative politicians, the professional social workers
who dominated the staffing of voluntary agencies and were
moving into government jobs, and others opposed to such
liberal programs, used a fall-back position: they successfully installed a whole series of qualifying criteria. Mothers'
pensions were not to be pensions at all; they were qualified

subsidies. Women who applied for and were granted these subsidies had their "cases" supervised. Since they were paupers, leading lazy, deceitful, intemperate, improvident, inefficient, extravagant, sexually promiscuous lives, society's interests had to be protected. Recipients were not to be trusted.

Mothers' pensions became common, direct governmental subsidies to one-parent families. But the out-of-home care of children remained primarily within the grasp of the private charitable organizations. Governments could build institutions for the young criminals, for the mentally handicapped, for the crippled and unwanted, but the care of homeless normal children was the closely guarded jurisdiction of charity, as long as the government would subsidize that care.

As the economy crashed into the Depression of the 1930s, unemployment and starvation were problems so large that no single state could handle the burden. Families were being torn apart. It was in this crisis that the first federalized Mothers' Pension Act — called Aid to Dependent Children (ADC) — was passed in 1935. Because welfare was considered the constitutional prerogative of state and local governments, the Congress devised a grant-in-aid system that provided the states with federal assistance, but only if the states, at their individual option, agreed to abide by some very general federal standards. The system was still controlled by state and local government. The infusion of ADC funds into the lives of disintegrating families was dramatic. In 1933, it was estimated that there were between 140,000 and 200,000 children in foster care. By 1938, the numbers were radically reversed, fewer children were in foster care, and it was estimated that 250,000 families were receiving ADC funds. Juvenile courts and social workers were no longer so quick to take children from fatherless homes. By 1950, there were only 100,000 children in foster care. ADC — later to be called

Aid to Families of Dependent Children (AFDC) — had a dramatic impact on single-parent homes; however, it did little to change the basic foster-care system. No federal funds were available to subsidize any form of foster care. State and local child-welfare problems were on the increase. The post–World War II baby boom and the rapid expansion of technology in the postindustrial society created damaging social and economic pressures on the family; the American peasants — blacks from the agrarian South, Puerto Ricans, and the poor whites from Appalachia — were dislocated, crowded into urban slums without the skills needed to compete in an already crowded job market. Just as the European and, later, the Mexican immigrants had existed in tiny, cold-water flats in decaying neighborhoods, these newer immigrants struggled for survival. Such desperate circumstances fractured thousands of families. The numbers of single-parent families on welfare were increasing, the declining trends in foster care became reversed, and by 1965 an estimated 287,000 children had been forced from their homes and were in foster care. By 1980, the number had increased to somewhere between 500,000 and 700,000; no one was certain of the total.

The rapid growth in these numbers was due in part to expanding populations, in part to increasing stresses on family structures, in part to the liberalization of government assistance programs for children. Some of these changes were mandated by new laws that qualified children who had been placed out of their own homes for federal foster-care funds, or laws that liberalized health-care programs to include aid to the mentally retarded and the emotionally disturbed children; some of the changes were due to litigation brought on behalf of specific clients, suits that resulted in radical changes in the laws as they had been interpreted. Children, the courts decided, had the right to individualized treatment according to need, and that treatment had to be provided in the "least restrictive" setting consistent with their needs. Each change, each new and expanded program, brought in more children, and with the growing numbers there were greater pressures on the bureaucratic structures of government. And there were crosscurrents. While the Congress and state legislatures might be pressured politically to be more liberal in their approach to the needs of foster care on a national basis, the local political and economic forces at the state and county levels created countervailing pressures.

At each step of the way conservatives worked against any liberalization of the welfare laws, including those reforms which would have increased aid to children. Even though it had been demonstrated that AFDC reduced the number of children in out-of-home placement by keeping them in their own homes, any increase in aid or services to the family has been strenuously resisted. And it is here, in these arguments and the resulting legislation, that the fossilized forms of the Elizabethan Poor Laws and the hypocrisies of welfare mythology are found. In the 1960s — three hundred years after the first residency laws were adopted in England — most states in this country would not help transient pauper families. Only the resident poor could receive assistance. What aid was available was geared to the local economies and the local wage structures. A comparison of the federal AFDC programs in the industrialized Northeast and in the rural South in the 1970s revealed that where industrial wages were high, AFDC benefits were relatively high. In New Jersey, where trade unions had long ago established a strong influence, the average AFDC family in 1971 was receiving $347 a month. In rural Mississippi, where workers were unorganized and wages were low, the AFDC family averaged $69 a month. A decade later, a General Accounting Office investigator reported a family of four in Jackson, Mississippi, was receiving $120 a month, plus food stamps, while the same family living in San Francisco would receive $487, plus food stamps.

Historically, in liberal states such as California, benefits seemed high by comparison, but the state's employers had imposed enough political regulations over the years to ensure that their workers would not lie around on welfare when they were needed in the work place. For example, in the 1950s California had both a residency requirement that kept the unemployed workers from leaving their "home" county and an "employability" standard that prohibited county welfare departments from giving relief to a family if there were any employable workers in that family. Use of this standard reached outrageous proportions in California's San Joaquin Valley. Mechanization of cotton harvesting had eliminated the fall and winter cotton-picking that once sustained eighteen thousand workers, giving them almost enough money to survive until spring farm work opened up. In the winter of 1958–59, heavy rains stopped all farm work. By spring, the families were literally starving, and spring work was delayed by the unseasonably wet year. The migrant farm-worker families had no money, no food; no work was available. In Tulare County — the third richest farming county in the nation — the welfare director ruled that because these workers were "employable," they were not eligible for aid, not even for the federal surplus food that had been warehoused for just such emergencies. Thousands of men, women, and children were hungry. Mothers were feeding infants sugar-water formulas, or boiling weeds and making potato-peel soup. A nineteen-year-old boy quit eating so that his eleven brothers and sisters would have something. His selfless act was discovered only when he collapsed and had to be taken to the county hospital. Only after a newspaper exposed what was happening did the local Board of Supervisors discover that it had had the authority all along to provide food for hungry people. The supervisors ordered the welfare director to open the warehouses filled with federal surplus commodities and feed the people.

Letting families starve because there was an employable

person in the family — even though no work was available — made no sense at all. The county did not have to pay for the federal surplus food. And Congress had made available a subsidized AFDC-Unemployment option available to states that would have provided aid to such families. However, it wasn't until 1965 that California included the AFDC-U provisions in its welfare programs. Even so, California was considered progressive. Most states rejected the option. As late as 1980 only twenty-eight states were providing AFDC-U benefits and then only if the families were truly needy. The historic concepts of providing public assistance only to the *truly needy* has its roots in the Poor Laws and remains an integral part of our national attitude toward the poor. As Ronald Reagan began his first term in the presidency he maintained his radical budget-cutting proposals would not harm those who were truly in need. Of course, he reserved the right to decide who was truly in need and then he was asking the Congress to help him make sure the poor worked for their welfare.

The task of trying to sort through the welfare system to get some concept not only of how it worked, but why it worked in such irrational ways, was frustrating. Even at the highest levels of government and in the Congress, those who genuinely wanted to bring about change, who were concerned about the serious and very obvious problems, could not find answers. For example, in 1975 Harrison Williams of New Jersey, then chairman of the U.S. Senate Labor Committee, and Walter Mondale, then chairman of the Subcommittee on Children and Youth, were worried about what was happening in federally subsidized foster care. According to Williams, "Programs for children are scattered among a variety of agencies. Joint actions among these agencies is the exception  . . one impact of this administrative fragmentation has been the very serious diminution of child welfare programs in the states . . ."

Williams asked Mondale to hold investigative hearings

to learn: How many children were in foster care? What were the costs? How effective were the programs? At Mondale's request, the Department of Health, Education, and Welfare sent over expert witnesses. The first HEW expert testified that "about" $700 million was being spent on foster care and "approximately" $500 million of this was federal money. There were "*about*" 350,000 children involved. The answers were troublesome, both because they were imprecise and because they conflicted with HEW's written responses to Mondale's questions prior to the hearings.

Mondale was getting the bureaucratic run-around, and he knew it. He asked for a more precise set of figures. A senior HEW expert fielded the questions and was off and running through the bureaucratic brambles, explaining this program and that regulation, carrying the subject beyond confusion into absurdity. Some of foster care was funded under one program, some under another. There were no totals, no summations. Mixed in with foster-care programs were Medicaid funds, special-education funds, programs for the developmentally disabled. To make the situation more confusing, there was within the HEW lexicon an ever-changing pattern of argot and acronym; nothing remained the same for long. One year there were programs for the Severely Emotionally Disturbed — called *Ess-Eee-Dees* — and the next the same recipients were renamed Minimal Brain Damaged and called *Emm-Bee-Dees*. And there were the *I-Wens*, Individuals With Exceptional Needs, who, under Public Law 94-142, passed in 1978, were guaranteed a free education in a setting that was as open and devoid of restraint as was consistent with the child's learning needs.

The problems of change and confusion were not limited to program titles. There has always been a pattern of shuffling offices and agency titles. In the spring of 1980 even the big, old Department of Health, Education, and Welfare underwent a radical change. Then President Jimmy Carter split off a new Department of Education and renamed HEW, calling it the Department of Health and Human Services. Because of the constantly shifting bureaucratic structures, the system has always been quite difficult to track. There has never been a strong national sense of direction in children's programs or services, there is no central focus, no good body of information. No one knows just how many children are in foster care. In 1978 Frank Ferro, associate chief of the Children's Bureau, told me that the "latest and best" estimates indicate there are seven hundred thousand children in foster care. The figure was twice the estimate given Walter Mondale just three years earlier. Not ten minutes after I interviewed Ferro, I was talking with Beverley Stubbee, then the designated foster-care expert for all of HEW, and she set the figure at five hundred thousand. Three years later, the Children's Bureau was using the lower figure, and one official explained, "We think that five hundred thousand is about right," but he admitted "no one really knows."

The inability of the Children's Bureau — or any other agency or bureau within HHS, née HEW — to come up with a more specific number for Mondale in 1975, or for me six years later, is indicative of a very basic flaw within the system that results directly from the political fights over all welfare issues. The liberals and humanitarians on the left would set national standards to force the conservatives, primarily in the southern and southwestern states, to provide a level of welfare services that could sustain a family and provide children with some chance of growing and maturing into productive, *independent* citizens. To counter the political moves from the left, the conservatives and fundamentalists on the far right rely upon a basic "states' rights" defense. Working through their powerful committee chairmanships in the Congress, the southern conservatives have historically managed to dissipate the power of the liberal forces, splitting the attacks, diverting individual efforts for reform into different jurisdictional directions. The so-called fragmentation of governmental services, bemoaned by so many critics of the foster-care system, did not come about by accident.

In the Senate, for example, it was okay for Mondale and Williams to conduct hearings on foster care, but if any legislation was to be passed, it had to get past Russell Long, then the chairman of the Senate Finance Committee. Why? Social Security *is finance,* and foster care is a part of the Social Security system. In the Senate Finance Committee, the efforts of liberals come up against the conservative, fundamentalist views of men like Long, who have always wielded enormous power. They have judiciously guarded states' rights and impeded what they saw as the intrusion of the federal government into issues that concern the welfare of people. It is not by chance that the states in the South provide the lowest cash grants for Aid to Families of Dependent Children or have the most stringent qualifications. Legislators like Long favor "work fare" proposals that would make welfare recipients work for their dole; they tend to take on issues one at a time and prevent sweeping changes. Within the Senate Finance Committee, funds are cut, amendments are added further to restrict recipient eligibility.

Long and the committee he headed stand as a symbol. Historically, the result has been a narrowly focused succession of fights over specific programs and issues. The resulting laws are compromises that create additions to the house of mirrors, room after crazy room, built one at a time into an expansive, expensive agglomeration. While something more than $1.5 billion was being spent yearly on foster care by the end of the 1970s, that expenditure was only a small part of the $10 billion being spent in the twenty-five to thirty different federal programs affecting children. The figures and program titles blur into meaningless confusion: Aid to Families with Dependent Children, $5.6 billion; AFDC Foster Care–Boarding Home and Institutions, $176 million; Title IV-B, Social Security social service funds, $56 million; Title IV-A, emergency services, $30 million; Indian Welfare Service for children, $12 million; child abuse and neglect, $18.2 million; Community Mental Health Center programs, $20.8 million; handicapped children educational programs under PL 94-142, $300 million.

The list is long. Each program has developed its own political constituency, its own bureaucracy, its own set of rules and regulations. Over half a century the liberals had fought hard, specific issue by specific issue, to build and maintain some semblance of a national child-care program, albeit a ramshackle construction that was seriously flawed. In the process each of the bureaus set up to administer these programs has grown and become more costly. Some have become ponderous, frequently inefficient, self-perpetuating bastions of special interests. Some programs, such as the 1974 Supplemental Food Program for Women, Infants, and Children, have proven a boon to the needy. By 1980 this program was targeting 2.2 million pregnant women, nursing mothers, and infants a year and was providing them with fruit, eggs, dairy products, and infant formula as a part of an effort to bring down the alarmingly high infant mortality rate in the United States. Other programs, such as the $12.4 billion-a-year food stamp distribution system, had grown unwieldy and were full of waste, abuse, and fraud. No one knew quite how to contain or direct such programs once the individual bureau or agency had established itself within the governmental framework. And public confidence in the government's ability to function in the public interest was at a low ebb as Ronald Reagan assumed power. Then, with Reagan's inauguration, the hopes of the conservatives and fundamentalists soared.

Just as he had done in California when taking over the governorship, the new president came into office in 1981 swinging a fiscal broad ax, determined to slash federal spending by $45 billion the first year. Reagan proposed cutting $1.8 billion from food stamps and $1 billion out of the school lunch program. The $1 billion a year Supplemental Food Program for Women, Infants, and Children was to be cut by a third, and eligibility for all forms of welfare was to be tightened. The budget cutting was to sweep across all departments of government. In the Justice Department, the Reagan team proposed eliminating entirely the $135-million-a-year Office of Juvenile Justice and Delinquency Prevention that was funding special services designed to keep youngsters out of kid prisons.

But President Reagan's goal was not just cutting back on spending. He also wanted to radically alter the existing relationship between the federal government and the states. His aim was to reduce the size and power of the federal government, primarily by undoing the social reforms that had begun with the Franklin Roosevelt New Deal in the 1930s. And to make this break with the past, Reagan proposed a very simple mechanism called the block grant. Where the New Deal approach had been to offer the carrot and threaten the stick, enticing and coercing states into expanding social services by offering federal dollars for following federal guidelines, the block grant was designed to return all decision-making power back to the states. The size of the block grant to each state or local governmental agency was to be determined by adding up all of the categorical aid programs and then cutting the total by 25 percent. The states and local governments were to be free to spend the money in any way they chose, to maintain services to children and their families, or to reduce the local tax burden by cutting back on services. In theory this would mean the big bureaus of the federal government would no longer be needed to ride herd on the states, so the size of the federal bureacracy could be radically reduced.

Reagan encountered surprisingly little resistance as he presented his budget proposals to the Congress  The mood of the country in the early 1980s was clearly self-indulgent. Big government was too big and taxes were too high. There was a feeling the government was no longer accountable to the people, and that feeling was not without foundation. In April 1978, for example, the Office of Inspector General investigated the old HEW and reported that the super-agency had misspent or wasted or had been bilked out of somewhere between $6.7 *billion* and $7.4 *billion* in the 1977 fiscal year. That amounted to five cents out of every budgeted HEW dollar. Much of this waste, fraud, and mis-spending happened within the children's programs year after year. The federal government paid precious little attention to how states were spending federal dollars on foster care. And, too often, the state had little interest in the children, or how they were being treated. In Illinois, during the early 1970s, the Department of Children and Family Services had been dumping its unwanted kids into private facilities in Texas without checking out the places, without supervising how the children, once placed, were treated. The results were predictable. The kid business in Texas was booming. Then, in 1973, the scandal was exposed by a law professor at DePaul University, Patrick Keenan. In a report entitled "An Illinois Tragedy," Keenan estimated the Illinois DCFS had spent $8 million sending troublesome children out of state, to private-care institutions in Texas. A large share of the money had come from the federal government. Many, if not most, of the children sent to Texas were placed in institutions that at best merely neglected their needs, at worst physically and emotionally abused them, according to Keenan's task force report.

Keenan concluded: "The children and the money were banished to and wasted in Texas by an efficient, responsive, mindless, heartless bureaucratic monster, inexorably grinding its way through children's lives . . . Everyone is responsible. No one is, or will be accountable. No one meant for it to happen, it just did."

I wanted to argue with those words. The system had to

be examined and held accountable. Nothing "just happened," not in Illinois or California or New York. But I could construct no logical, rational explanation of what was happening.

Then something occurred that enlightened me. I was interviewing Hilmi Fuad, the welfare director of a rural California county, a Cypriot who had been schooled in England before World War II and who had immigrated here after serving in U.S. Army intelligence. He was a trained, skilled bureaucrat, and he was trying very hard to explain how "the system" worked, jumping up, darting around the room to grab a binder full of regulations, or a report, or a letter from Sacramento, to make his point. But he was confusing me all the more, and I told him so, explaining my general frustration with my whole project. He interrupted me: "Ron, you're trying to be logical, and you *can't* do it."

His hand slapped the table between us to emphasize the words "*can't* do it." I was more puzzled: "Can't do what?"

> *Can't* be *logical*. It *won't* work. Ron, there is no clear-cut way to find accountability. There is no way to make sense out of this [foster-care, child-welfare] system. It is a quagmire. The only way to put the system into effect is to *muddle through* it. I am not trying to be heartless, but I just don't know how to deal with such a situation, so I *muddle through* it. The basic problem is that you can't deal with the problem, there is not enough money to solve the problem, so the bureaucracy makes rules that cannot be followed because there is never enough money to implement and enforce the rules . . .

I tried to argue with him, but the welfare director was determined to make his point:

> Look, most of the people [bureaucrats] you have dealt with so far have been reasonably intelligent, they were trying to be helpful, and yet the way the system works you can't be rational and you can't be systematic and you can't solve the

problem . . . What I am saying to you is that the people who say they want certain things done for the poor don't really want those things done at all. We as a society operate on two levels; one is the good, kind, moral Christian level, where we owe our neighbor help, and on this level we pass laws. We pass certain laws and regulations that say we want to do certain things for our neighbors. All right?

He paused for emphasis.

*But we don't mean it.* If you look at the way programs are run, you will find only a very small percentage of the people who are eligible for any welfare program actually get welfare . . . And that is the thing that saves these programs, because if everyone eligible had applied, there wouldn't be enough money to run them . . . Only about one half of the people who are eligible for food stamps apply, because the program is run in such a way that it is just too complicated, too undignified, too clumsy, too something, for them to benefit. Now the politicians pass a law saying that everybody should have food stamps, but these same politicians complain at the tremendous cost . . . If we ran the program efficiently and properly, the cost would double, and now they can barely afford it . . . So I get the feeling of this two-level business; you want to have laws that sound reasonable and compassionate, at the same time you put roadblocks against these laws. That way you can function as a society, as a government; otherwise you couldn't do it. Our hearts cannot rule; our heads have to rule. But our hearts get in the way, so we pass laws with the heart and we operate them with the head and *the system doesn't work as we say it should.*

I walked out of that interview in late 1977 shaking my head. What he had said *sounded crazy,* but in the weeks that followed, this man's words echoed through much of what I was finding. In Washington, D.C., I interviewed Arabella Martinez, then the Assistant Secretary for Human Development Services in the Department of Health, Education, and Welfare, and she said almost the same thing. Martinez had begun by talking about how fragmented the child-welfare system appeared: "I have used the word *frag-mented* a lot [but] . . . I am beginning to realize that we never had a whole system . . . There never was a rational system out there. Nobody ever thought about that. What they did was just respond to the critical needs that they saw and they wanted to take care of the children who were being abused and neglected." Although she did not say "muddled through," she was describing that process of responding to a situation crisis by crisis. A few sentences later: "The real problem is a lack of resources. You are never going to meet the needs of all of those people out there. We meet the needs of twenty-five percent of the children who needed Headstart, that's all. Fifteen percent of the elderly who are eligible for nutrition get served . . ."

In Massachusetts in 1978, where the emphasis on deinstitutionalization had received national attention and recognition, Mary Jane England, then the assistant commissioner of the Department of Mental Health, proudly described how troubled children were being treated closer to home, how children no longer had to be institutionalized in reform schools or state hospitals. She explained that ten years ago, Massachusetts had stopped admitting very small children to mental hospitals, four years ago, the state had stopped admitting kids to the kid prisons. What institutional care remained was modernized; there was, for example, a specialized twelve-bed autistic unit, with a network of family-care services and respite care to help families once the children were back in their homes. There were early-childhood intervention programs developed to help keep families from breaking up, to help parents deal with developmentally disabled or mentally disturbed children.

It all sounded very good. Question: Did Massachusetts have the resources to deal with all of these programs? "No," England said, explaining, "currently, we have resources to deal with half of the early intervention programs,

which means we cover about one half of the need . . .
Right now we are looking for ways to finance keeping the
children in their own homes. But there are barriers to
keeping kids at home."

Alexander Sharp, then commissioner of the Massachusetts Department of Public Welfare, was asked the same
question after he had described the full range of "preventive services" available to families. Did he have the resources needed? "Ahhh, not to the extent we would like,
because there are so many areas of crisis in social services:
a group-care kid who has run away and you literally can't
find a place for him, or a jurisdictional dispute between
whether the kid ought to be delivered to the Department
of Mental Health as opposed to the Welfare Department."

The echoes of Fuad's words persist. I've never been
able fully to reject them; they haunt me: "Our hearts and
our ideals are so far ahead of our pocketbooks. We want
to help, but we [as a society] cannot or will not face the
fiscal consequences . . ."

The words had a bureaucratic ring to them, and I had
quickly pointed out that much of the money spent on welfare was wasted, was ripped off, was misspent intentionally
or by accident. He responded:

Sure, you can find abuse and fraud and poor administration.
At any one time, anyone can come in and pick the system
apart, can find glaring horror stories. Licensing doesn't have
enough money, placement doesn't have enough money, you
find something wrong and it's my fault [as welfare director]
for not doing this, or doing that, not following the rules. So
what? Look at the crazy way we make regulations. If we are
to give aid, a person must be *thoroughly* eligible, and this
takes time to check, but the law also says we must give immediate aid to the needy. We can't do both. We are wrong
if we give aid to an ineligible person, and we are wrong if we
don't give aid immediately to the needy, so what do we do?
The average government worker is conscientious and tries

hard to make the system work. But there is no way to make the system work. You can't do it. The welfare programs in this country do not have a plan. It's like a house. If you want to build a house, you have a plan and then you build it. Okay? But the welfare systems in the United States were built without plans . . . We are trying to be all things to all people but without a definite plan.

Gilbert Steiner, in his book *The Children's Cause*, wrote much the same thing: "Child development policy is uncoordinated. Public involvement in the field is a federal-agency-by-federal agency, congressional-committee-by-congressional committee, state-by-state or city-by-city assortment of unrelated decisions that are as likely to be contradictory as complementary . . ."

The process has produced a structure tilted this way, leaning that, nothing quite fitting. The system and the structure it produced seem to defy logic, but I was bothered by Keenan's words in "An Illinois Tragedy": "Everyone is responsible No one is, or will be accountable. No one meant for it to happen, it just did."

Why? Nothing "just happens." And therein lay the challenge. I wanted at least to understand what had happened, what was happening. The key word had to be *accountability*. The focus of the inquiry had to go beyond the horror of children's lives. I wanted to learn how the bureaucratic structures worked, to get at the *why* of it all. So I set about taking apart the crazy house and examining it, bit by bit — first the foster-care system, then juvenile justice and the various forms of institutional care and community care — never quite sure of what I would find.

# 4

## Juvenile Justice

DURING THE LAST HOUR of 1980 a thirteen-year-old Los Angeles boy armed with a rifle fired seven bullets into an old man who had come next door to protest the noisy New Year's Eve party. But for the fact that this killing was the final homicide in what had been a very violent year in the city, murder number 1042 went virtually unnoticed in the media. In a year when the homicide rate jumped an alarming 25 percent, this single killing did not measure up to the crazy violence of two sixteen-year-olds gunning down four robbery victims at a bus stop, or of three shotgun-wielding youths blasting away three helpless restaurant patrons. Nor did the victim have a recognizable name like Sarai Ribicoff, twenty-three, who was shot down by two young robbers as she and a friend left a restaurant.

Los Angeles, like most metropolitan areas, was caught up in a wave of senseless, terrifying violence. In reaction, the citizens were arming themselves and politicians were joining the vigilante cries for law and order. Only two weeks into 1981 the Los Angeles County Board of Supervisors called a special hearing on criminal violence to provide officials with a law-and-order forum. One witness,

Juvenile Court Judge Art Gilbert, told supervisors, "I see kids packing thirty-eight-caliber revolvers and magnums and shotguns . . . what I've observed is a children's army out there."

The *Los Angeles Times* headlined the story, CHILDREN'S CRIME "ARMY" PROWLING L.A., and quoted the judge as saying the army of violent children showed "no sense of empathy" for their victims. "It's almost like they are programmed robots out on the prowl to kill."

Throughout the last half of the 1970s there was a growing apprehension across the nation, a fear of what *Time* magazine, in July 1977, called "The Youth Crime Plague":

> Many youngsters appear to be robbing and raping, maiming and murdering as casually as they go to a movie . . . A new, remorseless, mutant juvenile seems to have been born and there is no more terrifying figure in America today.

In Chicago, one third of the killings were committed by youngsters under twenty. In Washington, D.C., a university law professor and a psychologist studied nineteen young murderers and reported that, although some of them might be rehabilitated, seven were "primitive, nonempathetic" killers who murdered strangers for no discernible reasons. Each had a record of numerous property offenses. They were all unpredictably violent youngsters who had no guilt feelings, no feelings of sympathy or compassion. In Southern California, the judge of the Orange County Juvenile Court said, "Kids nowadays are becoming more violent . . . I have three teen-aged boys I just certified downtown [to adult court]. They had agreed to kill their robbery victim . . . stabbed him seventeen times and they got less than fifty dollars."

California crime statistics seem to bear out the judge's contention: the number of violent crimes against people has tripled, and the murder rate has doubled. There is more violence in the schools. In Los Angeles, for example, in five years (1975–1980) the number of assaults on teachers and students rose from 1802 to 3028. And the same violent trends are being reported nationally. The Federal Bureau of Investigation uniform crime reports indicate that just over two million kids under the age of eighteen are being picked up by police each year, and about half of them are being processed through the juvenile courts. A federal census showed that on any one day there were seventy-four thousand boys and girls confined in 2151 public and private juvenile detention centers and correctional institutions. By 1980 the entire juvenile justice system was costing in excess of $1 billion a year, yet media reports revealed the situation in the cities was getting worse.

In reaction, the voices of law and order were calling loudly for tougher laws and harsher punishments and asking that more violent juveniles be treated as adult offenders. In 1977 *Time* magazine contended: "The evidence suggests that a tough policy toward violent crime reduces crime." It was a popular, if unproved, theme. By early 1981, Chief Justice Warren E. Burger, in his annual address to the American Bar Association, worked on the flip side of the "get tough" theme. He warned, "Today we are approaching the status of an impotent society whose capability of maintaining elementary security of the streets, in schools, and for the homes of our people is in doubt . . ." The reason? The chief justice explained, "We have established a system of criminal justice that provides more protection, more safeguards, more guarantees for those accused of a crime than any other nation in history . . . yet fail[ed] to provide elementary protection for [our] decent, law-abiding citizens . . . Day-by-day terrorism in almost any large city exceeds the casualties of all reported international terrorists in any given year . . . Are we not hostage within the borders of our own self-styled enlightened, civilized country?"

While Burger acknowledged that he held a belief that

"poverty and unemployment are reflected in crime rates, chiefly crimes against property," he warned, "We must not be misled by clichés and slogans that if we but abolish poverty, crime will also disappear. A far greater factor is the deterrent effect of swift and certain consequences . . . Deterrence is the primary core of any response to the reign of terror in American cities."

The problem with such law-and-order rhetoric is that it is a subjective, simplistic reaction, a romanticized fitting of bits and pieces of information into glib solutions to wonderfully frightening situations. However, to establish that a youth crime plague in fact exists, and then to create effective changes in our social fabric, is a bit more difficult. The first chore, of course, is to measure the problems when there are no reliable sources of information, no accurate national statistics to provide a sense of measurement and proportion. No agency provides the leadership or the expertise to bring together the bits and pieces of the national puzzle and sort them into meaningful order. Result: What statistics are available can be warped to support almost any point of view. In California, for example, statistics could be used to show that judges were getting tougher in the late 1970s. The state prison system was filled beyond capacity. By 1981 there were 24,600 men and women locked up in the state's prisons, a gain of five thousand in just three years. In the California Youth Authority institutions — designed for 5174 inmates — there were 5400 youngsters, some of them sleeping "double-bunked" in small cells, or on cots in hallways, or, in some cases, on mattresses on the floor. And officials reported that generally the inmate populations were getting tougher. Comparative CYA data show that over the past decade (1970–1980) the proportionate numbers of youngsters sentenced to CYA institutions for robbery, rape, assault, and murder had risen 44 percent.

Though it is popular to use such statistics to show that

disproportionate numbers of children are committing violent crimes, such claims present a distorted view that ig-
nores, for example, the fact that the law no longer allows
the CYA to receive "status offenders" whose only offenses
— truancy, liquor-law violations, sexual promiscuity, or
running away — would not have been violations of the law
if they were of age. Such a factor weighs heavily in any
comparison. Without status offenders in the CYA population, the percentage of violent offenders would quite obviously be higher. On a national basis, it is possible to
show that 22 percent of the violent crimes reported were
committed by juveniles or to show that less than 4 percent
of the two million juveniles picked up each year were
charged with crimes of violence.

True, the sensational acts of murderous teen-agers and
the use of selected statistical information can be shaped
into frightfully persuasive arguments for a tough law-and-
order crackdown. But such arguments fall short because
not only do they fail to examine the basic social and economic structures that contribute to juvenile delinquency,
they also fail to examine the juvenile justice system itself.
Juvenile justice in the United States is, at best, an archaic
machine that creates as many problems as it solves. At
worst, it is cruel beyond belief. Children who are made
wards of the juvenile court, no matter how helpless or
blameless, are at considerable risk. Until the late 1960s
and early 1970s, children had no legal status, no legal rights
in juvenile court proceedings. Homeless youngsters could
be locked in jail or juvenile hall to prevent them from
becoming criminals, or they could be locked away simply
because the city, county, or state had no other place but
a jail cell to hold them. Too often in the course of gathering
information for this book, I came across the lives of troubled, violent teen-agers who had grown up within the foster
care–juvenile justice system. They had been made wards
of the juvenile court because their family environment had

shattered and they had been cast out. Through their records, I could trace the tragic progression of their escalating misconduct and, at each step of the way, I could see the court reactions, the recommendations and observations of the welfare and probation department workers.

If it is too harsh to say the juvenile justice system shaped these violent criminal careers, it is certainly fair to say the system did little to rehabilitate or reform them. And it is precisely this failure that needs to be examined, because the primary functions of the juvenile court are rehabilitation and reformation. The juvenile courts in this country hold a unique place in the judicial system. They are not involved in criminal justice or civil litigation. The juvenile judges do not conduct court trials to prove innocence or guilt. In the legal sense of the word, children are not convicted, nor are they sentenced as criminals. These special courts were set up to act in *parens patriae,* as parent. And it was believed that, if these courts were to act as parent *in the best interest of the child,* it was necessary for them to be free of the traditional legal constraints imposed on the courts by the U.S. Constitution. As a result, juvenile court proceedings are closed to the public, there are no jury trials, and since no one is convicted in the process, there are no demands upon the state to prove guilt "beyond a reasonable doubt." Each juvenile court is an independent entity. And though many states have enacted uniform juvenile justice laws to guide counties and cities, there are no systems to guarantee these laws are uniformly administered by the local juvenile courts. No two judges are quite alike, either in training or temperament. Few jurisdictions outside the big metropolitan areas have the resources to create full-time juvenile judicial positions. More often, judges are rotated in and out of the juvenile courts; probation officers are moved in and out of their departmental juvenile divisions; welfare social workers never remain long in the divisions that take dependency and neglect cases into court. Politically, it has been difficult to appropriate enough funds to run the system well at any level. The tendency was — and is — to overload the system, force as many cases through the juvenile courts in as short a time as possible.

The same thing is true in the juvenile correctional system. The costs of constructing separate juvenile halls, correctional camps, and kid prisons are high. As a result children wind up in adult jails. In 1977 the Children's Defense Fund surveyed 449 jails in nine states and found that 38 percent of the city and county jails routinely held children as a matter of juvenile policy. Another 14 percent indicated that they "sometimes" held children in adult jails. The CDF investigators interviewed 350 children being held in jails and reported that the "overwhelming majority" of these youngsters were a threat to no one, not themselves, not the community. Only 11 percent had been charged with serious crimes; the rest were status offenders or were charged with property offenses or minor crimes. The conditions in most of the jails were "abysmal." One of the youngsters interviewed was a fifteen-year-old boy who had been arrested for burglary and had been locked up for forty-one days, waiting for his juvenile court hearing. He begged the Children's Defense Fund investigator to get him out of the jail because he was having to fight off homosexual attackers: "This morning a guy started to come at me . . . a little guy. He must have been seventy years old and he was standing there holding on to himself looking at me like I was some chick . . . This ain't no place for a kid, man."

When the boy's case finally came to hearing, the juvenile court judge found him guilty and sentenced him to time served. *The youngster had been punished first, then tried and found guilty.* It was marvelously like something out of *Through the Looking-Glass*, where Alice and the White Queen are talking about the king's messenger:

"He's in prison now, being punished; and the trial doesn't even begin 'till Wednesday; and of course, the crime comes last of all," the White Queen explained.

"Suppose he never commits the crime?" Alice asked.

"That would be all the better, wouldn't it," the Queen said.

Alice had stepped through the looking-glass into that juvenile court world where backward living is quite normal, where the bureaucrats and judges talk of yesterday and tomorrow, but never quite deal with today, where children who commit no crime are locked away, while children who do rob and steal are allowed to go free. Once you follow Alice into the backward-living world, the arguments of the White Queen, the juvenile judges, and the politicians become wisdom. Then it isn't too hard to accept the validity of the argument that, by exposing delinquent teen-agers to the horrors of the penal system in places like New Jersey's Rahway State Prison, we can deter them from lives of crime. In a television documentary entitled "Scared Straight," New Jersey authorities seriously argued that eight thousand youngsters exposed to the brutal existence of adult convicts — who described how they raped, buggered, and killed each other inside prison — were deterred from a life of crime. What a marvelous, simple solution: all that it requires is that several hundred men be caged and treated like animals and allowed to act like animals, and then, periodically, teen-agers be passed through the cages for a brief experience of prison.

It is difficult not to ridicule simplistic attempts to solve complex problems after you have examined the lives of several juveniles who have developed long histories of troubled, deviant, antisocial behavior and after you have examined the patterns of bureaucratic reaction by the juvenile justice systems that have dealt with these children. Consider one case, that of a black seventeen-year-old who was convicted of murder in an adult court and sentenced to a life term in the California state prison system. While no single example can stand as proof absolute that the system is flawed beyond repair, the juvenile court records and probation reports on this one youngster — call him Tommy A. — come as close as any to showing how shallow, how mechanical, how lacking, the juvenile justice systems can be in any given metropolitan area.

Tommy's case involves the police, the juvenile courts, the probation departments, and correctional systems of both Los Angeles and Orange counties. Tommy's records — made available by a judge of the Orange County Juvenile Court — report a brief, violent career of deviant, delinquent behavior that links the ghettos of Watts and Santa Ana, a career that moves through the endless, ugly city streets and speeds down the freeways that tie the two counties into one urban sprawl. Tommy's record began when he was nine years old and was caught by Los Angeles police throwing rocks at cars on the freeway.

At the time, he was living at home with his mother and father in south-central Los Angeles, but there were problems in the family, and his parents soon separated. Mrs. A. moved south into Orange County, taking her children with her. When Tommy was twelve, the Santa Ana police caught him trying to break into a building. During the next six months he was arrested three times, for stealing cigarettes, for knocking a boy from his bicycle and stealing it, and finally for purse-snatching. He was locked up in the Orange County Juvenile Hall in October 1973. The county Probation Department filed a "petition on the minor's behalf" alleging petty theft; a juvenile court referee found that Tommy was a "child in need of supervision" under Section 601 of the California State Welfare and Institutions Code and ordered that he be made a ward of the court. Tommy was placed on probation and returned home.

Tommy's mother had remarried and the family was living in a lower-middle-class neighborhood in Santa Ana. Tommy didn't get along at home. He ran the streets, was a poor student, frequently truant. In April 1974, Tommy's mother died. The boy moved back to Los Angeles to live with his father, and within four months the Los Angeles police had arrested him twice for vehicle theft and joy riding. Apparently, the cops and the Probation Department didn't have time to work Tommy's case through juvenile court. Each time they picked him up, he was placed on "informal" probation and released. In the spring of 1975, Tommy was arrested on burglary charges that were dismissed for lack of evidence. By the fall, he had been arrested again, for petty theft. This time the Probation Department filed a petition against Tommy, and the juvenile court found him delinquent under state law. He was placed on formal probation and for a year he lived at home with his father and got into no more trouble. Then, his "rap sheet" shows, he was picked up for petty theft and released once more on informal probation. Why that arrest did not trigger court action on his formal probationary status is never explained. While Tommy was sixteen, the record shows, he was twice arrested and charged with assault with a deadly weapon — and he was once caught riding in a stolen car. Curiously, the records show no disposition of these cases. Not long afterward, charges of auto theft were dropped, but he was once more placed on informal probation.

There is no indication in all of Tommy's juvenile court "package" that anyone tried to work with this boy or his family. Yet all the signs of trouble were there: Tommy was a black street kid who was growing more wild and aggressive with each succeeding year, but the police, the Probation Department, and the courts didn't have time for Tommy, not until he and three other boys were accused of killing someone in March 1977. Police said the four teenagers, armed with sawed-off shotguns and pistols, drove from Los Angeles south into Santa Ana. There, they tried to rob a market. The owner of the store grabbed for a hidden handgun and, in the wild shoot-out that followed, a woman was killed. Police captured all four youths soon afterward. Tommy was locked up in the Orange County Juvenile Hall again, this time charged with murder. He didn't stay long. Records show that he and another boy overpowered a guard, and Tommy escaped. For two weeks he was a fugitive on the streets of Los Angeles. One evening, L.A. police arrested him and three other youths cruising in a stolen car. Officers reported that they found a pistol on the floor under the seat. An identification check revealed that Tommy was wanted for murder and escape. He was returned to Orange County. In juvenile court, the Orange County Probation Department reported: "It is quite apparent that probationary supervision in the community has been totally ineffective; while institutionalization has not been tried previously it is obvious from the fact of the minor's escape from juvenile hall that he could not be contained in a county facility . . . thus it appears the only possibility which would insure his containment or rehabilitation is the California Youth Authority . . ."

Sentencing a youngster to the CYA is normally the juvenile court's last resort, the alternative that is used after all else *fails*. Orange County is an urban part of the Los Angeles metropolitan area, a county rich in resources. Before the passage of Proposition 13, the county had created a big, modern, complex, and well-financed juvenile justice system, complete with a three-hundred-bed juvenile detention and correction center and a penal system that included therapeutic guidance centers, youth prison farms, and a series of "open" or "nonsecure" group homes. The juvenile court had one full-time superior court judge, who sat as juvenile court judge for a two-year term. The judge, in turn, appointed five referees to act as primary hearing officers in his stead. The judge and the hearing officers had at their disposal full-time psychiatrists, psychologists, psychiatric social workers, registered nurses, and a full range of detention, diagnostic, and correction facilities, some

operated by the county, some by private agencies contracting their services to the county. Yearly, the juvenile
justice system in Orange County handled about seventeen
thousand youngsters. Half of them passed through the juvenile hall. The other half were processed by the police
and the Probation Department on an informal basis. Those
youngsters who were petitioned formally into juvenile court
were automatically defended by one of the seventy young
attorneys working in the county public defender's office.
Plea bargaining had become a normal part of the juvenile
court routine: first offenders went home, repeaters went
to camp or to a group home, some were ordered into treatment, some released under close probationary supervision.
Only the worst offenders with long records went to the
California Youth Authority.

At least, that is the way Orange County Juvenile Court
and Probation Department officials described the system.
But that wasn't the way things happened in Tommy's case,
not according to his records. From the time he was nine
he was repeatedly picked up by police, quickly processed
through juvenile court, and released on probation. There
was nothing in Tommy's juvenile court records to indicate
that any of the various county agencies attempted to help
stabilize the family home; there was no indication that
Tommy had been placed in counseling; no decision was
made to place him in a group home where he might have
received therapy. Like thousands of other kids from low-
income neighborhoods across the country, he was trapped
in an overloaded, bureaucratic system that kept sucking
him in and spitting him out. Only when he became too
violent did the Probation Department act, and then it was
to recommend that Tommy stand trial for murder as an
adult because he had become "a criminally sophisticated
youth" who "evidenced very little respect for the property
of others."

The juvenile court judge agreed that sending Tommy to

the California Youth Authority wasn't the thing to do; the boy was seventeen and the CYA could not detain him past his twenty-third birthday. Six years would not be long enough to punish or rehabilitate Tommy, so it was decided his case should be transferred to adult criminal court. The juvenile justice system had failed. The seventeen-year-old who had been under the guidance and supervision of the juvenile courts and probation departments of two metropolitan counties for eight years was tried as an adult and sentenced to life in prison in an adult penal system as notorious as New Jersey's Rahway Prison, a prison dominated by racial gangs and predatory convicts who delighted in sexually attacking young boys. Any seventeen-year-old who could survive ten or fifteen years in the California state prisons would be more than streetwise when he was paroled.

Was Tommy's case unique? And were Orange County and, to a lesser extent, Los Angeles County the exceptions rather than the rule? No. In California in 1978 there were twenty-eight teen-agers in state prisons, scores of juveniles doing time in local county and city jails, all sentenced under the same legal processes; and the results of the Children's Defense Fund survey made it obvious that the practice of jailing children was not confined to California.

The problems and attitudes in California at the close of the decade were reflective of a changing national mood; people were reacting to runaway inflation, crime in the streets, violent teen-agers, exorbitant gasoline prices, and runaway profits for the oil industries. They were frightened, angry, frustrated, and in California the voters reacted precipitately, passionately to the Jarvis-Gann antiproperty tax initiative, saying "yes" to Proposition 13 and "go to hell" to government and politicians. Across the country, the people were listening to the voices of law and order. Justice had to be swift, harsh, painful, vengeful. The pendulum, it was argued, had swung too far. Young killers were being coddled and turned loose with nothing more than a slap on the wrist. It was time to set things right. New laws had to be passed to impose — in the words of *Time* magazine — "adult" punishments for "adult" crimes. Youngsters fifteen or sixteen or seventeen who committed crimes should be and were being sent to state prisons.

It was uncanny. The thirst for retribution, the self-indulgent mood that demanded severe punishment for youngsters like Tommy rather than spending the time and the resources before the murder at least to attempt to help such children, was disconcerting. The very primitive instincts that once prevailed in the criminal justice system had been rediscovered. The processes that put Tommy away in state prison in 1978 were little different from the actions taken against the child pickpockets picked up from the London streets and hanged, two or three centuries ago. The same mood that prompted New York City judges to sentence seventy-five to one hundred youngsters a year to state prisons in the 1820s had returned.

The poor, the orphans, the neglected youngsters who ran the streets of New York and London ended up in the almshouses or the jails. The line between poverty and criminal act was drawn exceedingly thin. And children like Oliver Twist were frequently pulled across that line from dependency and neglect into criminal conduct as much by happenstance as by intent.

Children were presumed bad, presumed guilty unless proven innocent. When Oliver was finally caught after a wild chase through London's back streets, he was sick and faint, both from the run and from the bashing he had taken at the hands of his captors. When he was taken before the magistrate, he asked for a drink of water.

The magistrate shouted, "Stuff and nonsense, don't try to fool me."

Oliver fainted.

The magistrate ordered the court attendants to stand

away while he passed judgment: "He stands committed for three months, hard labour, of course."

Although Oliver had not stolen the handkerchief, he had been caught running from the scene of the crime and therefore he was guilty and had to be punished. That same sort of court scene was being repeated in the 1830s in Boston. But there were pressures to change, to improve the system. Conditions in the Massachusetts prisons were scandalous. Reform groups were demanding that children be removed from the prisons and placed in special Houses of Refuge or Reform Schools. In 1846, the Massachusetts legislature appropriated funds to construct the Lyman School for Boys. Within a decade, it housed five hundred youngsters and had become the prototype, the first big kid prison.

At about the same time, a Boston shoemaker was concerned about the way the courts were treating street children who had been picked up by the cops and who were in jail pending court action because they could not make bail. John Augustus interceded on behalf of these children, offering to stand their bail if they, in turn, would promise to behave and remain within his supervision. The judges cooperated, postponing sentencing while Augustus worked with the youngsters. If the shoemaker reported that the child behaved well, the case was either dismissed or the judge imposed a very light sentence. Thus was the idea of probation put into effect. The concept spread to other areas, other states, and was haphazardly added to the judicial processes. Each state, each county, each city, operated its judicial systems more or less independently, each creating and adapting its own procedures for handling children to suit local custom and myth.

During the 1890s in areas like Chicago, there was a growing concern about the way children were being detained in jail before the disposition of their cases. If it wasn't good for youngsters to be locked away with adult convicts in the state prisons systems, wasn't it equally harmful for them to be locked up with adults in the jails before they came to trial? There was also a growing sentiment against processing young delinquents through the same criminal courts, where the judges were bound by the Constitution and the state laws that hindered efforts to order rehabilitative efforts for young offenders. In 1899 a law was passed by the Illinois legislature establishing the Cook County Juvenile Court, and funds were made available to construct the first juvenile detention center.

Those were the beginnings, the creation of specialized institutions, of special juvenile courts and a probation system, all held together by *parens patriae*. To protect the children's reputations, the juvenile court proceedings were closed to the public. Judges could act on their own, in Star Chamber–like sessions, without fear of judicial review or appeal. They could lock children up, take children from their parents, order harsh punishments for disobedience, all without public review. Civil libertarians challenged the closed hearings and the lack of due process, arguing that to lock any person up, even a child, without first conducting an open trial was unconstitutional. But for decades these arguments fell on deaf judicial ears, because it was ruled that a state reform school *was not a prison,* it was a place of reformation; youngsters *were not being punished,* they were being trained in industry, their minds were being imbued with the principles of Christian morality. The defenders of *parens patriae* argued, "May not the natural parents, when unequal to the task of education, or unworthy of it, be superseded by the *parens patriae,* or common guardian? The right of parental control is a natural, but not an inalienable one."

That kind of thinking prevailed until 1967, when the U.S. Supreme Court finally broke with tradition with its decision in the case known as *In Re: Gault.* Gerald Gault was a fifteen-year-old Arizona boy who had been accused of making an obscene phone call to a woman neighbor. An adult convicted of such a crime could have been sentenced to pay a $50 fine and to spend two months in jail. The boy was sentenced to serve six years in the state reform school, even though he was never given a hearing. The only "evidence" presented to the judge was the probation officer's petition alleging that Gault was under eighteen and in need of the protection of the court because he was a delinquent minor. The probation officer orally explained the "facts" to the court, using a police report of the complaint and his own notes taken during a phone conversation with the complaining witness. At no time did the complaining witness appear in court or provide any sworn testimony. The boy denied the offense. The judge ordered him confined to the state reform school until he was twenty-one years old.

On appeal, the Arizona Appellate Court upheld the sentence, but the U.S. Supreme Court reversed the decision, holding:

> It is of no constitutional consequence — and of no practical meaning — that an institution to which Gault is committed is called an Industrial School. The fact of the matter is that however euphemistic the title . . . an industrial school for juveniles is an institution of confinement in which the child is incarcerated . . . In view of this it would be extraordinary if our Constitution did not require procedural regularity and the exercise of care implied in the phrase "due process." Under our Constitution the condition of being a boy does not justify a kangaroo court.

The *Gault* decision established for the first time that the Fourteenth Amendment to the Constitution applied to children as well as to adults. The U.S. Supreme Court ruled that children facing charges that could result in their being confined in a state correctional institution had a right to due process. Both the children and their parents had to be provided with a "notice" of the charges that was detailed enough to allow them to prepare an adequate defense. A youngster had a right to counsel, and if he or she could not afford to hire an attorney, one had to be appointed by the court. Kids could no longer be required to testify against themselves, and they were granted the right to confront and cross-examine witnesses. *Gault* was a limited decision, however, applying only to those youngsters who were charged in proceedings that could put them in state institutions. Because the case was narrowly focused on institutional placement of a delinquent, it did not provide the same safeguards for the 150,000 to 200,000 nondelinquent youngsters who were appearing before the courts as "dependent" children.

Even so, *Gault* was the first of several important cases that began to extend constitutional protections to persons under eighteen years of age. *In Re: Winship* (1970) made it necessary for prosecutors in juvenile court cases to prove *beyond a reasonable doubt* that a crime had been committed. In *Baker* v. *Hamilton* (1972), it was ruled that children could not be held in places of punishment during the predispositional portions of the case being heard. In other words, it was illegal to lock up a kid in a county jail. In *Breed* v. *Jones* (1975) the Court outlawed the practice of trying a youngster in juvenile court and then, if the results weren't to the judge's liking, retrying the youngster again, in adult court. It is unconstitutional to try adults twice for the same offense, and that rule against double jeopardy was extended to children. But not all of the decisions were going in favor of the kids. In *McKeiver* v. *Pennsylvania* (1971) it was held that juveniles did not have the right to a jury trial, that imposition of the right to a jury trial would take the authority of *parens patriae* away from the juvenile court and force the proceedings into an adversary contest to prove guilt or innocence. Justice Blackmun expressed the unwillingness of the majority of the Supreme Court justices to give up the traditions of the juvenile court system "despite the disappointments of grave dimensions" that were felt and acknowledged — disappointments caused by the troubled history of the juvenile court system.

Just how far the closed-door juvenile justice system can go was demonstrated in the courts of Illinois and Texas, where two lawyers fought against flagrant denials of due process, and, more shocking, against the cruel and abusive treatment of incarcerated youths. Patrick Murphy, a legal-aid attorney, was doing battle with the Illinois juvenile system in the late 1960s and early seventies. His primary focus was on Sheridan, the maximum-security unit for boys within the Illinois Department of Corrections. Kids as young as ten and eleven were being sentenced by the juvenile courts to St. Charles — then a medium-security kid prison — and those who screwed up in St. Charles were sent to Sheridan, where guards used psychotropic drugs and solitary confinement as routine correctional techniques. Many of the kids in Sheridan were the runaway, truant, beyond-the-control-of-parent kind of status offenders, or they had committed misdemeanors, which, had they been adults, would have netted them a few days in the local jail. Like Gerald Gault, they had been sentenced to the state kid prison system instead. Murphy filed a series of suits on behalf of four such boys.

Playing a complicated legal chess game, the aggressive lawyer maneuvered the issues into federal court. There, he contended that the boys had been denied due process; they had not been given equal protection under the law; the use of drugs and solitary confinement was cruel and unusual treatment; and, finally, the State of Illinois was in violation of its own statutes requiring juvenile jailers to use discipline "similar to that which a parent would provide." He argued that Illinois's juvenile justice system routinely scooped up kids who had done nothing more serious than break a window, that the kids were not given hearings, they were forced to plead guilty, placed on supervision, and then automatically, with each succeeding police contact or offense, were pushed upward through the system, from probation to custody in St. Charles and then to Sheridan.

Murphy prevailed. Judge James B. Parsons ruled that:

> . . . Sheridan was a penitentiary-type institution, one that had its foundation in the history of those prisons into which persons were placed in cells that were like dungeons, under the idea that by so being placed they would contemplate upon their sins, they would ask forgiveness and be absolved and possibly be released . . . No adult could ever be required to spend the same amount of time in a penitentiary-type institution for the same conduct of which these four petitioners before me have been required to spend . . . because of their age they have been discriminated against . . . The state system has not been a benevolent one, as intended by the statute; else how could it in its benevolence utilize Thorazine for purposes of punishment of a child, for purposes of control and punishment . . .

The judge released the four boys and ordered that "the custody into which they are released be such as will provide a parent-child relationship . . . if not in a home, in an institution that provides that type of relationship."

The State of Illinois fought back, appealing the decision, but Murphy's position and the judge's decision were upheld, clearing the way for a class-action suit in the state courts to close down Sheridan. The matter never came to trial. An out-of-court settlement was reached. The Illinois Department of Corrections announced to the press that it was closing the Illinois Industrial School for Boys at Sheridan.

At the time Murphy was fighting to close Sheridan, a young legal-aid lawyer from El Paso, Steven Bercu, was asking for help from the Youth Law Center, a San Francisco–based Legal Services Corporation back-up center, because he wanted to shut down the entire Texas Youth

Council reform school system. Bercu, in the course of representing a teen-ager who had been locked up in a TYC institution, had stumbled onto one of the most brutal kid prison systems in the nation. It was as though the *Gault* and *Winship* cases had never been decided. Thousands of youngsters were being physically and emotionally abused by guards. Youngsters who had committed no crimes were sentenced without hearings, then were placed in the cruelest prison system the legal-service lawyers had ever heard of. With the help of Youth Law Center attorneys William Hoffman and Peter Sandman, Bercu filed *Morales* v. *Turman* on February 12, 1971.

The *Morales* case developed out of a simple dispute between minor TYC officials and Bercu. Bercu had been investigating his own client's problems when several other youngsters who were locked up in the same facility asked if he would represent them. The TYC officials balked, saying they would not allow the legal-aid attorney even to interview these other youngsters. Bercu's efforts to gain access to them created so much resistance within the TYC that Bercu began to realize he was onto something much bigger than he had first imagined. Because the federally subsidized legal-aid offices in El Paso were not staffed or funded for a major class action, Bercu asked for help from the back-up center. Working in both the state courts and the U.S. District Court, the attorneys first obtained injunctions ordering Texas officials to grant the juvenile inmates their constitutionally protected right to be represented by counsel and to make the inmates available for consultation with their attorneys.

Once he had access, Bercu set about developing *Morales* v. *Turman*. The federal court case took its name from Alicia Morales, one of the girls confined by the TYC, and James Turman, then director of the TYC. The filing of the case in the U.S. District Court opened the way for the plaintiffs to begin extensive discovery proceedings. Bercu,

Sandman, and Hoffman recruited a small army of law students, equipped them with a specially designed question-
naire, and sent them through the TYC system to interview
all twenty-five hundred kids then being held in the six
reform schools. The U.S. Department of Justice agreed to
enter the case on the plaintiff's side, as a "friend of the
court," and this gave Bercu access to several civil rights
lawyers and a staff of paralegal assistants to help develop
the case.

It was discovered that between 1967 and 1971 more than
five thousand Texas children had been sent to TYC reform
schools without due process, and that in 1971 there were
863 youngsters serving time who had not been represented
by a lawyer. More shocking, it was learned that *280 had
been sent to prison without any hearing at all.* And that
wasn't all of the surprises. Half the youngsters in TYC
reform schools came from just seven of the 254 counties
in Texas. While population distribution would account for
some small part of this imbalance, this was a dramatic
example of how uneven the juvenile justice system could
become. The only discovery that was not surprising was
the racial make-up of the reform school population: 56
percent were either black or Chicano; 43 percent were
Anglo.

By December 1972, the litigation team had amassed
enough evidence to convince the Texas Court of Civil
Appeals that it should order the release of all those youngsters who had been imprisoned without due process or
representation. However, the lack of due process had become but one of several issues. Perhaps the most pressing,
the most discouraging, issue was the widespread use of
cruel and unusual punishment. During the course of the
investigation, the litigation team uncovered massive evidence of unbelievably harsh and frequently sadistic treatment within the TYC institutions. The TYC operated six
facilities, three for boys, three for girls. As the investigators

soon discovered, the worst problems were in the Gatesville State School for Boys, a century-old kid prison that held 1560 inmates, and in Mt. View, a maximum-security unit that housed 480. Gatesville was known as a tough place to do time, a place where the most troublesome kids were sent. That was true only in part: 20 percent of the kids in Gatesville were status offenders; 60 percent were in for misdemeanors and nonviolent thefts. *Only 9 percent had committed violent crimes.*

If a kid messed up in any way in Gatesville, he was sent to Mt. View, where any infraction of the rules, any misconduct at all put him in the Special Treatment Center. The STC was "the hole," the place where kids were locked away in tiny steel cells and where guards were extremely cruel, even by Texas standards. One case demonstrates the point. A skinny black teen-ager named Albert was transferred into the STC and put on a work detail. In depositions and testimony, the STC guards contended that the youngster refused to work: "He was hollering and crying and taking on and trying to run off . . . When we started talking to him he went to cussing and saying he wasn't going to work." Refusal to work is a cardinal sin. Court records show that three guards, each standing six feet tall, each weighing nearly two hundred pounds, dragged Albert from the work detail into the STC cell block, threw him bodily into his six-by-twelve-foot cell, and slammed the steel-plate door. Albert continued to cry and yell and tear up anything that was loose in his cell. The guards telephoned a supervisor and asked for permission to tear-gas Albert. Permission was granted. In a deposition, a supervising guard explained: "I think we used the big spray [can] first, and it was just about [empty] and so it didn't slow him up, what we put in there. So we put one of the other [grenade] type in there, we pitched the can of that in there [through a small opening in the steel door]." The six-by-twelve cell was nearly airtight, the door was closed, and the dry powdered chemical exploded all over the boy, sticking to his skin, burning his black skin pink. He screamed in pain, and was rushed to the infirmary, where the nurse treated him. She later told attorneys, "Well, of course, he smelled like gas, you know. We could smell gas on the boy. We bathed him and shampooed his hair . . . and put some medication on his eyes . . . There is an ointment which we can put on burns . . . There were burns on his face, neck."

James Turman, director of the TYC and a named defendant in the suit, was questioned about the use of tear gas in the STC unit. At first he avoided answering the attorney's questions directly, but finally admitted that tear gas was used by policy "to stop serious problems before they get out of hand, the destruction of property, the endangering of the life of either the student or someone else . . . We will not tolerate and cannot tolerate one youngster completely disrupting a large group . . . If you have, if you allow mutiny, if you have ten youngsters, say, in STC you cannot permit mutiny, you cannot permit any person to completely refuse to carry out his assignment . . . Tear gas is not used as a punishment, force is not used as a punishment . . . But by the same token you cannot permit mutiny or a complete disruption of everything this particular group is involved in."

By whatever name, punishment or treatment, the inmates at Gatesville and Mt. View were treated harshly, painfully. After six weeks of trial, U.S. District Court Judge William Wayne Justice ordered Gatesville and Mt. View closed down. He concluded: ". . . in the sordid parade of evidence brought before the court showing incident after incident of physical abuse, two particular incidents stood out . . . one involving a corrections officer interrogating a boy who had just attempted suicide." The officer knocked the boy to the floor and sprayed tear gas in his face for refusing to answer a question. The second incident involved a homosexual boy who had screaming fits. A guard punched the boy, then tied his hands behind him and blind-folded him. After twirling the youngster around and around to make him lose his sense of direction, the guard ordered the boy to *run* to his cell. The kid tried to obey, slammed headlong into steel doors and walls, got up and tried again, struck his head, and fell to the floor, screaming and crying.

Judge Justice's seventy-three-page opinion quite graph-ically detailed the horror of life in the Texas kid prisons. In the section on *disciplinary procedures,* he described "certain degrading, make-work tasks" ordered if the boys talked back or talked in food lines or failed to eat all the food on their plates. One of these extra-duty tasks was grass-pulling, a torture wherein the guard required the boy to bend at the waist, without bending his knees, and pull weeds hour after hour. The judge wrote:

> While on grass-pulling duty in March 1973, J. became tired after three hours and bent his knees. For this he was kicked in the back and punched in the mouth . . . and told to go back to pulling. When he again became tired and started to stand up a [corrections officer] kicked him in the head with his booted foot . . . Apparently desperate, J. escaped from the work detail and ran to the superintendent's office. There he was met by [another corrections officer], who pulled the boy into the office by the neck. After slapping J., the officer told him to get up against the wall and put his hands in his pockets . . . [the officer] struck the boy many times in the jaw and stomach with his fist and open hand and kicked the boy when he fell down . . . late that evening J. was placed in STC for running away from work duty.

By the conclusion of the trial it was obvious to Judge Justice that one of the primary problems was the failure of the TYC's top administrators to set policy and to reg-ulate the operations of the six kid prisons:

> Practically every decision related to employment, treatment, education, discipline, institutional life and allocation of re-

sources in an institution is left to the superintendent of that
institution, who may in turn delegate the decision . . . to an
even lower echelon staff member . . . Superintendents of training schools in the TYC system exercise wide discretion in
formulating the programs, services and ground rules in their
respective schools . . . There are often major differences between the rules of the various institutions . . . Furthermore
the rules may vary from dormitory to dormitory, or cottage
to cottage within the same institution . . . In fact almost *any*
action, however arbitrary, by an employee . . . is probably
*consistent* with TYC policy because that policy is so vague
as to be nonexistent."

In addition to remedying the immediate problems by
ordering Gatesville and Mt. View closed and instructing
the TYC to treat juveniles humanely, Judge Justice ruled
that once a juvenile is committed to an institution, he or
she has a constitutional right to receive humane, professional, individualized treatment based on his or her specific
needs. Children held against their will have the right to a
good, clean, healthful environment, the right to some pri-
vacy, the right to be treated like human beings, not animals.

In effect, the U.S. District Court was forcing the State
of Texas to do what it should have been doing all along,
to do what state laws intended. In the process, the court
established "new law" and expanded the rights of children
all across the nation. Cases like *Gault* and *Morales* prove
that the system can be forced to protect the rights of the
individuals, but not without the work of aggressive lawyers
like Steve Bercu and Patrick Murphy. And then the change
is never lasting. The State of Texas or Illinois may shut
down a facility or two, Massachusetts may close all of its
big kid prisons and trumpet its intent to deinstitutionalize
the juvenile justice system, but such disruptions of the
normal, bureaucratic rhythms don't last long. In 1977,
Murphy said during an interview in Chicago that he saw
a "great deal" of change, that the juvenile courts in Cook

County were now much more aware of the juvenile's right to due process and individualized treatment, that there was less use of psychotropic drugs and solitary confinement as behavior-control techniques in the state reform schools. However, though the system may have improved from Murphy's perspective, the problems hadn't gone away; they had just moved.

St. Charles, the medium-security facility during Murphy's crusade to shut down Sheridan, had been made the maximum-security facility. In 1977, *Chicago Sun-Times* reporter Mike Anderson began a series of stories on juvenile justice that focused on St. Charles. The headline: HUGE COVER-UP AT ST. CHARLES JAIL, OVERCROWDING, DRUGS, HOMOSEXUAL RAPE, STAFF SHORTAGES. And the lead on Anderson's story began: "It is more important to curry bureaucratic favor than rehabilitate youngsters at the state's largest prison for children . . ." The stories indicated that bureaucratic concerns over jobs and promotions were more important than what happened to kids. One former St. Charles administrator told Anderson, "The task is not to rehabilitate kids; the task is to keep everybody happy. And basically [administrators] worry about if something happens, how will it look in the newspapers? That's how decisions are made."

While *Gault, Morales,* and similar cases have provided children with more protection, juvenile court proceedings remain closed sessions, where the combined authority of the judge, the district attorney, and the probation officer are aligned against the juvenile defendant and his or her counsel. Even if the officers of the court and the defense counsel are all in agreement, there are unbelievably complex bureaucratic obstacles to overcome if the youngster's best interests are to be served. In each of the nation's major cities, the juvenile justice system — with all of its educational, therapeutic, and community-care appendages — has come to resemble nothing so much as a gigantic

machine made up of hundreds of cogged wheels of varying
sizes, each turning at different speeds. Sometimes the cogs
are meshed and the machine grinds out justice; too often
the wheels are out of alignment, the cogs unmeshed.

In New York, the Family Court in each of the boroughs
had installed a Rapid Intervention Program (RIP) that was
supposed to do complete diagnostic work-ups on all kids
to help move them through the court system quickly and
get them into proper placement, instead of having them
waste months in the overcrowded system. However, the
highly publicized RIP system itself soon became so impossibly bound with red tape that it was impeding juvenile
justice, not expediting it. Problem: Funding cutbacks in
the RIP and in court staffing reduced the number of typists,
and the lack of typists slowed preparation of "dispositional
plans" for each child, plans the judge had to have before
any decisions could be made. An investigation of the
jammed-up legal machinery revealed: "Cutbacks, freezes
and controls have hampered the effective operation of the
Family Court and have seriously prejudiced the lives of
young children . . . Because of unconscionable delay caused
by the lack of a typist . . . the life of a child hangs in limbo.
For want of a typist a child may be lost." The RIP system
was abandoned not long after, and when asked why, the
court administrators said that they could not talk about
what had happened; judge's orders.

The problems were the same all across the country: tight
budgets, short staffing, heavy case loads in the courts, in
the probation offices, and the juvenile halls. Mike Goodman, a reporter for the *Los Angeles Times*, first exposed
the overcrowded conditions in the Los Angeles County
Central Juvenile Hall, the largest in the nation in 1974. At
the time, as many as five hundred to six hundred runaways,
status offenders, petty thieves, hustlers, robbers, rapists,
and murderers were all crowded together; every bed was
taken; scores of kids slept on the floors. Most stayed a

week or two, waiting for their cases to come up in one of the thirty-three juvenile courts. (Los Angeles County has ten juvenile judges and twenty-two juvenile referees who sit as judges. They hear twenty-five thousand cases a year.) Some of the kids stayed longer because they were sentenced to do time in the hall, rather than in one of the county's "camps" or in the California Youth Authority kid prison system. Some stayed in the hall much longer simply because the court could find no place to put them. One seventeen-year-old black girl spent nearly two years in Central Juvenile Hall because she was emotionally disturbed and so aggressive that no state institution or private psychiatric hospital would take her. Eventually, with the help of L.A. County Supervisor James Hayes, the girl was placed in a private hospital, at a cost of $2000 a month, and after extensive treatment, she was able to return to junior college, complete her education, and find work.

Goodman's periodic articles between 1974 and 1976 made it clear that juvenile gangs, not the corrections officers and counselors, were the dominant force within the Central Juvenile Hall. Streetwise young blacks called the place "Disneyland." They liked the hall because they were in the majority; it was a place where they had power, not the whites, a place where they could find self-esteem in violence against whites. Chicano youths moved in packs for protection and recognition. Even the staff was polarized: Chicano counselors and probation officers reported racial tension between them and their black counterparts. Months after his first exposé, Goodman once more reported, "Violence, sexual attacks, inadequate medical facilities and an atmosphere fostering anger and hatred still plague Central Juvenile Hall, seven doctors charged in a protest letter to the Los Angeles County Board of Supervisors." Two years later, Goodman wrote: "Unsanitary conditions and overcrowding — a situation Los Angeles County officials promised two years ago would never return

— were discovered at Central Juvenile Hall in a surprise visit early Thursday. Children were found sleeping on the floors in the infirmary and some dormitories."

The repeated exposure of the problems by the *Times* created pressures on the courts, the Board of Supervisors, and the Probation Department. Angry politicians ordered the Probation Department to "do something" to take the heat off while plans for a new $23 million juvenile prison at Sylmar were rushed to completion. To relieve the pressures on the Central Juvenile Hall, the Probation Department hastily reorganized its camp structure and began moving kids out of the hall into its juvenile prison farm system. Camp Glenn Rockey, in the San Dimas foothills, was converted from medium to maximum security, and the toughest kids from the hall and from the other camps were transported in and locked up. The same black and Chicano gang structures that existed downtown were transported along with the kids. The pressures inside Glenn Rockey began to build as each gang began to establish its own turf inside the wire. A fight between a black inmate and several Chicanos was triggered by an argument over the use of a weight-lifting area. The bad feelings carried over into the mess hall, and a general riot broke out. During the fracas, club-wielding juveniles tore the mess hall apart and tried to overpower the guards. Fifteen juveniles and five probation officers were injured. *Nine inmates escaped.*

In a postriot press conference and in information releases, the Probation Department denied that anyone had escaped, and officials played down the seriousness of the situation. Probation officials covered up the mess, and the press went off to cover other stories; but the pressures built back up, and another riot broke out in July. Again there was the attempt to minimize the problems. But this time *Los Angeles Times* reporter Dorothy Townsend set about reconstructing what had happened in May and again in July, and in the process she discovered not only that several inmates had escaped, but that some of them were still at large. Her story detailed how the May riots had started and how the politics of the county juvenile corrections system had contributed to the problems. During a hearing investigating the causes of the riots, one probation officer testified that the switch from minimum security to maximum security at Glenn Rockey was

> extremely poorly planned, slipshod, unprofessional . . . When there is a whole lot of kids at juvenile hall and you have got to move them out to a camp program, you just put kids where the empty beds are because the Board of Supervisors is complaining that there is overcrowded conditions at the hall . . . When you take all of the failures of the probation system on the street and put them into a camp . . . something's got to give . . . They [court and Probation Department] take and transfer [any boy] to Glenn Rockey where he is locked up in a security dorm . . . You have an extremely wide range of delinquent history [in the dorm]. The only real criteria, when it comes down to it, is "Is there a bed open at that camp?" and if so, put that body in that camp.

Find a bed, any bed, and place the kid, shape the kids up, make them fit the circumstance, mold and twist them to suit the system's needs and its shortcomings. For a while the new juvenile jail in Sylmar, at the northern end of the San Fernando Valley, solved the overcrowding problems, but not for long. With the increasing emphasis on law and order, the juvenile courts were ordering more youngsters locked up. By early 1981 there was serious overcrowding in all of the county's juvenile halls and the state was warning that if something was not done, quickly, the county would be taken into court. The state was threatening to close down the juvenile halls if the county did not comply with health and safety standards.

The problem was the same everywhere. Like the seventeen-year-old black girl who did two years in the Los Angeles Central Juvenile Hall because there was no place else to put her, a fifteen-year-old girl named Cathy was placed in the Illinois State School for Girls at Geneva because the Illinois Department of Children and Family Services could find no other bed. The Cook County Juvenile Court had ordered the DCFS to find counseling for Cathy, possibly in a group home. The girl's social worker wrote in such careful detail how seriously disturbed and aggressive the child really was that no group home or hospital administrator would touch her. These private or voluntary agencies are notoriously selective, and they shy away from the tough cases. The caseworker went back into court and asked the court to declare Cathy a Minor in Need of Services — a MINS — and then had her placed in Geneva, pending alternative placement. She had been there nine months when Patrick Murphy discovered the case. He filed contempt-of-court actions against the DCFS bureaucrats, contending that they had not followed the court's orders to place the girl in counseling. The judge ordered the girl released to her parents and demanded that the DCFS find her counseling, as he had first ordered.

Why hadn't the court followed up the case before Murphy's action? That was the job of the DCFS, acting for the court. The court delegated most of its responsibilities for follow-up investigations and case supervision to DCFS social workers or Cook County probation officers. Murphy said the DCFS social workers were frustrated, overworked, and trapped in snarls of red tape and bureaucratic bungling, and that the nine juvenile courts were all so overcrowded that they were pushing cases through at the rate of one every five to ten minutes. The courts, the prosecutors, the legal-aid lawyers, and public defenders were all part of the treadmill, Murphy said, adding, "The simple fact is that the juvenile courts are a failure."

One of the saddest casualties of this national bureaucratic nightmare called juvenile justice is a girl named Jerri. I met Jerri in 1978, when she was facing an eighteen-month "fall" for car theft. Then sixteen years of age, Jerri was a pretty girl with soft features. She didn't look like a cell-block tough who would fight guards or inmates at the drop of an insult, but that was her reputation. Jerri's mother agreed, said her daughter was tough, very tough, and it worried her: "I can see her walking into a gas station with some boy and him saying, 'Okay, we're going to rob it, and if the guy moves, shoot him,' and if that boy yells 'Shoot him,' Jerri will pull the trigger. I mean it. It scares the hell out of me. I know that if she doesn't get some help it will happen. I can see it. You call it pessimistic or whatever, I call it knowing my daughter . . . This girl is sixteen years old and she has spent most of the last five years locked up . . . Every birthday since she was eleven she has spent locked up in juvenile hall somewhere."

As Jerri's mother talked, she was slumped in the front seat of my car, smoking one cigarette after another, waiting for visiting hours to begin in the big, urban juvenile hall. There was a hardness about her, a toughness that showed life had not been easy. As she talked about her daughter, there were both traces of sorrow and hints of pride: "I got a letter from her the other day saying she was going to have to knock some heads around [in juvenile hall] because the guards think they can still walk all over her. If anyone crosses Jerri, or if they tell her something she doesn't like, then she's going to fight."

Jerri has a long record. Her juvenile files date back to June 1974, when she was first locked up for making obscene phone calls and for being beyond the control of her mother. Jerri and her stepfather didn't get along. He frequently beat her. Her mother said, "Seems like I was always defending her, trying to cover up for her, which may not always be the right thing to do, but he was just a little too violent. I never did interfere with his correcting [four children] when they needed correcting, but when it came to hitting her over the back with a cane, then I stepped in."

That marriage broke up. Jerri was rebellious at home; she skipped school, stayed away from home, was disobedient. In the early summer of 1974, Jerri's mother told authorities that her daughter was beyond her control. The probation officer reported:

> Appearing before the court for the first time is an intelligent, but very insecure and unhappy young lady, twelve years of age. Jerri has indicated she is a troublemaker; she does not want to be, but it seems to just happen. The minor appears to have no impulse control whatsoever . . . The girl wants friends, desperately. She craves attention and structure at home, but the mother is working at two jobs . . . Jerri has a very negative self-image — and is searching for love and attention. Apparently because of the mother's own lack of nurturing, she has not been able to provide emotional nurturing for Jerri . . . Jerri would benefit from twenty-four-hour, maximum external structure, institutional placement, but because of her age she would not be accepted. The next alternative is a special supervision [probation] unit . . . Supervision of Jerri would require maximum time and patience. She is eager to please and is searching for acceptance and attention. Jerri's mother is searching for support as well. She appears to be receptive to counseling for Jerri and herself . . . Since Jerri is reflecting much of the mother's negative perceptions of men, inappropriate coping mechanisms, etc., working with the mother would benefit indirectly Jerri's behavior . . .

It was all there — the problems, the diagnosis, the willingness on the part of the mother and the girl to accept some kind of help. It was all there — except for the help, except for the counseling. Jerri was returned home, there was some attempt at "family counseling" through a community mental health clinic, but the county did no substantial casework, made no sustained effort to shore up the family structure. Mother and daughter went once a week, for an hour, to a psychology student who was completing her training. "We were in counseling for about six months; then Jerri got busted again, for fighting in school, for assault and battery. She beat up this girl pretty bad and they put her [Jerri] away.''

Jerri was placed in a big, modern kid prison run by the county; there was a strong emphasis on education and group therapy. Jerri's mother went once a week, sometimes twice a week, for counseling. The mother explained, "Jerri was not only the youngest girl there, she was thirteen then, but she was there longer than any other girl. She was there a year." Inside, Jerri fought with other girls, the guards, the police who were summoned to take her back to juvenile hall until she calmed down. She cut her wrists, jabbed a big needle in her arm, and broke it off. Her mother recalled, "Every time a release date would get close, she would screw up. She would try to run or she would get into a fight. *She didn't want out . . .* They [counselors] told me she was afraid to come out, but they didn't tell me why . . . Just like right now, the trouble she's in right now. She knew it would happen, she's not a stupid girl, but she did it anyway."

Jerri's current problems had started with a sequence of events that had landed her in the California Youth Authority's girls' unit. She had been before yet another juvenile court judge on assault charges, and the judge, noting her record, ordered that she be sent to the CYA for a ninety-day diagnostic observation period. She went through another round of diagnosis, received no therapy or counseling, then was paroled to an "open" (unlocked) setting in a group home in a city a hundred miles from her home. Jerri stayed a week in the group home; then she and a boy from the home ran, swiped a car, and drove to her home. She was caught almost immediately, and was back in juvenile hall.

If that had been the end of what I had learned about Jerri's case, hers would have been just another very sad story, a case where the system had expended its best efforts but the girl, for whatever reasons, had failed to respond. But then something happened that lifted the case out of the ordinary, and in the process provided a quick glimpse of some serious flaws in the juvenile justice machine. At the time Jerri was sitting in juvenile hall — certain she was headed back to one of the state's big kid prisons — Daniel C. was routinely handed her case file. He was working in the juvenile division of the public defender's office; his assignment was to handle the initial court proceedings, where he could either plea-bargain the case with his counterpart in the district attorney's office or could recommend the girl's case for a full-scale, contested hearing. If he decided Jerri should have a hearing, he would ask the court for a hearing date and then turn her file over to another assistant public defender, one who was assigned to try contested matters.

Daniel C. told me: "Her case looked just like another commitment to state reform school, and she was agreeable to copping a plea rather than contesting the case. But the story she told me was disjointed; something didn't fit. Here was a sixteen-year-old who, by her record, had spent most of the previous five years in every facility this county had, and nobody had done a bit of good for her. It didn't make sense. It was strange. So I had the case assigned to me, permanently."

By asking for the case, Daniel had stepped out of the routine and undertaken a task that grew to such proportions that it nearly overwhelmed him. "I began to spend a lot more time on that case; I knew the system, but even I didn't really understand what it was going to take to get that girl the help she needed." His first task was to get the girl's probation officer to agree with his plan of action.

Unless you have the P.O. on your side in one of these court hearings, you're not going anywhere, but it took me almost two months to convince the P.O. that Jerri was a good risk, that she did not belong in reform school. With the P.O. on our side, we were ready to fight the case. I was prepared to subpoena all of the officials needed to show that Jerri had not received treatment at [named county facility] and [named county facility], as they tried to indicate. I had talked to all of them, and it was obvious these facilities hadn't done their work. Everyone was recommending treatment, but no one was providing treatment. Even at [reform school] she had been kept ninety days without treatment. They had some excuse or other, but *they didn't do anything at all.* Nothing. I was set for a contested case, but the assistant district attorney assigned to the case was an understanding person, too. She didn't fight me  So the only real problem left was the court.

The court agreed that Jerri could be placed in a closed community-care facility if Daniel C. could arrange placement and financing. The one private school Daniel knew about was charging between $1200 and $1400 a month, depending on the type of case. The Probation Department told him it did not have that kind of financial resources. Daniel did not know how to qualify her for mental health funding or welfare funding that might pay for such a placement. Finally, he found a private psychiatric hospital that would take Jerri, if he could qualify her for a Medicaid card. He explained, "We worked out a myth, procedurally, to qualify her for Medicaid. Technically, she was made a ward of the court — actually, this procedure is used for children who have no parental involvement, who have been abandoned — but it was stretched to cover Jerri, even though she was technically already a delinquent. Medicaid accepted her case. Then it took *three weeks* to get her a Medicaid card."

And that wasn't the last of the bureaucratic surprises. The Medicaid card was good for only ninety days of psychiatric care, even though it was estimated that Jerri would need at least six months of help, six months in which she and her mother would receive the intensive kind of therapy they had been seeking for years. It was decided by the public defender, the district attorney, and the court that they should chance the ninety-day Medicaid commitment and hope that they could find additional funding. After nearly three months, Jerri was placed — at a cost of $80 a day.

It would be simple just to end the story there, but cases like these never have such endings. After a few weeks, Jerri ran away from the hospital, was easily found, and placed in juvenile hall again. Daniel C. had been transferred to another section of the public defender's office, but the young woman who took over the case continued to work in the girl's behalf. The girl was placed in an adolescent program in a state hospital, she escaped, and was replaced. When she was placed a second time, the judge told me, "Here were my alternatives. She still is only sixteen. I could let Jerri go back to the state hospital or send her to reform school — she is very bright, quite a bit higher I.Q. than average . . . I think she is a product of circumstances . . . I don't know if it is too late for her or not. If anybody can help straighten her out, it's got to be with a kind, understanding approach."

If there is one quality the juvenile court justice system lacks it is "a kind, understanding approach." The cases of Jerri and Tommy are proof enough of this fact. But why the failures? After all, we're spending $1 billion or more each year on the elaborate machinery set up to assist the government in its role as parent.

The answers are found in our national attitudes, of course. We are essentially a conservative nation founded upon a socioeconomic system that places little value on individuals who are not productive. We say we love our children and we give lip service to the fact that the very young are helpless and dependent. We pass laws, appropriate money, create great bureaus to provide help and care and, where need be, reformation, but we begrudge the expenditure of public funds for the economic and social services that could have altered the lives of children like Jerri and Tommy. Welfare is viewed as a negative influence and welfare agencies have become the regulators of the public largess, set up more to police the poor than to serve the needy. We also have a deeply ingrained belief in a punitive law-and-order system that relies on rituals of pain and death to deter crime. In concert, these attitudes pose a great and costly irony. While we are unwilling to commit ourselves to a national social policy that could have given Jerri and Tommy some better chance of survival, we have loudly called for a swift and sure system of justice to deter such children from a life of crime.

The system has failed and this failure has proven very costly. Calculate, if you will, the cost of a violent young person who spends more time in institutions than out; consider the loss of lives and the destruction of property. Each time a violent youngster kills someone his or her act of violence stands as evidence of just how bankrupt the current system of juvenile justice is, the editorial views of *Time* magazine and the rhetoric of Chief Justice Burger notwithstanding.

Would a swifter, more sure system of justice have stopped the thirteen-year-old Los Angeles boy from committing murder number 1042 at 11:15 P.M. on December 31, 1980? Hardly. The youngster was attending a party and had been drinking, according to police reports. The party was noisy and a neighbor, a seventy-four-year-old man, came over to protest. An argument ensued, possibly including some pushing and shoving. The thirteen-year-old armed himself with a rifle and police say he killed the old man.

Phil Kerby, a columnist for the *Los Angeles Times,* used the final murder of 1980 to bring some perspective to the public outcry for more law and order. Kerby explained that the boy was a member of a gang, his father had died in prison while serving time on a narcotics conviction, and the boy no longer lived with his mother. Then Kerby wrote:

> He had access to a deadly weapon in a society that refuses to impose any rational restraints upon the spread of firearms. Since birth he had lived in a nightmare world of chaos, vio-

lence, and drugs. He was manufactured for violence, just as surely as the rifle he used was manufactured to kill. In his nightmare mind, the human connection did not exist between him and his victim, and it was easy for him to pull the trigger . . . The ominous truth is that the conditions that spawn such violence are beyond the power of the police to control.

That truth seems so obvious. And the basic flaws in the juvenile justice system seem so simple to comprehend: We don't see the child as a complex individual who is an integral part of a family structure; we have no national children's policy, no basic commitment to help children in need. Instead we have taken a narrow, compartmentalized view that focuses on the bits and pieces of children's shattered lives and fails to recognize that juvenile dependency and juvenile delinquency are only threads in a much larger social fabric, inseparably entwined with the threads of unemployment, poverty, hunger, sickness, disability, and dislocation. No noisy cries for more law and order, swift and sure justice, and harsher penalties can solve so complex an issue.

# 5

## Out of Sight

To his mother his name is Joseph, not Joey, and as she talked about her teen-aged son it was with a great sadness, mixed with deep anger: "He's a good boy. He's not un-controllable. He'll listen as long as I'm here, but he won't stay in school. He got mixed up with the police, with some other boys . . . That child is so mixed up."

Joseph's mother is a big, strong woman who has worked hard to make a life for herself and her children, against great odds. Her anger is directed at a system that took her children away from her just because she was poor. That was in 1964. Joseph was three. She explained:

My husband left me with all those babies [five children, ages nine months to six years] and I didn't have no way to support them, no other way of gettin' money other than goin' to welfare. At that time they [the state] had a system where you had to be separated for six months before you got any money, so they told me the best thing they could do for me was to put my kids in foster care and let me work and then, when I was able, I could take 'em back . . . I could visit my kids only once a month, for an hour, that was all . . . and when I would go see Joseph, he would scream and holler [as she was leaving] and you couldn't get away from him . . . He didn't see why he had to leave home.

It took Joseph's mother nearly two years to get her life back together. She got a job, remarried, and then asked for her children:

> The welfare authorized for them to come home, but at that time they said Joseph [then five] was emotionally disturbed. They said he was running around, he took roach poison, he was cuttin' other little children's hair, he run away, all kind of stuff like that, and he was hard to control. So they told me he needed some kind of schoolin' for emotionally disturbed children. So they told me they didn't have no place for him in New Orleans, that they had to give him a place that was a good distance away . . . They told me the only place they was able to get him in was in New York [State, and said] . . . I had to go to court in order for them to send him to New York, to make him a ward of the state, in order for them to pay for it, because if I kept him in my custody I would have to pay for it and the tuition [in 1967] would be seven hundred dollars a month . . . I understood that I was puttin' him in a home for children that were emotionally disturbed, for at least a year, and that he would be able to come home as soon as he got better and I would be able to handle him.

Joseph was in the New York private school for four years. Records show that each year the school's administrators informed Louisiana bureaucrats that the boy was not in need of continued care and treatment, and they recommended he be returned to his parents. If that was not possible, they suggested that he be placed in foster care in New Orleans. Louisiana officials never responded to the recommendations. The monthly cost of care in the New York facility had increased year by year until it reached $1100 in 1971. Louisiana officials decided cheaper places might serve as well. They transferred Joseph to the East Texas Guidance Center in Tyler, Texas, but they failed to notify the boy's mother of the move.

She told me:

I would ask them if Joseph could come home yet, and they was tellin' me that he wasn't ready to come back. They said when he was ready, they would let me know. I ask them maybe twice a year . . . They didn't tell me they was bringin' him to Texas . . . I found out later. About six months after they moved him they sent me a letter and told me I had a new social worker, and she would call to introduce herself to me and she would tell me some things about Joseph that I might want to hear . . . but she never came, so I called them. And finally they sent her out and she told me Joseph was in Texas . . . She thought I knew, but I told her no, I didn't know that.

According to Joseph's mother, the social worker's visit was the first personal contact she had ever had with the Welfare Department. She had *never* seen the caseworker who handled Joseph's placement in New York. She said, "I used to talk to him on the phone."

How often had she seen the new social worker? "She came that one time. Then she called me and told me she had tried to arrange it for Christmas [to have Joseph come home], and she even told them [East Texas Guidance Center] that she'd come and pick him up herself . . . and they told her no."

From the time Joseph was taken to New York until he was finally returned home from the East Texas Guidance Center, ten years later, his mother was given no opportunity to visit him. She was contacted only the one time by a social worker. No one had ever developed any kind of family-reunification plan. After Joseph was placed in Texas, his mother received letters from him, and occasional phone calls: "He was about twelve or thirteen then, and he used to call me and ask me why he couldn't come home. This man in Texas had told him he would be there until he was an adult, that I didn't want him . . . I wanted him, I did . . . [She was crying at this point] . . . I wanted him

home. That place was no good. He told me he was gettin'
whippin's with a belt, whippin's with a board.''

Joseph's mother wanted him home, but she didn't know
what to do, how to go about fighting for his release. Then,
by coincidence, the lives of an underground journalist —
Edith Bierhorst Back — and a New Orleans private attorney — William Rittenberg — crossed with those of Joseph and his mother. Edith Back was in the process of
exposing the horrible conditions in many of the private
residential facilities in Texas. Her work, combined with
the legal actions brought by Rittenberg on behalf of Joseph
and two other youngsters, resulted in a class-action suit
in federal court that ultimately freed more than eight
hundred Louisiana children who had been similarly placed.

What had happened to Joseph was not unusual. In the
late 1970s most state and county placement agencies across
the nation were exporting their most troublesome cases.
The Children's Defense Fund investigated and reported
*only four* of the fifty states neither shipped kids out nor
took kids in from other states. One measure of just how
far into the house of mirrors the various bureaucrats had
wandered was revealed by CDF investigators, who found
that twenty-seven states were receiving children from
states to which they were sending children. In states like
Texas and Florida, where licensing laws and quality control
regulations were extremely lax, increasing numbers of entrepreneurs were willing to take in problem children of all
kinds, from anywhere, as long as the states and counties
were willing to pay their price. A thriving kid business was
developing in these states. Children's Defense Fund investigators also discovered that only one third of the states
that shipped children out of their official sight sent caseworkers to check on how the children were being treated.
Caseworkers in Chicago or Trenton or New Orleans simply
assumed all was well with the children unless they heard
otherwise.

No one was quite sure how many children were being shipped across state lines. The Children's Defense Fund estimated ten thousand a year; the *New York Times* set the number at twenty thousand; and CBS-TV's Mike Wallace reported on "60 Minutes":

> The interstate commerce of kids: fifty thousand children shipped across state borders every year. These are the difficult, hard-to-handle youngsters sent to institutions, treatment centers, psychiatric or disciplinary facilities, public or private. They're shipped out — for pay — because their own families, their own states don't have homes or adequate facilities for them. So New Jersey kids wind up in Florida, or Ohio kids in Pennsylvania, Illinois kids in Texas . . . [Taking in children] is a big business . . . close to a billion dollars' worth a year.

Wallace singled out New Jersey — the state then placed two hundred youngsters out of state, at an average cost of about $8000 a year — and one private, for-profit institution, the Montonari School in Hialeah, Florida, for examination. The Montonari School is a cluster of twenty-seven group homes, an adminstrative unit, and a maximum-security residential institution that housed the toughest, most difficult youngsters. The school's total enrollment was 320, and Aldelio Montonari, founder of the school, charged between $12,000 and $25,000 a year in tuition, according to Wallace.

On camera, Wallace asked Montonari: "You make between $400,000 and $500,000 a year, out of $4 million [gross] and your own salary for 1974 . . ."

MONTONARI: "Was very good."

WALLACE: "Was $57,000."

MONTONARI: "Very good."

WALLACE: "And now it's more?"

MONTONARI: "A little more, yes."

A few questions later, Wallace got Montonari to explain how the $400,000 a year in rent was paid by the school to Montonari himself and to another corporation that he controlled. He was operating a lease-back operation, renting his property to the school corporation that he operated. Montonari denied that he was simply warehousing children and making a lucrative business of the operation. However, teachers in the Montonari School who were interviewed told Wallace there was no remedial reading program and they were unaware of tutorial programs. A teacher in the maximum-security unit said he had met only one psychiatrist and one social worker in the facility in six months. The impression left by the Wallace exposé was of a large facility that paid low staff salaries, a facility that was understaffed and ill-equipped. In short, the Montonari School was a business venture that dealt in tough, hard-to-place kids from other states.

At the time the Wallace show was aired, the Virginia Departments of Welfare, Mental Health, and Mental Retardation had 560 children placed in twenty-nine states, at a cost of $5 million; 109 of these youngsters were in Florida facilities, eighteen of them were in the Montonari School. The Virginia House of Delegates was investigating the whole issue of out-of-state placement, and the "60 Minutes" program focused attention on the Montonari School. The commonwealth's Welfare Department officials ordered an investigation of the school, in a self-protecting action. The resulting report teeter-tottered up and down, but reached no conclusions. While the cottage house parents appeared "very dedicated," they were generally "unqualified and untrained." However, "earnest efforts" were being made to provide in-service training. In the area of treatment, "useful treatment plans were not developed," but the "rudiments" of good treatment planning were present. "Some programmatic areas were extremely understaffed," but "management staff, teachers and medical staff were well qualified and competent . . . the strength of Montonari is in its education program."

The subject was controversial, and state officials were

reluctant to take a stand on this one school or on the subject of out-of-state placement. In the Virginia legislature, Delegate Frank M. Slayton, a conservative Democrat, was leading the investigation of the entire system, questioning why so much was being spent to send so many children so far away from their home communities. Delegate Slayton's subcommittee concluded:

> The current system for dealing with these unwanted and unloved children is harsh, dehumanizing and often cruel. In many instances, for economic reasons, parents are required to surrender custody of their child to an agency of the state. [To qualify for federal funding, parents must voluntarily give up custody, or the juvenile court declares the child a "ward" of the court.] Even after the state has acquired custody . . . either by court action or entrustment agreements, the services provided are sporadic or nonexistent . Current policies and practices dealing with children in out-of-state placement . . . are calculated to more nearly produce the "battered child" than to achieve any positive result.

The problem was pervasive. Where Mike Wallace had zeroed in on New Jersey and Montonari, I had looked at Virginia, Illinois, and then Louisiana. Between 1963 and 1973, the Illinois Department of Children and Family Services had placed somewhere between eight hundred and one thousand children in private for-profit and nonprofit childcare facilities in Texas. Pat Murphy's work defending the children caught up in the DCFS system led ultimately to the exposure of the horrors of the kid business in Texas. Murphy explained, "We often heard rumors about various abuses at the Texas places, but we had been too busy with other matters to really investigate . . . [Then] we uncovered several unsettling facts that prompted us to file suit challenging Illinois's right to place neglected kids in Texas."

One of the unsettling facts was the unauthorized and unnecessary hysterectomy performed on a teen-aged girl who had been banished to Texas. Murphy said the DCFS listed the operation as an appendectomy. While working on the girl's case, Murphy learned that a dozen or more private kid businesses in Texas specialized in Cook County delinquents and neglected children. Some of these youngsters were placed in facilities that increased the number of children they could take by sending some on extended "camping trips," camping trips that lasted as long as three years. The kids lived outdoors, under military discipline, receiving little or no education or treatment.

Murphy's court actions attracted the Chicago press. A *Sun-Times* article read, in part: "State admits it lost track of 55 wards. Lawyers for the Illinois Department of Children and Family Services conceded Tuesday that they don't know the whereabouts of 55 youngsters who are wards of the state. The admission drew expressions of anger and disbelief from the chief judge of the Juvenile Court, William S. White . . . [who said], 'We only know about the missing children who are parties to this suit, but how many others must there also be missing we don't know about?' "

Murphy's work and the resulting media attention to the subject prompted the state government to create a task force to study the problem. Professor Patrick Keenan of DePaul headed the task force. In "An Illinois Tragedy," he reported, "The placement of hundreds of Illinois wards at Texas institutions was a tragic mistake. A large part of the [$8 million spent between 1963 and 1973] was wasted. A large part of the child-care services rendered were of unacceptable quality. The State of Illinois did not get all it paid for. The children did not get the care and help guaranteed them by statute and court order."

According to the Keenan report, three children had died in Texas, hundreds were abused. He described the DCFS bureaucratic structures: "No one in DCFS ever willingly made a decision . . . Individuals at all levels attempted to make every action appear as if it were ordered from higher up or at least had originated elsewhere." According to Keenan, the DCFS bureaucracy was designed to prevent investigators from finding anyone who was responsible or accountable. The lines of communication between social workers in the field and their supervisors wound their way so tortuously through one layer of the bureaucracy to the next that no decisions could be made and responsibility for inaction could not be traced.

The Keenan task force report stood as an indictment of the national practice of placing children out of state. However, it wasn't until Bill Rittenberg was contacted by Joseph's mother, and the mothers of Gary W. and Elizabeth M., that events that would fully expose the culpable bureaucratic systems began to take shape. Edith Back's journalistic investigations in Texas had put her in touch with these three teen-agers in various private institutions, and she had asked where their homes were. Through the children, Edith Back found the parents in Louisiana and then helped them find an attorney who could help them get their children back. The resulting lawsuit, filed by Bill Rittenberg, was called *Gary W., Joey G., and Elizabeth M.* v. *William Stewart* (Commissioner of Louisiana Health and Human Resources).

The suit, known simply as the *Gary W.* case, was filed in U.S. District Court in New Orleans. The charges detailed in very human terms how children were affected by being shipped out of state and how incapable the state and local agencies were of acting in the best interests of such children.

Like the *Morales* case before it, the *Gary W.* case had its beginnings in the early 1970s with a single lawyer responding to what had seemed, at the start, a relatively simple matter. Bill Rittenberg, four years out of law school and practicing privately in New Orleans, had begun to earn a reputation as a lawyer who would take on children's rights issues, especially if they involved constitutional questions. It was this reputation that brought Edith Back to his office. Posing as a social worker from Louisiana, Edith Back had talked to youngsters from New Orleans, obtained their parents' addresses, and was now seeking help for both the children and the parents. Many of these youngsters were black; many were from broken homes and had been arbitrarily taken from their mothers by social workers and by the juvenile courts without hearings, without any attempt having been made to keep their families together. She said some of these children were being abused, drugged, and worked without compensation. Some had been misplaced. Normal children were in facilities for the retarded, ambulatory mentally retarded children were confined to cagelike cribs and not allowed to move about, a deaf child was placed in a facility for emotionally disturbed children. Edith Back asked Rittenberg to meet with some of the parents and listen to their stories. He agreed, and then began his own investigation.

Rittenberg said, "It soon was obvious that the issue wasn't how terrible these Texas kid institutions might be — and many of them were horrible — the issue was that Louisiana didn't know shit about any of the places where they had put these kids."

No state official, at any level, whom I contacted later in Baton Rouge or New Orleans had an idea of how many children had been sent to Texas or how much money was being spent keeping them there. There were no quality controls on placement or care; social workers were not inspecting facilities to see how the children were being treated. There wasn't even a list of the private for-profit and nonprofit institutions being used. Part of the problem was the structuring of the state's health and welfare systems under the umbrella of the Louisiana Health and Human Resources Administration. The HHRA had the overall responsibility for all child-welfare and social-service programs; under the HHRA, the Office of Family Services (OFS) handled welfare and child custody, and the Division of Youth Services (DYS) handled predelinquent and delinquent children. The HHRA also comprised the Department of Mental Health, the Office of Mental Retardation, and the Exceptional Children's Act. The ECA was both a law and a bureaucratic structure responsible for the placement and funding of children within its jurisdiction. It had one caseworker for every four hundred children on its books, and was responsible for several hundred children placed in private Texas facilities.

Edith Back had told Rittenberg about the Louisiana and Illinois children she had seen, and he knew that many of the facilities identified in "An Illinois Tragedy" had also taken in Louisiana children, but he paid little attention to that report, at first. His primary focus was on the New Orleans children, and the deeper he got into the subject, the more frustrated he became. The case was obviously too big for him alone, so he wrote to Marion Wright Edelman, the director of the Children's Defense Fund, asking for help. For weeks, he heard nothing in response to his plea.

Rittenberg focused his attention on the two or three cases he felt he could help. He arranged with one of the HHRA agencies to have Gary W., a teen-ager from New Orleans, brought home for the Christmas holidays. Then Gary's mother, on Rittenberg's advice, refused to allow the boy to be returned to the Dyer Vocational Training School in Leona, Texas. Rittenberg explained:

> Gary was one of the three kids whose mothers had come to me. He'd been in the institution in Texas for five years, since he was twelve. He had committed a burglary and he'd been sent to state reform school, then transferred to Dyer. At Dyer, we found that Gary was put on drugs, on Thorazine, for five years . . . Our investigation showed that there was literally no treatment at Dyer. There was no indication that the state seriously considered any alternative placement, nor did they determine that Dyer had anything to offer Gary. While he was

there they ignored him. He was excessively drugged. He was physically beaten. He was forced to work at menial jobs under substandard conditions. He wasn't given any meaningful educational or vocational opportunities.

In a tape recorded interview, Robert Dyer denied that he had physically beaten children placed in his institution. When asked if he had used a paddle on Gary W. — as both Rittenberg and Gary had said — Dyer responded: "Did I use corporal punishment? Yes. Just a paddle . . . just like they use in the public schools." The court found that Dyer did use excessive amounts of psychotropic drugs to control residents and that Dyer offered no training for its inmates. A court-appointed psychiatrist substantiated Rittenberg's contention that the state had failed to consider alternative placements.

As Rittenberg prepared to fight legally for Gary's freedom, his plea for help from the CDF was finally brought to Edelman's attention. During a discussion of "An Illinois Tragedy," Edelman said the subject interested her. Someone mentioned to her that she had received a letter from a New Orleans lawyer indicating that Louisiana was still shipping kids into Texas, a letter that was asking the CDF to get involved. She read Rittenberg's letter and sent two CDF attorneys south to help out. Even with the help of the CDF lawyers, the task was awesome. The initial investigation had to cover all of the foster-care and social-service delivery systems in two states; scores of private institutions had to be checked out; hundreds of case files had to be located and inspected. But the first job was to develop a legal strategy and set out the causes of action.

The original *Gary W.* suit was filed in the fall of 1974 in the U.S. District Court in New Orleans. The class action asked $1 million in damages for Gary W., Joey G., Elizabeth M., and all others similarly situated. The suit contended that Caspar Weinberger, then secretary of the U.S. Department of Health, Education, and Welfare; William

Stewart, then commissioner of the Louisiana Health and Human Resources Administration; several lesser state bureaucrats; and forty private Texas schools had denied the plaintiffs "and their class" their constitutional rights to due process and to individualized treatment in the least restrictive setting. The suit further complained that plaintiffs and their class had been denied equal protection under the law and had been subjected to cruel and unusual punishment. Weinberger was named in the suit because federal foster-care funds were being used to finance the Texas placements, and because Rittenberg and CDF attorneys needed a bargaining chip. Once the case had been filed, negotiations were begun with the U.S. Department of Justice — Justice lawyers had to defend Weinberger in the suit — in an effort to bring the federal government in on the side of the plaintiffs. Information developed in the preliminary investigations by Rittenberg and CDF lawyers was convincing. What had happened in Texas did not appear defensible. Agreement was reached: Weinberger's name would be dropped from the case as a named defendant, and the Justice Department's Office of Special Litigation agreed to come in on the side of the children as plaintiffs' intervenor. This provided the plaintiffs with a total of eighteen attorneys and a staff of skilled investigators. Before the trial began, the lawyers and investigators gathered forty-seven thousand pages of exhibits and thirty-three hundred pages of depositions. This material constituted a library of horror stories, a body of evidence that would indict and convict the foster-care and juvenile justice systems in two states.

Of all the Louisiana children, the case of Joseph stands out. The *Gary W.* case complaint reads: "Plaintiff Joseph G. was adjudicated a neglected child *because of his mother's poverty* [emphasis added] . . . While confined at East Texas Guidance Center, Joseph suffered severe harm. He was excessively drugged; he was physically abused;

he was forced to labor at menial jobs . . . The report for the Illinois Attorney General, 'An Illinois Tragedy,' documented the horrible conditions in the East Texas Center . . ." The complaint referred to page 101 of "An Illinois Tragedy" for a description: "East Texas Guidance and Achievement Center was, during the time Illinois wards spent there, the worst of the Texas places."

The facility itself was located in an old set of Negro high school buildings, ten miles outside Tyler. It was revealed in court that the buildings were never adequate for residential use: the sewer system was chronically malfunctioning, the roofs leaked, the place was filthy. Former teachers and employees told investigators that the facility was operated on a behavior-modification system of fines and punishments, a "point system" or token economy in which the students were kept in constant debt. Two small, concrete toolsheds were used as isolation lock-ups, where kids were kept in solitary confinement. Children were swatted with wooden paddles.

"An Illinois Tragedy," and that state's withdrawal of children, sent shockwaves throughout the State of Texas. A Texas legislative investigative committee reported:

> The problems in both public and private out-of-home caring in Texas are of crisis proportions. The quality of care provided to children and young people in both public and private out-of-home settings is frequently substandard and sometimes inhumane . . . The observation and regulation of such care by the state has been sadly deficient, allowing questionable, objectionable and even illegal practices to go unchallenged. Children have . . . become economic pawns in private attempts to gain wealth or [in] governmental attempts to save money . . . The blame must be shouldered by every Texan.

Those were the conditions in Texas when Louisiana was placing children there in 1973–74. Louisiana officials responded to the Texas-Illinois controversy by sending out a task force of their own. The Louisiana investigators found little wrong with the Texas facilities. Louisiana's child-welfare workers argued that they had nowhere else to put the children. The state had only seven institutions for the retarded, and they were overcrowded. Private institutions were always full, and, in every case, they were very selective in their intake. Three of the state's hospitals for the mentally ill had children's units, but these took only short-term patients. Louisiana officials explained they were deinstitutionalizing the big hospital-warehouses, but their words had an empty ring. In fact, state policy worked against the development of much-needed private care, especially foster-home care. Time and again, administrators of community-care facilities complained that they had been treated shoddily, even criminally, by the state. State agents had bargained and contracted for services, then arbitrarily backed away from the contracts, according to people like the Reverend Michael S. Haddad, executive director of the Associated Catholic Charities. Too often Louisiana's regulations seemed to make no sense at all. Father Haddad cited an example: Louisiana could purchase out-of-home institutional care, but administrative policy kept the state from contracting with institutional providers for foster-home care.

> The state was supposed to be in the business of providing foster homes . . . but what happened was the state failed to recruit sufficient numbers of foster parents . . . In 1973 a five-year-old girl was placed in St. Elizabeth's by state welfare. She stayed two years then was placed in a state foster home, and she went to community schools. Five years later, when she was twelve, her foster parents were retired [by the state] because they were over the age limit . . . the state [because it had no other foster homes available] sends her application back to Catholic Charities, asking us to put her back in St. Elizabeth's.

Father Haddad suggested that if the state did not have foster homes, Catholic Charities had foster homes, and the girl could be placed in a good home, rather than the institution, at a cost of $150 a month, instead of $360 a month. "The state told us they did not purchase any foster care, so they would not purchase foster care from us. So the Louisiana Office of Family Services paid $360 a month rather than $150 a month because of an administrative policy, and we took care of the child in St. Elizabeth's."

At the time, St. Elizabeth's was staffed to care for emotionally disturbed or mentally retarded youngsters. The facility had the use of special teachers, speech and physical therapists, psychologists and psychiatrists. Father Haddad's voice rose in exasperation as he talked about this problem: "Now at the same time they would pay us $360 a month, and no more. They would say, 'Okay, here's Susie Jones, who is retarded, and there's no institution in Louisiana that will take her. So we'll send her to a place in Texas and we'll pay them $600 a month because they will not take less than $600.' It didn't make sense!"

Such bureaucratic maneuvering through the house of mirrors discouraged private, nonprofit charities from creating more foster homes, group homes, and institutions for children. By the end of 1973, Louisiana's various agencies were paying for the care and treatment of 1812 children. Of these, investigators found, 725 were placed out of state. Louisiana was paying an average of $254 a month for in-state care; the average payment for out-of-state care was $414. But that figure went as high as $850 in Joseph's case. Testimony during the trial revealed that many of the children had been misplaced, mistreated, abused, or neglected. Some Texas facilities caged mentally retarded children. Many of the places used drugs to keep inmates in a stupor while they were forced to do menial work. Few places had adequate staffing, appropriate therapy, or educational programs. Children who should have been in foster care were in $70-a-day psychiatric hospitals; others, who were really in need of psychiatric services and therapy, were placed in $25-a-day facilities that were not staffed adequately.

On July 26, 1976, Judge Alvin B. Rubin ruled the "Texas Children" as a class had to be returned to Louisiana and that the HHRA agencies had to evaluate each child's needs and make appropriate placement within the state, near that child's home community. Placement had to be in the least restrictive setting consistent with the child's need. Judge Rubin held that every child had an absolute right to individualized treatment, each child had a right to due process prior to any form of commitment or placement, each child had a right to an education, to humane treatment and care, and the Constitution required that each child had to be protected from cruel and unusual punishment. Further, Judge Rubin ordered that Louisiana had to pay private institutions within the state at least as much as it paid out-of-state facilities.

To be sure that his orders were carried out in the best interests of the children, Judge Rubin took an extraordinary step. He formed a special team of behavioral experts and ordered this team to evaluate each of the Texas Children and make recommendations to HHRA on how each child should be placed and treated within the state. Rubin named Dr. R. Dean Coddington, director of Louisiana State University Medical Center's department of psychiatry and behavioral sciences, to head the "Texas Children Project" evaluation team.

The established bureaucrats within the Health and Human Resources Administration didn't like the order. The HHRA director, William Cherry, who took over after William Stewart resigned, commented:

> Our people are really shook up over a federal judge's order. See, that was a stupid-ass rule. Not the fact that the judge ruled like he did . . . but he set me up an independent bird like Coddington whom I don't know and I don't know what his capabilities are. I don't know him personally and I have no evaluation that I can do [on Coddington]. Up in New York with the Willowbrook Case, at least the judge was wise enough to set up an overview to the problem . . . I mean this [the

Gary W.] situation is like a monopoly . . . I don't know what kind of job Coddington is doing. I have no right to look at it . . . The goddam judge says he [Coddington] does it. I've never heard of such a ruling. So those children pretty much go where he says . . .

Well, maybe. But not without resistance. The agencies under Cherry's big umbrella made excuses, shuffled paper, fussed and fiddled to avoid recognizing Dr. Coddington's authority. The midlevel layers of civil servants saw themselves as scapegoats and victims of unfairness, subject to the rule of an outsider. Dr. Cherry did little to disabuse them. Nowhere was this bureaucratic petulance more obvious than in the actions of the Exceptional Children's Act people. During the course of the trial, it had become obvious that some of the Texas institutions were worse than others, that the children's lives were more threatened in some facilities than others. The judge ordered that quick action be taken in those cases where jeopardy was most acute. Dr. Coddington's team did rapid evaluations on one hundred children in the facilities Judge Rubin had ordered evacuated, and recommended relocation plans. However, the ECA bureaucrats resisted taking orders; they left the children in Texas and asked for a more detailed evaluation report.

On November 10, 1977, sixteen months later, Dr. Coddington reported to Judge Rubin, "Our efforts toward the very rapid evaluation of the children in the least desirable institutions last fall were for naught." The report went on to detail the team's work and the state's responses:

The evaluation team has sent final evaluations to the state in 221 cases and preliminary evaluations in 43 additional instances . . . We have discovered a small but definite number of children who have been clearly misdiagnosed . . . Similarly, we have found a few families that have been mislabeled as being inadequate, but who are successfully parenting other children . . . [Some children] are in "holding facilities" for

months because of the state's inability to find permanent placements that fit the children's needs; and since the holding facilities are full, approximately 43 children remain in Dyer
Vocational School [one of the facilities the judge ordered
evacuated].

I asked Dr. Coddington to cite instances in which state
officials circumvented the team's recommendations. Dr.
Coddington recalled the case of a ten-year-old boy who
had been placed in Dyer. He said the boy had been seen
in October 1976 as part of the effort to get kids out of Dyer
as quickly as possible. A good foster home was found. The
foster parents had two natural children at home, plus a
foster child who was mentally retarded. Dr. Coddington
said:

They had experience and they wanted one of the Texas Children. We responded, saying that was great . . . The [state]
caseworker evaluated the house and family. She recommended
this family wait until final placement recommendations were
made. Now I don't know if that is what the state is still waiting
for [a year later] or not, but the fact is that the child stayed
in Dyer Vocational Training School until November 1, 1977.
Then he was put in a place called Howell House, which is
some kind of group home in Baton Rouge, which I haven't
seen and where his hyperactive behavior was unacceptable
to them, so, on November 2, 1977, he was moved to Greenwell
Springs Hospital, a state facility that has just been changed
from a tuberculosis hospital to a psychiatric unit for children
. . . The staff knows nothing about children, and he was there
until he was brought in last week for final evaluation. We again
recommended foster-home placement. Now that means the
whole [expedited] process developed in the judge's office a
year ago was just absolutely undermined. The idea was the
repeated placement was bad for a kid, so we wanted to avoid
that by making preliminary recommendations. The other thing
was to get him out of Dyer in a hurry, because that was a bad
institution, and this little guy spent six extra months in Dyer.
Then they placed him in Greenwell Springs. That kind of

craziness I don't understand. What scares me is that the grass-roots caseworker's will won out. There was absolute disregard of court orders.

The slowness of the whole process was brought home to me, coincidentally, the following day, when I met with Dr. Cherry in his office in the Charity Hospital. The meeting took place on the day the last of the Texas Children were arriving in New Orleans by bus from Texas. It had taken sixteen months for the state to obey the court orders, and still the officials were scrambling for beds, any beds, anywhere. There was a growing criticism of the HHRA and its slowness, and Dr. Cherry had been reluctant to see me, but he finally agreed. The director's offices were on the eighteenth floor of the massive, old concrete hospital building. It was raining hard and the mood in the tiny, overcrowded lobby on the main floor was wet and sour. Umbrellas were popping and folding; coats were dripping. Visitors, nurses, janitors, doctors in smudged white smocks, their stethoscopes stuffed in patch pockets, moved grimly, quickly about, or stood crowded near the elevator doors, waiting, waiting. One of the elevators was out of order; the others were slow. Guards with heavy guns sagging on Sam Browne belts stood by indifferently.

Up on the eighteenth floor, the same dreary scene was made somewhat bearable only because there were fewer people. The halls were dingy, poorly lighted, and empty. In the lobby by the elevator doors were two rocking chairs, usually occupied by staff persons waiting for an elevator. The pace was slow. A receptionist sat behind an old desk, working through a high stack of form letters, using a pink-highlight pen, marking one paragraph, folding the letter, and stuffing it in an envelope, repeating the process over and over. When the phone rang, she answered in a bored voice. She called my name and told me I could go on back, waving in the direction of Dr. Cherry's office.

Dr. Cherry was quick to explain that when he had taken

over the HHRA in the early summer of 1977, the shape of the Texas Children's Project was already cast. The tape-recorded interview in his wood-paneled office went smoothly, at first. Dr. Cherry was trying to give the impression that he was candid: "Frankly, I'm embarrassed to say the state had to be sued before it would do something, but they [the children] are all back now. They haven't all been evaluated, but we've made space in our institutions, and we're waiting for Dr. Coddington's team to evaluate them and make recommendations . . ."

I asked Dr. Cherry how many children had been involved? How many had been brought back? He did not know. I asked him to describe the organizational structure the HHRA had established to bring the children back and to place them according to Dr. Coddington's recommendations, but his mind was not on the question; it was on the fact that Dr. Coddington had the power to tell him what to do: "We don't have any choice at all; it was all spelled out by the federal judge . . . See, Coddington's team even went out of state and evaluated the children, and even recommended institutions, private or otherwise, for the [children] to come back to, for holding."

When I read him parts of Dr. Coddington's report and excerpts from my interview, parts that were critical of the HHRA's slowness and its failure to follow recommendations, Cherry snapped, "He's a liar . . . There's not very much of that because that son-of-a-bitch tells you exactly where to go . . . They [the Texas Children] are placed wherever he said."

I asked why, according to Dr. Coddington's report, it was taking — on the average — 145 days to get the children back into the state, once Dr. Coddington's evaluations had been made?

Dr. Cherry's answer was confusing: "I haven't heard that [criticism], but I'm not denying it's true. I was the guy that gave the order; I had my mental health director in

. . . [and] said let's get those children back into the state,
in a nice holding situation . . . I wanted 'em back."

QUESTION: But why so slowly? Until yesterday you still
had thirty-three children in Dyer.

DR. CHERRY: I was told it was due to the slowness of
the LSU evaluation team.

QUESTION: But Coddington says he did immediate evaluations on a preliminary basis to at least get the kids home
quickly, as the judge ordered. Is that wrong information?

DR. CHERRY: Let me tell you, if that son-of-a-bitch says
that in fifteen minutes he can evaluate a kid and tell you
what he needs, I don't believe it. I'm unhappy with that
evaluation. Okay?

QUESTION: Why?

DR. CHERRY: Because I don't think it is accurate, and
it is too dictatorial. The judge gave him too much [pause]
. . . One man in this whole state can evaluate children?
For the state?"

He then lapsed into silence, trying to control his temper.
Obviously, he was reacting to the loss of authority, to the
intrusion, the imposition of an outside expert. I tried again
to determine the bureaucratic structure set up within the
HHRA to deal with the court orders. Was the Exceptional
Children's Act in charge? Did the Office of Family Services
and the Department of Youth Services place their own kids
after return?

Dr. Cherry seemed to have only a vague sense of the
*Gary W.* case and the impact it was having on the agencies
under his command. He acknowledged that the state did
not have enough places for the children, but he said his
people were working hard to remedy the situation. He
referred me to Anne Stewart, in the ECA, for specifics.
I asked if he had budgeted special funds for the return of
the eight hundred or more Texas Children, and got another
nonresponsive answer: "Some of the kids will wind up in
our state institutions. We believe that is the answer. It is
a temporary-permanent answer, if you know what I mean.

It is obvious the kids ought to go back into a homelike atmosphere, their own home if they can. The technical questions I can't answer; it's just too big a department for me to know the answers . . ."

At Dr. Cherry's suggestion, I talked to Anne Stewart of the ECA. She explained that the ECA had been designated as the agency to direct the return of the children, even though some had been placed by Youth Services or Family Services. She said, "I was hired specifically to design a program that would expeditiously return children to the state . . . Most of the people I come in contact with feel the court order was the best thing that ever happened. We have succeeded in establishing a core of really fantastic programs within the state just within the last twelve months. And that would probably have taken five years . . ."

Anne Stewart's view of the whole process was surprisingly positive, despite the complexities of her task and the problems she faced. When the court decision was rendered, ECA had had a staff of only seven people to supervise the cases of all handicapped children placed anywhere in or out of the state. Then each caseworker had a case load of from four hundred to five hundred children. As a result, the work was more of an accounting procedure than social service. Following Judge Rubin's order, the HHRA increased the ECA's budget so that it could employ seventeen more caseworkers, bringing the case load down to about 150 kids per worker. This was still far more children than one worker should have to handle, but it was a step. According to Stewart, the primary problems in bringing the Texas Children home involved the coordination of the evaluation processes and the placement processes. The ECA had contracts with seventy-eight private programs, she said, and Youth Services and Family Services had contracts with another twenty-five or thirty facilities within the state. Stewart contended that the entire process was "moving fantastically fast," and she said that Dr. Coddington's criticisms were based on a lack of understanding of the realities of the bureaucratic world.

I asked her about Joseph's case. After being kept away from home for ten years, what kinds of things were happening with the teen-ager?

Her first response was defensive: "He was a child placed by the Office of Family Services. He was not nor has he ever been placed by this [the ECA] program. We have assigned about six people to see what we can do for Joey . . . First of all, the young man is on probation; the person who will make the ultimate decision on that young man is the juvenile judge."

Joseph had been back in New Orleans, with his mother, for more than a year. Rittenberg had secured his release, and the release of a dozen other youngsters, not long after the trial had started. Joseph's mother talked about his return: "Everything was so new, and so strange. Even I was. With the other children he [pause] . . . he would sit by hisself, and he wouldn't say nothin' to 'em. Couple of times he run away. He just wouldn't let me tell him nothin'. He didn't want nobody tellin' him nothin' . . ."

Joseph was on the streets more than he was home, running with a tough group of street kids. The state government that had taken him away from his mother because she was poor, the state that had been willing to pay $700 a month to a New York private institution rather than $24 a month in welfare aid to a mother wanting her child, that same state government no longer wanted anything to do with him. After spending approximately $100,000 for keeping Joseph in institutional care, the state of Louisiana abandoned him.

Joseph's mother is angered by the whole process. She has seven children, and in 1978 was living in a housing project on $246 a month, yet strangers in Texas had been paid three times that much, and they had mistreated her son. At the time of our interview, she was struggling to get off welfare, to get an education and find work. She had recently completed her high school education and was en-rolled in a junior college, taking typing and accounting. She said, "I'm tired of livin' in this ghetto area and I believe that this environment contributes to Joseph's be-havior . . . If I could get the other children out of this environment, while they are little, show 'em how the other people live, how the other side lives, they might be better . . . This is a place that will get to young minds. This project area is not a good place to live, but I couldn't do no better . . ."

Joseph was not attending school, and this disturbed his mother. "He won't stay in school. He got mixed up with the police, shopliftin'. A lot of things I get mad with him about, but he's so mixed up . . . If they'd just sent Joseph home [when he was five] and not off to New York . . ." Her voice trailed off.

According to Dr. Coddington, Joseph had been in more serious trouble than his mother had indicated.

She has no control over him. He comes and goes as he pleases. Our feeling was that if the juvenile court judge wished to incarcerate him in a penal institution, that would have been his decision, but we do not feel that would be therapeutic. But there is a question of how therapeutic one can be for a boy like this. The only choice is to put him in an intensive ther-apeutic program that would either be psychoanalytical or would be an intensive behavioral-modification program that would have to continue for at least two or three years . . . So we recommended three places, George Junior Republic in upstate New York, or the Oaks Unit of the Brown Schools in Texas, which is based on the Menninger Children's Service Model, or we could try the Menninger Unit itself. The last two would cost around $2000 a month. We sent these rec-ommendations to [the ECA] and to the judge . . . The judge put him on probation, but did not assign a probation officer, saying simply, "We have too heavy a case load and we just don't have any probation officers available. We will assign one as soon as possible."

The irony was awful. Because Joseph had been sent to New York and then Texas, instead of being left with his mother, the boy had become so disturbed that a full evaluation by a team of experts had to end with the recommendation that Joseph be sent to specialized therapy programs existing only outside Louisiana. Yet the judge ignored the recommendations of Dr. Coddington and the orders of the federal court, and put the boy back on the street, without a probation officer.

What had the ECA done? Anne Stewart answered: "We don't have a case file on him. We don't know anything about the situation. It is a little difficult to do anything when you don't have the records."

This, despite the fact that she had assigned six caseworkers. According to her, the evaluation team report to the ECA consisted only of three "pieces of paper" that named three suggested places of treatment, reported the results of a physical examination that was not as thorough as the ECA required, and gave an account of a conversation one psychologist had with Joseph. Anne Stewart said: "That was not enough information for us. Again, we are at the mercy of the private provider. Most of them would throw that [file] in the garbage can."

QUESTION: Does Family Services have a file on Joseph?

STEWART: Family Services has a file on the child. They have attempted on several occasions in the last year to provide services for that young man. The boy is sixteen years old now and still under parent's custody.

According to Stewart, the boy's mother was uncooperative: "So you see, our problem is that we [the ECA] cannot legally force her to do anything . . . They [the OFS] do not have the legal authority to place the child in residential placement. Certainly not into the most restrictive residential placement setting available, not in the face of the [judge's] order that says we are to place the child in the least restrictive setting."

Stewart apparently did not pick up on the inconsistency of her statements. At the outset, she had said the person who must make the ultimate decision was the juvenile judge. Joseph was a ward of the juvenile court. The judge, acting as *parens patriae,* was deciding the boy's future, not his mother. Be that as it may, it was obvious that Joseph, Gary W., and hundreds of other children in Louisiana were once more pawns in a crazy game. Because the state was moving so slowly, Rittenberg and the CDF lawyers went back into court in September of 1978 and asked for the appointment of a "special master" to supervise the state's compliance with Judge Rubin's order. At that time, Rittenberg presented evidence showing that 57 percent of the Texas Children had not yet been fully evaluated — four years after the case had been filed, two years after the decision rendered — and that half of the children evaluated had not yet been placed. A year later, Dr. Coddington said the evaluation process had been completed, but the state was lagging from twelve to eighteen months behind in the placement processes.

Rittenberg, not trying to hide his frustration or his anger, commented:

> *Gary W.* has been hailed as a victory for deinstitutionalization of child care. Yet what has the State of Louisiana done for children's needs since the court order? While admitting there are placement problems because of inadequate community services, group homes, and foster care, they have expanded the beds at the state institutions for the retarded and proposed to build three new psychiatric hospitals for Louisiana's children. It doesn't seem to matter that none of the children need to be in a hospital or that the large rural institutions for the retarded are an outmoded idea. The *Gary W.* case was not a failure. There are more community services in Louisiana, but the point is, you can't just win a lawsuit and go away. State bureaucracies don't change easily. If you go away, they will just rename the institutions "community-care facilities" and claim they agree with you.

# 6

# Deinstitutionalization

DEINSTITUTIONALIZATION is a buzz word, impressively long and sufficiently vague; a political word; an adaptable word that provides a sense of action and progress. In theory, deinstitutionalization means that all children who are in need of care, treatment, and / or rehabilitation will be helped either in their own homes, in foster care, or in some form of specialized care in a small, private institution near their own community. The placement of last resort is the state hospital or kid prison. The word itself is of relatively new coinage, but the processes of deinstitutionalization are as old as institutionalized care. In the ebb and flow of politics and governmental reactions to scandals, children have periodically been pushed and pulled in and out of institutional settings. Juvenile delinquents were removed from adult prisons and placed in special reformatories, and when conditions in these kid prisons were exposed, the youngsters were removed to "camps" or "farms" or group homes. As early as 1909, a White House conference on children and youth recognized the desirability of keeping children in their own homes whenever possible. But this recognition extended only to normal children in one-parent households or to orphans who had no outward deformities or mental problems. Delinquents, retarded children, the emotionally disturbed, and the physically handicapped were best cared for in big, specialized institutions.

This was the collective wisdom until the late 1950s, when experts in the various fields of child welfare began to recognize the limits and liabilities of institutional care. Over the next fifteen years, the reactions to problems within institutional care created enough pressures to force a move toward what appears to be something like a national policy calling for deinstitutionalization. But this is a policy forged not by design so much as by unplanned responses to circumstances. Legal decisions like *Gault*, *Morales*, and *Gary W.*, combined with similar class-action suits brought against big hospitals for the retarded in Pennsylvania, Alabama, and Washington, D.C., have given children new rights. Youngsters can no longer just be locked away in institutional care, even by court order. States have to provide children with the kind of care and treatment that will help them, rehabilitate them, educate them. Congress passed laws reforming the mental health programs and created new programs for the developmentally disabled. The Juvenile Justice and Delinquency Prevention Act of 1974 provided federal funds to assist states in developing community-care facilities for runaways, truants, and other status offenders, but only if the states agreed not to lock up such children in juvenile halls or jails. By 1978, Public Law 94-142 was passed, guaranteeing suitable education for all handicapped children.

Through these court decisions and legislative actions, the skeleton of a new deinstitutionalization policy was emerging, but it was a disjointed policy, without a national mandate, without a constituency powerful enough to force its implementation. The political climate did not favor the creation of a logical, soundly conceived set of policies or goals in juvenile justice, mental health care, or programs for the developmentally disabled, all under the unifying flag of deinstitutionalization. But politics did advance the buzz word use of *deinstitutionalization*, and the politics of deinstitutionalization created an interesting, if bewildering, chain of circumstances that put liberals and conservatives on parallel courses. People from both ends of the political spectrum liked the word and its implications, for their own, disparate reasons. Liberals and conservatives borrowed each other's rhetoric to advance their own views. One side argued against continued use of large institutions because, experts contended, the institutional setting per se was harmful to children, and, coincidentally, these big institutions were costly burdens on the taxpayer. The other side reversed the order of argument: government was inefficient, so the care and treatment of children was better placed in the hands of free enterprise. The cost would be less; the result, more humanitarian.

In states like New York and Massachusetts, politicians and child-care advocates talked authoritatively about the move away from the big, costly state reform schools and hospitals toward the more economical, more humanitarian community-care systems. Much of the argument for deinstitutionalization rested on the alleged economies of shutting down big institutions. But, as alluring as these arguments were, the economics of deinstitutionalized care are illusory. The full costs of care and treatment are not always seen, because they are spread across the whole range of board and care, therapy, medicine, and education, and so are not totted up on a single ledger. But the price tag for adequate diagnosis and delivery of all needed services to a child in his or her own community is at least as costly as institutional care, because the emphasis is on a wide array of individualized care and treatment programs performed by private individuals who contract their services to public agencies or to private-care facilities. And any economies in deinstitutionalized care must come at the expense of the children.

Nowhere are the economic facts and the political truths of this more evident than in California. Because of its size, its complexities, because of its liberal reputation in the field of social welfare and its pre-eminence in institutional care, the Golden State makes an ideal laboratory for studying the political and economic forces at work in deinstitutionalization. Through the 1950s, the California progressives had worked long and hard to put the finishing touches on the big, efficient California Youth Authority, the state hospitals for the mentally retarded and the mentally ill. As the political career of Governor Edmund G. (Pat) Brown was ending and that of movie actor Ronald Reagan was beginning, California was proudly operating fourteen state hospitals. By reputation, these hospitals — which housed forty-seven thousand men, women, and children — were the finest of their kind anywhere in the world. But there were problems within the system. Most of the wards were overcrowded, and the legislature was balking on providing funds for expanding the system. Because of the overcrowding, there were staffing problems. Programs for the patients suffered. Sensing the new mood, the Democratic leadership in the legislature and Governor Pat Brown began to look for alternatives. New community mental-health programs were developed and funded. People who needed help could find it in their own communities. Fewer patients were being admitted to state hospitals initially, and the hospital administrators were able to release patients back into community-care programs.

By 1967, when Ronald Reagan took over the governorship, there were ten thousand fewer people in the state mental hospitals. The overcrowding had been relieved, staffing ratios were back to normal, and the crisis had been relieved — but only temporarily. Governor Pat Brown's deinstitutionalization efforts had worked with the mentally ill, but he ran into trouble when he tried to take the pressure off the hospitals for the retarded. In the early 1960s, there was no way he and other proponents of community-based care could assure the parents of retarded children that their youngsters, once out of the hospitals, would receive the kind of care and treatment that was essential to their well-being. The politics of caring for these developmentally disabled youngsters remained weighted in favor of institutional care until new ways were found to deliver the needed services to retarded children in the community.

With the help of the legislature, Pat Brown created twenty-one private, nonprofit "regional centers" to serve as the diagnostic and placement agencies for developmentally disabled children. These regional centers were funded directly by the state, but they operated as independent businesses. Each center's staff developed its own network of resources, contracting purchase-of-service contracts with vendors of mental health services, physical therapy, and speech therapy. The centers developed funding sources, evaluated clients' needs, placed the children, and supervised their cases.

The processes of deinstitutionalization were well under way when Reagan was inaugurated in 1967. As Brown, the New Deal–style builder, was replaced by the conservative voice of corporate interests, the politics of deinstitutionalization were twisted about to serve the Reagan point of view. One of Reagan's first acts was to order a 10 percent across-the-board budget cut for every state agency. Then, casting about for a big, dramatic target, Reagan seized on the state hospitals. He argued that the system was wasteful, and slashed $40 million from hospital appropriations. Reagan closed three state hospitals; then, using the rhetoric of the liberals who had worked to build community-care delivery systems, he vowed he would close the remaining eleven hospitals and transfer the patients into community care. In Reagan's simplistic view of the world, the free enterprise system would move in and take up the reins.

It became painfully clear that this was not the case. Reagan and his cliché-talking advisers never understood the complexity of their task when they shut the first three hospitals down. The primary problem was that there were not enough beds of any kind out in the communities, and the Reagan deinstitutionalization delivery schemes soon became overloaded; the pipelines were clogged. Without money, design, or leadership, the entire system quickly broke down, but not before the Reagan procedures had dumped nearly twenty thousand men, women, and children into the unprepared communities.

In the meantime, the budget cuts in the remaining eleven state hospitals created another serious problem. The seventeen thousand people left in the state hospitals — including several thousand children — were the most difficult to handle. They had the most intensive care needs. They were the most troubled, the most troublesome. But they couldn't be helped because there weren't enough doctors or nurses or therapy technicians or nurses aides. The system was thrown into chaos. The most qualified people quit to find work elsewhere; those who remained faced impossible workloads in rapidly deteriorating conditions. A 1974 report by a state senate select committee that studied the effects of these Reagan cutbacks first described conditions in the hospitals and then pointed out that most of the community-care facilities were in trouble too:

> No single responsibility is fixed for follow-up care. Most operators of board-and-care homes lack training . . . There is no one to serve as either agent for continuity or as an advocate of the patient . . . to see that a comprehensive and coordinate effort at resocialization and rehabilitation occurs. Operators of board-and-care facilities [group homes, foster homes, and such] are reimbursed on a bare-bones basis which discourages any attempt to create a truly therapeutic environment . . . in this setting patients are inactive, bored, tranquilized and vulnerable to exploitation.

In other words, under the Reagan administration, the state hospitals had been emptied of another seventeen thousand men, women, and children, but very little of the money "saved" in state hospital budget-cutting was transferred to fund the vital services for patients or clients who required much more than a bed and something to eat. The advantage, politically, was obvious. Once out in the communities, these people were lost from public view, and the once very costly state hospital system had been pared down to a size that allowed the conservatives to point to their economies.

By the time Edmund G. (Jerry) Brown, Jr., became governor in 1975, the bureaucracies responsible for the administration of the state hospitals and the community-care systems were located in the gigantic Department of Health, a $3.3-billion-a-year, twenty-one-thousand-employee superagency created by Reagan. It was Reagan's theory that, by bringing all the separate health and welfare services in under one administrative structure, he could streamline government and make it more efficient by the application of the management techniques used in private industry. As awkward and inefficient as the several old departmental systems may have seemed to the Reaganites, their efforts to fold the Departments of Social Welfare, Public Health, Mental Hygiene, Health Care and other lesser agencies into one efficient superagency proved futile. Each of these old departments had a functioning history, complete with its own rules, regulations, its own policies and goals. Social Welfare simply didn't do things the way Mental Hygiene did things, and Public Health was another system altogether. Each operated its own network of group homes and institutions; each had different clients, funded through different sources. The merger into the DOH resulted in a "loose federation of independent programs without substantial coordination at the state level and little integration of services in the community." The words come from the report of the state's independent "Little Hoover" Commission, created by the legislature to act as the watchdog of government: "Overcentralization of administrative support functions has disrupted health programs . . . superfluous layers of bureaucracy have encouraged unproductive procedures." The list of problems went on and on:

> The style of administration is hectic and crisis-oriented. Troubled programs are subjected to extensive, serial reviews, following which little corrective action is taken. Marathon staff meetings are held at all levels with loosely drawn agendas. Task forces are appointed almost daily as problem-solving devices and consume large blocks of time . . . The total number of task forces is unknown . . . off-site staff seminars, retreats and conferences generate position papers, action memoranda and conference reports but little substantial change . . . All of these activities are conducted in an atmosphere of great urgency and give the appearance of productive activity but, in fact, they represent the administrative equivalent of cardiac fibrillation . . . a condition in which the heart beats fast and irregularly but does not effectively pump blood.

The Little Hoover study, made during the first year of Jerry Brown's administration, seemed like a good opportunity to those fighting to save the state hospitals and bring some order into community care. The Little Hoover Commission report was an indictment of the Reagan superagency theories and of the DOH handling of the state hospitals and community care. If not a blueprint for change, it was, at the very least, the needed record of the Reagan administration's failure to bring about change. And Jerry Brown was seen as the fellow who would change things. Brown was a liberal, a new kind of liberal, maybe, with strange ideas, but a liberal nonetheless. But Brown was a surprise. Although he talked and acted the liberal intellectual on environmental and consumer issues, though he flirted with Cesar Chavez and the United Farm Workers, Brown proved the conservative on fiscal matters. He shunned the official trappings of luxury that Reagan had built into the job. Jerry Brown declared small was beautiful; he drove an old Plymouth and settled into a pad near the capitol, instead of riding in a limousine and living in the $1.3 million governor's mansion built by Reagan on the banks of the American River.

Perhaps more important, Brown was a new kind of politician, the wired media candidate. Brown's sharp intellect, his ability as a quick study, his extraordinary mastery of buzz-word rhetoric made him a political sleight-of-hand artist to be reckoned with. He clearly sensed the angry, self-indulgent mood of the middle-class electorate, not only in California, but in the nation, as well. Brown, the fiscal conservative, positioned himself expertly on economic issues: he declared that his administration operated in an era of *limited expectations*, and he offered only mild opposition to the Jarvis-Gann Proposition 13 initiative. When California voters overwhelmingly approved the tax-cutting initiative, Brown deftly jumped the fence in time to help the voters throw the babies out with the bath water. Brown had no commitment to state hospitals or to children caught up in the horrors of community care. Nor did he really understand the processes of government and bureaucracy. Unlike his father, Jerry Brown had a deep mistrust of the traditional ways of party politics and government bureaucracy that Pat Brown understood and had used so expertly as governor. In his appointments to fill top jobs of government, Jerry Brown rejected the experienced bureaucrats and selected instead "spirited leadership" of people who had "new and imaginative ideas."

Brown appointed Dr. Jerome Lackner to head up the $3.3 billion DOH superagency. Lackner had absolutely no experience to qualify him for such a job; he had been in private practice — Cesar Chavez was one of his patients — and he was considered a brilliant man who had strong humanitarian instincts. He had never been in government, had never run for office. In the Brown antiestablishment scheme of things, these shortcomings were virtues. Lackner's appointment was critical to the issue of deinstitutionalization. Not only was he boss of the state hospitals, but he was in charge of quality control in community care, through licensing. Within the DOH there was the Licensing and Certification Division, a conglomerate responsible for the inspecting and licensing of the forty-two thousand community-care facilities then in operation. Of these, fifteen thousand licenses covered child-care facilities ranging from day-care and preschool programs to foster care, nonprofit and for-profit group homes, institutions, and nursing homes. There were fifty-six thousand children in some kind of out-of-home placement when Lackner took over, twenty-seven thousand of them either in group homes or in institutions.

When Lackner took over the directorship of the Department of Health, a psychologist employed by the state Department of Education was just completing a study of the effectiveness of deinstitutionalization and its impact on children. Question: Were emotionally disturbed children receiving the kinds of care and treatment that would help and rehabilitate them, facilitate their growth and maturity? Working through Napa State Hospital's children's unit, the psychologist selected the cases of 115 youngsters, each of whom had been in Napa from one to two years and had been released into community care. The children in this study were not psychotic, nor did they have brain damage or similar developmental disabilities. They were not retarded. Most of them were socially maladaptive youngsters who had been in some kind of out-of-home placement for at least three years before being admitted to the state hospital. Some were aggressive, troublesome kids from broken homes who had not adjusted to care in their local communities. Some had been thrown out of foster care and had been rejected by group homes and institutions. All of them had been placed in Napa by court action. On their release, 70 percent of these children were discharged with "treatment complete" on their records, but with a rec ommendation that they be placed in settings that provided minimal behavioral freedom and constant supervision. Making such recommendations was a futile gesture. The study revealed that once the youngsters were back in the community, they were back in the system that had rejected them a year or two earlier, a system of "inadequate community accommodation plans, inadequate communication and coordination between service delivery systems, inappropriate placement, lack of service delivery and inadequate monitoring; California service delivery systems are not reaching these children and their families."

The words were those of Stuart Greenfeld, the psychologist who had conducted the study for the Department of Education. Greenfeld, writing to Dr. Lackner, warned: "Although the California Departments of Health and Education have repeatedly affirmed their intent to meet the needs of children in this state and have expended great amounts of money, professional time and energy, the needs of these children and thousands like them within the state go unserved."

Though Dr. Lackner was new to the job, he had already begun to realize that the DOH was more seriously flawed than he had anticipated. He responded to Greenfeld, "The conclusions of your study support my beliefs that the system is not doing an adequate job . . . at least half the findings outlined in your letter indicate these children needed help long before they entered the hospital." Lackner wrote to Greenfeld that he wanted to learn more about what was happening to the children and said he turned the matter over to Don Miller, manager of the DOH state hospital division, and Dr. Richard Koch, manager of the DOH community-services division. Miller and Koch were career bureaucrats in a system that was influenced more by budget ledger sheets than humanitarian goals. Greenfeld was an outsider pointing to the shortcoming of their divisions. They saw him for fifteen minutes, accepted his report, and filed it. Two years later, Greenfeld told me he hadn't heard from them, or from Lackner, since.

Not only were the needs of these children going unserved throughout the 1970s, but there were strong indications that children were actually being mistreated. The shortage of "beds" in all kinds of foster-care and community-based treatment facilities was causing serious problems. Emotionally disturbed children were ending up in facilities specializing in the treatment of autistic children; mentally retarded kids were winding up in group homes licensed to care for delinquents on probation. One mentally retarded youngster was found chained to a tree in a nursing home for the aged, where he was treated — and teased — like a pet dog.

The situation was so bad in Southern California that James Hayes, chairman of the Los Angeles County Board of Supervisors, and his staff made an unannounced series of inspections through twenty-one different group homes and institutions used by the county and reported that "far too many placement homes for delinquent, mentally ill or neglected children are unfit." He ordered a crackdown on those "filthy hell-holes" that he said were offering up poor food in run-down, unsafe buildings. Many of the facilities, he said, offered little or no rehabilitative services. While arguing to get the Board of Supervisors to make changes, Hayes explained, "This used to be a charity and the homes were well run, but since it became corporate big business there has been a determined effort by some operators to extract as much money as possible from the misery of children."

Supervisor Hayes's comments were found to be right on the mark by federal investigators from the General Accounting Office. In 1977 GAO investigators inspected eighteen group homes and private institutions in four of the

five states included in the study and found children were
sleeping on mattresses on the floors; windows and screens
were missing; living quarters were cramped, ill-kept, and
dingy; there were dirty bathrooms and unsanitary sleeping,
living, and eating areas. Kitchens were dirty. Children were
without adequate, clean clothing. Placement agencies were
not providing needed social services for children or their
families. Federal regulations were encouraging rather than
discouraging institutional placement. There was no fiscal
accountability, no placement accountability, no coordination of services in many of the areas the GAO looked at.

In response to this and the similar conclusions of other
federal and state investigations, Arabella Martinez of HEW
created a task force to study the problems and develop
some national perspectives. The task force was headed by
Peter Schuck. In the spring of 1978, after five months of
work, Schuck told me:

> There is a tremendous dearth of information. Basically, all we
> know is that vast numbers of people have been emptied out
> of institutions over the past fifteen years and that a *small*
> number of community-care facilities have been developed. So
> the question is: "Where *are* the rest of the people?" People
> talk about deinstitutionalization without much thought to
> where the participants or clients are going. That's the real
> problem. We didn't find an answer [but] . . there's a clear
> sense that something is wrong . . . You have deeply en-
> trenched interests which, for the best of motives, liked the
> programs the way they were.

The interview was brief because Schuck explained that
nothing in the way of a report had yet been assembled.
The material was still being gathered. A year later I telephoned, and Schuck was gone. The people occupying the
offices where he worked hadn't heard of him, nor could
they say where he could be found. Several phone calls
made over the course of the next few weeks could produce
no information on Schuck's whereabouts or the work of

the task force. No one had heard of it or of any report it might have produced. Schuck and his work were gone: Puff. But his question remained, haunting: "Where *are* the rest of the people?" What has happened to those children turned out of state hospitals into community care in counties that are hopelessly short of "bed space" and services? No one knows. There are no statistics, no overall evaluations. There are no answers. Like the kids, Schuck had disappeared in the national house of mirrors, where there are no route maps, no policies, no sense of direction or purpose. No one was keeping track. No one was in charge.

From the outset, the attitudes of the industrialized nations toward the poor and the deformed within their midst have been predicated primarily on expediency, leavened only by a miserly portion of Christian duty. Historically, the churches created institutions as a matter of convenience. It was much easier to gather the poor, the halt, and the convicted criminals in centralized institutions than to do God's work on a case-by-case basis. And from the outset, the church deacons and beadles preferred working with normal children. It has generally fallen to the lot of government to confine the criminals, the retarded, and the insane. At first, such public institutions were only generalized warehouses, with appropriate dungeons for the criminals and the insane. Work places were provided for the rest. But generalization gave way to specialization; it was more efficient. Penitentiaries were built, then reform schools and orphanages. By 1848, Massachusetts constructed a small, highly specialized facility for the "idiotic and feebleminded" youths of the state. New York City took specialization another step, creating a special Colored Orphan Asylum, which housed six hundred black children in an old four-story building.

The specialization, the construction of more and more sophisticated institutions, continued through the end of the nineteenth century. It is important to understand how deeply rooted the wisdom of institutional care or punishment is within the American socioeconomic system and how difficult it is to change, to understand the dilemmas faced by those who tried to bring about some form of deinstitutionalization. The construction of a prison or a state hospital requires the parallel development of large administrative structures and of political constituencies. Once in place, bureaucracies and political constituencies create a formidable force. Nowhere is this more obvious than at Forest Haven, twenty-two miles outside the nation's capital, in the Maryland countryside. Originally purchased as a "poor farm for the feeble-minded," it was converted by the District of Columbia to a full-fledged institution in 1925. During the next fifty years, Forest Haven underwent the same stultifying institutional processes that have so deeply entrenched similar facilities across the nation, processes that ultimately led to scandals. By 1975, Forest Haven housed more than a thousand mentally retarded men, women, and children. A congressional hearing on conditions in Forest Haven revealed that the patients lived in old dorms and large residential buildings euphemistically called "cottages." Forest Haven's thirty buildings were run-down, badly in need of repair; the food-delivery system was neither safe nor sanitary; there were never enough funds to provide even the basic necessities, like warm clothing, soap, toothbrushes, toothpaste, or toilet paper. There was a serious shortage of doctors, therapists, and nurses. Staff morale was low; absenteeism was high. Most of the patients were black and from the low-income neighborhoods of D.C. A third or more were only mildly retarded and were capable of living outside the institution in far less restrictive settings. Some of the children in Forest Haven *were not retarded at all, but had been placed there because no other educational or therapeutic residential facility was available*. Forest Haven was a convenient dumping ground for a society that could not or would not provide for the needs of its children.

The conditions in Forest Haven were exposed by the media after the parents of a girl named Joy forced the issue into public view. Theirs was the dilemma faced by every parent of a severely retarded or grossly handicapped child: they loved their daughter and they wanted to care for her, but as the girl grew older the kinds of pressures and demands on the family became unbearable. They needed help. None was available. There was no respite care, no way for them to escape even for a few hours. Medical costs climbed, and the family's economic situation was severely strained. There was never enough money to care for the rest of the family's needs, but Joy's mother could not work because she had to stay home with Joy. Finally, a decision was made: Joy would have to be placed out of the home.

Forest Haven was the only option. In 1967, the girl's parents visited the old institution, and they were impressed. Nearly a decade afterward, they testified before Congress that it was only later that they learned their tour "was quite selective, shielding us from the areas that can only be described as snake pits . . . We were told Joy would receive appropriate educational programming and that in general her experiences would be directed at maximizing her growth potential."

To get Joy admitted to Forest Haven, a public institution, the parents had to go through a legal charade that would make her eligible for public funds. They had to agree to give up their daughter; she was made a "ward" of the court on the premise her parents could not or would not care for her. During the court proceedings, Joy was seen briefly by a psychologist and a court clerk; each matter-of-factly signed the necessary documents. The judge, acting in *parens patriae*, glanced only briefly at the paperwork before making Joy a ward of his court. She was committed. Her father said later, "At that instant a nursing attendant came over, took Joy by the hand, and told us to say good-bye. She was taken from the courtroom as we stood helplessly watching and feeling that the separation could have been handled in a more delicate and sensitive manner."

The nightmare had started for Joy, and for her parents. Because of staffing shortages and other problems, Joy was repeatedly injured in falls; she was attacked by other, more aggressive patients. Because she was severely retarded, she was transferred to Dogwood Cottage, a facility housing eighty patients who spent most of their time sitting or lying around a dayroom. When the parents later spoke before the congressional committee, Joy's father described the scene: "The odor of urine and feces was pronounced . . . The room itself was bare and stark, with only a few benches . . . We were stunned at the existence of this human warehouse where not even minimally acceptable custodial care was being conducted."

The shocked parents brought their daughter home and tried once more to care for her there, but again they could find no help. Her father said, "The massive burden of Joy's care at home resulted in the gradual deterioration in the emotional climate of our family . . . There was no choice but once again to return Joy to Forest Haven."

The D.C. administrators had been attempting to remedy the Dogwood Cottage situation by replacing the outmoded structure with a new facility. The new building was completed, but it stood empty because, as Joy's father explained, "there were insufficient funds to provide staff. This was so outrageous, we decided to seek public help. With the assistance of the Antioch Law School and the Urban League, the Forest Haven Task Force was developed. Through the task force we were able to bring the deplorable, inhumane conditions existing at Forest Haven to the media attention and thereby to public scrutiny."

The media exposure created enough political pressure to force the funding of staff for the new Curley Cottage, and to cause a congressional inquiry in 1976. Joy's father testified that the staffing of the new cottage had been only a token gesture: "Despite the superficial physical appearances, there are numerous negative factors which simply have not changed. Many of the programmatic promises have never been fulfilled and were obviously nothing more than empty rhetoric."

In other words, despite the task force's work and the media pressure, not much had changed. Roland Queene, the superintendent of Forest Haven, told the subcommittee, "It has become very apparent that the institution . . . is not only failing in its mission, but in many instances it is contributing to the handicap of retardation for its residents."

An investigation by the Department of Health, Education, and Welfare revealed that Forest Haven was the worst of thirty-one comparable institutions within HEW's Region III. Investigators found conditions so intolerable and efforts to correct such conditions so lacking that they recommended all HEW funding be withdrawn. It was their view that only huge infusions of money and staff could correct the deficiencies. The investigators' testimony, the testimony of the task-force members and other critics, angered Joseph Yeldell, director of the Washington, D.C., Department of Human Resources. Yeldell, who was Queene's boss, testified: "The innuendo in this room is stifling . . . We are not going to solve the problems of Forest Haven by exposé hearings, but rather by recognizing the ills of the past and making the total commitment required, including a massive infusion of resources, to correct these problems . . . Forest Haven has been neglected for forty-five years, and now the social consciousness of this community is aroused. But this consciousness does not extend to opening the pocketbook to provide the funds needed for Forest Haven."

The focus was on dollars for Forest Haven, on patchwork remedies, not on the basic problems, the lack of support for families in need. At a time when the collective

wisdom of society was stressing the move away from the
institutional care toward the kind of community-based services needed by Joy and her family, the Congress and the
district administrators were bickering about how much to
spend to patch up Forest Haven. Yeldell contended that
the bureaucratic structures, given the limited resources,
were attempting to do the best they could with what was
provided. As Yeldell talked, he sounded like administrators
in other areas, from other hospitals. The problems in Forest
Haven were the same as those found in the Partlow State
Hospital in Alabama and in Pennhurst in Pennsylvania and
Fairview in California. No matter what the state policies
and political goals of each state or each locale, the bureaucratic resistance to change was remarkably the same.

Federal court records in Pennsylvania show that the state
legislature had authorized the expenditure of $21 million
in 1970 to plan and construct community-care facilities for
nine hundred people who otherwise would be warehoused
in the state hospital at Pennhurst. Clearly, the policy was
to deinstitutionalize, but the agencies of the state, for whatever reason, had spent *only* $3 million of the authorized
amount by 1977, and the terrible conditions within Pennhurst were the subject of a court action. At the end of the
trial, the judge found there were children in Pennhurst who
could and should "be moved immediately into the community and who would be able to cope with little or no
supervision . . . the primary limiting factor has been the
failure of the Commonwealth and its subdivisions to provide sufficient living units, vocational and day facilities and
other support services at the community level."

But even if the Pennhurst patients had been transferred
into a fully developed community-care service system —
as the legislature had ordered seven years earlier — the
experiences in other states revealed there were no guarantees that deinstitutionalization would provide a better
therapeutic environment, nor even a more humane envi-

ronment. The record in states like Illinois shows that the problems are only being shifted from one or two big institutions into dozens of smaller, private for-profit and nonprofit boarding homes and institutions. Two separate reports filed by the Illinois Legislative Investigation Commission in 1975 and 1977 revealed that twenty-two persons had died because of mistreatment and/or neglect in private nursing homes in the Waukegan area. Although the institutions were not staffed for the care of severely retarded patients, these nursing homes were admitting such retarded persons. State hospital patients were being transferred into private care to keep the nursing home beds full and profits up. In 1975, the commission commented on the death of a nineteen-year-old, profoundly retarded girl: "During the four-day period of her [terminal] illness, insufficient staff observation and treatment, unacceptable and unprofessional [staff] attitudes and general irresponsible nursing performances were the rule." The girl — one of seven patients who died in this one institution during the previous year — died of pneumonia. She was never seen by a doctor, according to the report.

Two years later, a similar series of deaths in another private institution prompted another commission investigation. According to the commission report, the operators paid themselves substantial salaries, took out dividends, arranged for kickbacks from providers of services and medicines, and created a management corporation that was paid to run the business. The commission reported that patients in the institutions were physically abused, sexually molested, and generally neglected. One of the patients who died was a severely retarded nineteen-year-old boy who had spent virtually all of his life in the Lincoln State Hospital and then had been transferred into this facility during Illinois's deinstitutionalization processes. The commission concluded, "The entire operation of this facility demonstrated the spectrum of abuses and deficiencies encoun-

tered in the industry; kickback arrangements with purvey-
ors, misappropriation of patient funds, physical and sexual
abuses, falsification of documents, deliberate understaffing
. . . One or more of the above problems exists in every
facility to a greater or lesser degree.''

The words were a strong indictment of the state and
local governmental systems that were supposed to be regulating and monitoring the deinstitutionalization processes
and ensuring that the men, women, and children placed
in community-care facilities were receiving humane care,
treatment, and education. The processes of deinstitutionalization were failing; the systems of government could not
protect even the children in their care. In the spring of
1977, two *Chicago Sun-Times* reporters, Edward T. Pound
and Pamela Zekman, investigated the operations of another
private for-profit institution outside Chicago and came up
with a series of stories that exposed just how the one
facility worked. Even more important, they reported how
the several state agencies that licensed, placed, and funded
the care and treatment of retarded children were operating.
The *Sun-Times*'s first-day headline read: RETARDED CHILD
ABUSE; GANG BITING, TONGUE BURNING CHARGED. Former
employees told Pound and Zekman how children were
bound to wooden potty chairs for hours, how hot sauce
was poured on their tongues, how they were held under
cold showers, how they were hit and slapped about. Experts told the reporters that such treatment was not acceptable behavior-modification technique, and the school's
owners denied they personally abused children. They acknowledged that children were tied to potty chairs, but
insisted that no children were abused. The story noted that
some parents supported the school and defended the
owners.

The second-day story: "The owners of Windgate Home
for mentally retarded children are making substantial profits and salaries while failing to provide adequate services

paid for largely with public funds, according to financial records and former employees." The Windgate Corporation, licensed to operate a group home by the Department of Children and Family Services (DCFS) for the care of fifty-two mildly retarded children, paid Robert and Pat Mariacher $49,000 in salaries to operate the school. They also received $66,300 a year in rent for the buildings they personally owned and leased to the corporation they had created. In 1976, the corporation showed a $13,968 profit, not, by Illinois standards, an unreasonable financial gain on invested capital, nor were the salaries or rents considered out of the ordinary. Most of Windgate's children had been placed by the Department of Mental Health and Developmental Disabilities (DMH/DD). Some had been placed by the DCFS, and, in the complicated scheme of things, others were DMH/DD wards turned over to DCFS custody. Each of the children received an Illinois Office of Education (IOE) grant of $2500 per school year. A state educator later admitted that the IOE had never monitored the Windgate School. After the *Sun-Times* exposés, she told me that the IOE investigation revealed that "Windgate had a grossly inadequate educational program."

The Pound-Zekman stories revealed just how little each of the several agencies had known about Windgate. By the time the third installment hit the streets, the Department of Children and Family Services was announcing plans to revoke Windgate's license. The *Sun-Times*'s continuing series also lighted a fire under the governor, who responded by creating a Windgate Task Force at the same time that DCFS lawyers took Windgate's owners into license-revocation hearings. The hearing officer concluded that the institution's staff had used hot sauce on children's tongues, had finger-flicked their noses and ears painfully, had given them cold-water showers, restrained them in their beds, tied them hand and foot to potty chairs, all in the name of behavior modification. The hearing officer found the education and recreation classes inadequate and the staff not well trained, and he ruled that "on numerous occasions [the staff] subjected residents to cruel, severe, and unnecessary punishment." A year's probation was recommended. The DCFS followed the recommendation.

The Windgate Task Force reported that there was

> sufficient reason to believe some abuse did occur at Windgate. [However] . . . the Task Force concludes that the systems of service delivery of the three agencies [DMH/DD, DCFS, and IOE] lacked the communication, coordination, cooperation, and resources to adequately discharge their mandated responsibilities. Further, monitoring guidelines and license standards are insufficient or do not exist at all for community-based residential facilities and therefore the process of measuring the quality of services is greatly impeded.

In short, there was a lack of accountability. And this failure was almost universal. In Los Angeles County, James Hayes's investigations revealed that one rural facility housing forty-eight county wards, at a cost of $700 a month, had lease-back arrangements generating $72,000 a year. Another entrepreneur was less sophisticated. Audits showed that, while his group home claimed to have spent $400,000 a year in operating expenses, $65,000 of this sum was actually posted for salaries and fringe benefits of maintenance and clerical workers who did not exist. The number of scams was almost limitless. The GAO investigations in California revealed that Los Angeles and Orange counties were paying $340,000 in federal funds to profit-making group homes, even though federal regulations clearly prohibit the expenditure of federal funds in places operated for profit. A subsequent audit by HEW revealed that another $600,000 in federal funds was going to group homes operated for profit in Los Angeles County alone. Combine these costs with the reports on the living conditions in these facilities, and an ugly picture emerges: the welfare and probation departments in Los Angeles and

Orange counties were spending nearly $1 million in illegally placing federally subsidized foster-care children in for-profit group homes, many of which were scandalously unfit to care for these children.

The patterns of deinstitutionalization were beginning to emerge in state after state. Big, public institutions were costly and troublesome. Years of budget-slashing politics had caused short staffing and a lack of maintenance, turning even the best state hospitals and kid prisons into horrible warehouses. Ironically, tragically, the deinstitutionalization quick-fix schemes being slapped into place were proving to be costly, problem-ridden solutions that were not helping children. Large amounts of money once spent in institutional care were being legislatively diverted into the free-market kid business. Even though conservatives were cutting budgets, the amounts of money going into community care still totaled in the billions of dollars. In New York City alone, $300 million a year was being spent on foster homes, group homes, and private institutions. Half of that funding came from the federal Aid to Families of Dependent Children–Boarding Home and Institutions (AFDC–BHI) provisions of Title IV of the Social Security Act, as amended. By 1978, the kid business in New York City was booming and the New York State Department of Audit and Control reported that real estate entrepreneurs had been attracted to the public honeypots. The profit potentials were enormous. Audit control revealed that 15 percent of the buildings used by the voluntary foster-care programs were controlled by real estate operators who recognized this profit potential. The *New York Times* headlined the story OWNERS OF FOSTER-CARE HOMES REPORTEDLY TRIPLE INVESTMENTS. The *Times* reported one example: a real estate corporation purchased a home in the Bronx that had a value of $53,000 in 1972. Backed by a twenty-year lease from the Department of Social Services, which set rent at $26,000 a year, the corporation secured a $140,000 mortgage from a savings and loan association. According to the paper, the city had leased fifteen such homes and operated them directly, housing 150 kids. Another private company was leasing thirteen single- and double-family homes to voluntary child-care agencies, grossing $118,000 in rents. Audit control inspectors reported that the corporation "apparently utilized the leases as security to obtain mortgages totaling $595,000." Even church organizations owning buildings were leasing them back to subsidiary nonprofit corporations created to operate an orphanage or hospital or group home. Such real estate manipulations were draining off local, state, and federal tax dollars that had been earmarked for child care.

Despite all of the problems, there is evidence that deinstitutionalization can work, that it sometimes provides the kind of help children need. Massachusetts, for all of its flaws and faults, has demonstrated this fact. The impetus for change, of course, was crisis. In 1965, the Massachusetts Department of Youth Services was running kid prisons that were still using very primitive, punitive training school methods developed more than a century earlier. In addition to the big kid prisons, the department operated reception centers, diagnostic centers, guidance centers, and forestry camps. Eighty percent of the DYS wards were institutionalized. The entire system was overcrowded. In reaction to a critical HEW Children's Bureau report, some reforms were made, a new state school for boys seven to twelve years old was built at Oakdale, and a "new" maximum-security unit was opened in the old Bridgewater State Hospital. By 1969, the DYS was operating ten institutions. There were more scandals and more investigations, allegations of a lack of leadership, accusations that there was an absence of diagnostic and treatment goals and an inadequate parole system.

Governor Francis Sargent brought in a new director, Jerome Miller, and gave him a mandate: reform the reform schools; create an environment that is both humane and rehabilitative. From the start, Miller was faced with the usual problems: lack of funds and an entrenched bureaucracy. The new director outlawed the use of physical force and of strip cells, and strictly limited the use of solitary confinement. Each new order brought more resistance from the entrenched administrators and guards. They hated what was happening, believed it foolish and wrong. By 1970, Miller concluded that he could not reform the reform schools. Change by adminstrative order was impossible. A very radical move had to be made. Miller decided to *eliminate* the entire state reform school system as quickly as he could and replace it with small, community-based treatment programs, family-support systems, and an effective parole apparatus that would help youngsters adjust to community life.

Miller ordered the Bridgewater unit closed; forty-nine of the boys there were paroled. A dozen of the most troubled kids were transferred to Lyman, the nation's oldest reform school, built in 1848. Next, Miller closed Oakdale and Shirley. Calling in the press, he swung a sledgehammer and destroyed the locks on the segregation-unit cells to demonstrate his determination to break with the past. Utilizing federal Law Enforcement Assistance Administration funding and state appropriations, Miller laid out the foundations for a community-based network of treatment programs. He was relying heavily on purchase-of-service contracts with private vendors. By 1973, the DYS had 250 youngsters in foster homes, 750 more in some kind of structured group homes, 120 of the most seriously disturbed youngsters in residential treatment centers.

The years between 1969 and 1973 were not easy. There were problems with the quality of care, and the lack of security within community care became a public issue. When kids escaped, people were outraged and fearful. Prosecutors and judges began transferring juvenile cases into adult court to bypass the "leaky" juvenile system. Then, in 1973, Miller quit to take a similar job in Illinois. His assistant, Joseph Leavy, took over, developed a decentralized regional administration system, and tried to cope with the controversy generated by runaways. By 1976, Leavy had had enough. He resigned, and Governor Michael Dukakis appointed John Calhoun to the troubled DYS directorship.

Calhoun said:

> When I took over the agency it was about to fall apart. It had been deinstitutionalized rather cataclysmically and — without demeaning my predecessors — it was an agency held together by rhetoric. There were no standards, no basic bureaucratic fiber left. Efforts were being made to demolish DYS or to merge it back into adult corrections. The real job was to keep the walls from falling in and get back to some basic structure and to address the problem of security, of what to do with the rapists, the murderers, the robbers, and the kids who were stomping old ladies.

The DYS had within its jurisdiction, on any given day in the late 1970s, about two thousand youngsters: three hundred were in some form of precourt detention, awaiting hearings; fifteen hundred were committed to some kind of community-care program; and the rest were "referred" to informal probation. Of those who had been placed in programs, one-third were living at home and were under the supervision of a parole agent, another third were living at home but were receiving more intensive parole supervision and were in some kind of counseling or job training or alternative school. The remaining 550 kids were in residential care either in foster homes or group homes or psychiatric treatment centers: seventy of these kids were locked up in "secure" units, twenty of them in intensive psychiatric programs operated by the Department of Mental Health. Calhoun explained that Massachusetts no longer sent two hundred or three hundred children out of state because the DYS and the DMH had enough treatment programs to care for all but about thirty of the most severely handicapped, disturbed children. At the time, the DYS had contracts with two hundred private-care programs. Most of them handled five or fewer children. All were nonprofit. The list included the traditional providers and a few aggressive young professionals who, Calhoun said, had developed new approaches to care and treatment. While Calhoun liked to talk about the DYS "turnaround" and its progress, he candidly admitted that some serious problems faced him: "Security is the most hotly debated issue in youth corrections . . . The paucity of secure care beds has threatened the very existence of the community-based movement . . . Everyone, whether liberal or conservative, Republican or Democrat, police officer or social worker, advised me that the state ought to create more secure beds . . . However, most agreed that the majority of the delinquents should be treated in the community."

To defuse this controversy over security, Calhoun created a task force headed by L. Scott Harshbarger, who was chief of the Public Protection Bureau, Department of the Attorney General. After months of study, the task force concluded that the "deinstitutionalized, community-based approach to juvenile corrections should be preserved and strengthened." Harshbarger told me, "Deinstitutionalization has worked. The public now accepts it as *the* only approach, but we face the difficult task of learning how to deal with ten or eleven percent who are violent and who need security . . ."

While Harshbarger felt the public, in 1978, had finally come to accept the concept of deinstitutionalization in the juvenile justice system, there was evidence three years and one governor later that public acceptance was not a foregone conclusion. Dennis Curran, assistant legal council to Governor Edward J. King, said bluntly: "Deinstitutionalization is not working."

At the time, Curran was part of a *new* task force studying the subject. The primary problem: "security." DYS had 110 beds in secure treatment facilities, and Curran said, "That's clearly not enough." To make things worse, he said the task force hearings had revealed that the system for transferring the more violent youngsters from juvenile to adult court jurisdiction was "clogged" by restrictions and administrative red tape. Giving voice to the law-and-order mood of the 1980s, Curran explained, "We [the state] have seen too much [deinstitutionalization] too fast. As a result, the system has not been able to deal with the violent young criminals." To make his point, Curran told how a young rapist had been sent to a secure treatment facility, and then, two weeks later, the horrified victim of the rape saw the boy sitting next to her at a rock concert.

Curran said his task force would recommend construction of more security facilities. Asked if he meant big kid prisons, he said no, the state was committed to the idea of keeping such facilities as small as possible. But clearly the mood in Massachusetts, as expressed by various people in the King administration, had swung toward a more aggressive, conservative, law-and-order position that openly ridiculed as "crappy" and "phony" some of the community-care programs developed and used by DYS in previous administrations, programs that did not provide swift, sure justice.

There is no children's policy, no national goal, no coordinated effort in juvenile justice, in foster care, in the programs for the emotionally disturbed or the mentally retarded. The politics of a Governor Sargent swing one way, those of a Dukakis another, and King's yet another. And Massachusetts is only an example. In Massachusetts, the problems of overlapping bureaucratic structures and the lack of consistency were labeled "The Children's Puzzle" by the University of Massachusetts Institute of Governmental Services in a 1977 study that revealed the Department of Mental Health (DMH), the Department of Public Health (DPH), the Department of Public Welfare (DPW), the Office for Children (OFC), and the Massachusetts Rehabilitation Commission (MRC) were all working on their own, frequently at odds with the work of the other agencies, and that the human and financial waste was "incalculable." For example, as the hospitals for the mentally retarded were being deinstitutionalized, the DPH was placing increasing numbers of children in pediatric nursing homes. This caused a rush by private operators of all kinds to get into the nursing home branch of the kid business.

"The Children's Puzzle" singled out the Department of Public Welfare as the most disorganized of the agencies, indicating that it had almost irreconcilable management conflicts. The DPW was then spending $63 million on purchase-of-service contracts for children's services, but $13 million of that amount went for administration. Even so, the DPW could not provide the institute's investigators with a current list of the private-care providers it had under contract. The report concluded: "Programs for children who need day care, foster care, group care and protective services are often successful only because individual social workers and administrators endure . . . They manipulate the agency disorganization to get some children services."

The problem with this, of course, was that there was no sense of direction and no accountability. The system was manipulated, and the result was a hodgepodge of programs and services, some good, some not so good, and a few that were far out on the fringes of acceptable therapy techniques. Individual social workers placed youngsters in programs that were of questionable value. Steven Bing, an attorney for the Massachusetts Advocacy Center, described two "concept therapy" houses that used what he called "attack" therapy through encounter groups. He felt that some of the techniques used by these concept houses "constituted assault and battery." Harshbarger, who, as an assistant state's attorney general, had investigated one of these houses, agreed.

Harshbarger said that the facility had started with twelve of the state's toughest kid prison inmates in 1972 and had expanded into a $500,000-a-year program handling forty such youngsters. Harshbarger said the expansion had been quick, that it had not been made so much on the basis of the needs of the adolescents, but rather on the needs of the system:

> They ended up with a mixed case load, but they were applying the same [treatment] system. They didn't have individualized treatments varying with each kid . . . Civil libertarians like myself believe that, but for the fact it was called therapy, it was punishment. The question becomes: What can you do in the name of treatment? Legally, you could never do this sort of thing in corrections as a form of punishment. The tendency today in such programs is to have a charismatic leader. They try to substitute the program for the family, break the kid down, bring him or her back up, but what was happening was that you had people who *believed* rather than those who were trained in the application of concept therapy . . . This led to allegations of physical abuse.

Harshbarger's investigation of the facility brought the whole system into question. Both the DYS and the DPW had been using the concept house for years, and for years the methods used in the facility had been controversial. As early as 1972, there had been recommendations that the place be closed, but such recommendations only triggered further studies and ambiguous reports. Neither agency took any definitive action until the issue had become so controversial that it was forced to refer the problem to the attorney general. Harshbarger said the agency administrators "should have either said, 'Yes, we support the place, some kids need this kind of therapy and to hell with the critics,' or they should have said, 'No, such treatment is too tricky, too difficult to control and we will not use the place because of potential problems.' They did neither."

While officials in both agencies avoided making any decisions on their own, both the DYS and DPW did withdraw the youngsters they'd placed in the facility, pending the outcome of the attorney general's investigation. In the end Harshbarger recommended that unless and until the DYS and DPW could ensure clinical safeguards for the children within such a program, the agencies should not place anyone there.

Harshbarger, somewhat disgusted, said, "They [DYS and DPW officials] never did take the responsibility; they just quit using the place."

This one controversy stands as an example of how, in state after state, bureaucrats failed to confront issues and make decisions. Time and again interviews with such officials started off well. They would talk in general terms, explaining how they controlled the system and ensured that the quality of care and treatment was topnotch, and their departmental operations sounded impressive. However, when the questioning became specific, the answers often tended to be evasive and the bureaucrats became reluctant. In this particular case, Alexander Sharp, then commissioner of welfare, was asked why DPW had put youngsters in this one facility. He couldn't think of an answer, but he kept talking anyway: "Ahhh, I think that behavior, ahhh, they were difficult kids, ahhh, you get, at some point, to problems which are so extreme, ahhh, that is, it is very hard to find any program that can adequately deal with them."

What he seemed to be saying was that troublesome kids are hard to place. The thought was a familiar one. For all of its progress, for all of the rhetoric, Massachusetts was then — and is still — having problems finding enough places and enough services in its various community-care programs for children in need. And Massachusetts is considered one of the leaders in deinstitutionalization, not only in juvenile justice and foster care, but in mental health and mental retardation as well. In the 1960s the state had been operating a dozen big state hospitals that were warehousing 27,000 people. Controversy closed three of the hospitals and the populations in the remaining nine were markedly reduced over the next few years as the emphasis swung away from institutionalized care. By 1970 there were 12,510 men, women, and children in state mental hospitals and 7554 in the state schools for the mentally retarded. A decade later, the numbers had been reduced to 2827 in the state hospitals and 4446 in the state schools. Another indication of the progress made toward deinstitutionalized care can be found in the budget figures. Dr. Robert Okin, commissioner of the Department of Mental Health from 1975 through 1980, pointed out that while the total departmental budget had risen from $200 million to well over $400 million in the past decade, the community-care share of that budget for both mentally ill patients and mentally retarded persons had risen 400 percent. By 1981 Massachusetts was one of the few states spending less for institutional care and more for community care, Dr. Okin said, with obvious pride.

Mary Jane England, former assistant commissioner of the DMH, and, in 1981, the commissioner of social services, explained that deinstitutionalization of the state hospitals and schools for the retarded came about in part because of state policy, set in 1966, and in part because of the class-action suits brought against individual state institutions on behalf of patients. These suits, brought by several legal-service groups on behalf of indigent clients, resulted in a series of consent decrees that required change. In effect, the various legal-service attorneys had proven that individual state hospitals and schools for the retarded were short-staffed and that the children and adults in these hospitals had been abused and mistreated and that they had not received the kind of care and treatment they needed for rehabilitation. The state then agreed to make those changes set out in the consent decrees. One of the decrees went much further than the rest in that it established a patient's absolute right to treatment in the least restrictive setting; for the first time, patients had a right to care and treatment in their own community and the state had an obligation to provide that care and treatment. Together, the several decrees required the state to make needed changes not only in the state hospitals and schools but also in community-care services.

The state, spurred on by these decrees and by the work of concerned citizens and experts who insisted upon a community-care approach, made remarkable progress toward deinstitutionalization, despite political setbacks caused by politicians like Governor Dukakis. In 1975 Dukakis, sounding much like California's Jerry Brown, impounded $40 million that had been appropriated for various human services. According to a Massachusetts Advocacy Center study, the Dukakis attempts to cut state spending eliminated a $169,000 delinquency prevention program budget for eleven towns, wiped out half the funds for a $1 million project to help establish group homes for retarded children, and cut another $430,000 from home teaching programs for retarded children. With the freeze on state budgets came losses in staffing. Vacant job slots could not be filled. In the Gaebler Children's Unit at the Metropolitan State Hospital, for example, the number of nurses authorized was eighty-five. At the time of the hiring freeze, sixty-nine were working, but by 1978 that number had dropped to fifty-four. The situation was so critical that administrators of the children's unit shipped twelve psychotic children home. Kids who needed help desperately had to be sacrificed to relieve the pressures on the unit so that other children might be saved.

The Massachusetts Advocacy Center, a nonprofit organization set up to take on a broad range of children's issues, attacked the Dukakis fiscal policies, in court and out. "Mass. Advocates" pointed out, for example, that by cutting corners on children's programs and other social services, Dukakis was accumulating a state surplus estimated at between $69 million and $72 million. The freeze had been imposed at a time when the state was taking in more than it was spending. In a detailed study of Dukakis's budget cutting, Mass. Advocates reported:

> The freeze severely damaged services for children and young people throughout the state, both in institutions and communities . . . Many programs which had already begun were cut back; others were terminated altogether . . . The state Office for Children lost $1.2 million in frozen funds appropriated for children not receiving help from other agencies . . . Programs killed by executive action included a lead poisoning screening program in New Bedford and a child-abuse program in Revere.

Steven Bing later told me, "We found that as the budgets were cut there was an increase in the use of physical restraints and seclusion in the hospitals. We found that state programs were warehousing children. Youngsters who had learned to walk had forgotten how, children who were partially potty-trained regressed." Through the courts and through public opinion, the Massachusetts Advocacy Center and others finally forced the issues. The freeze was lifted and some of the budget cuts were restored, but not before the processes of deinstitutionalization had been severely disrupted.

Changing the subject, I asked Bing in 1978 if deinstitutionalization generally was working. Setting aside the controversy over the impounding of the $40 million and the hiring freeze and budget cutting, was the emerging system of community-based care working to the advantage of the children?

Bing replied, "Nobody really knows how good community-based care really is. The basic problem in the purchase-of-service system is that there are a whole lot of independent contractors and the state has little or no capacity to monitor these programs or evaluate them. The private providers run the show.''

Three years later, John Gillespie, director of communications for the Human Resources Agency, the parent bureaucracy overseeing those departments using community-care facilities, acknowledged the criticism was still valid. ''We still do not have good quality control,'' he said, agreeing that some of the twelve hundred private contractors used by the state were not licensed or monitored regularly, as the law required. The problem, he and others explained, was the seemingly never-ending struggle with budgets, with legal consent decrees requiring expenditures of ''hundreds of millions of dollars'' to upgrade existing state institutions, and with finding and keeping contract services. According to Gillespie, the state was still committed to the policies of deinstitutionalization. One of the problems under study in 1981, he said, was the fact that foster care was not returning children to permanent homes, as intended. Recognizing that far too many children in foster care were being deprived of permanent homes, Gillespie said budget planners were then trying to estimate how much it would cost for the state to move into an accelerated program that would place foster-care children back in their own homes, or, failing that, to find them adoptive homes.

However, in 1981 there was one huge, overriding problem: the fiscal uncertainty of the times. From the White House, Ronald Reagan was calling for $45 billion in budget cuts. And Massachusetts voters, following California's lead, overwhelmingly had approved a tax reform measure that was called Proposition 2½ because it limited the property tax rate to 2.5 percent of real value and imposed a 2.5 percent ceiling on local tax revenue increases. Under such fiscal restrictions, city and town politicians were frantically warning the voters that police, fire, and educational services were going to be radically cut, if the state did not come up with another $300 million in aid to local governments. It was obvious services were going to be cut. The only question was: Which services?

Dr. Okin, who had just resigned from the DMH, summed up the pessimistic mood: "If I'd stayed on, I think we could have worked around two-and-a-half somehow. Through the years, we'd managed to keep moving toward our goals in community care. But two-and-a-half, plus Reagan? That's awfully tough. I'm worried."

Steven Bing talked in more catastrophic terms: "The combination of the state and federal governments taking the same budget-cutting courses will be disastrous."

In the short run, the blasts from such a double-barreled-shotgun approach to cutting spending may prove disastrous. Sadly, it is the children who will suffer, despite all the "safety-net" rhetoric coming from the White House. But the effect of Proposition 2½ and Reaganomics will generate counterattacks by legal-services attorneys in the courts and by those special-interest groups lobbying for various children's causes. If these attacks are made on an individual, cause-by-cause basis, their effectiveness will be seriously weakened. If some sort of children's coalition were formed to bring all these special interests into a co-ordinated battle group, the impact could be considerable. And it must be remembered that the changes that have come about in Massachusetts — and elsewhere — did not occur in an atmosphere of calm, reasoned debate and rational actions. The move away from big institutions toward community care was born in outrage, and it has survived and grown in an environment of controversy.

# 7

# Licensing

EARLY IN THE SUMMER of 1973, a teen-aged girl died in one of the many private, for-profit kid businesses licensed by the State of Texas. The death of the girl in Artesia Hall attracted the attention of Liberty County officials, who took the case to the grand jury. The investigation, in turn, attracted the media and then the state legislature. The Artesia Hall incident is significant not for the details of the case, but because the following investigation revealed just how insensitive and indifferent the legislature and the various bureaucracies had been to the scandalous problems within the kid businesses then flourishing in Texas. Thousands of children from Illinois, Louisiana, and a dozen other states had been shipped to Texas and placed in private group homes and institutions with pleasant-sounding names. But Texas had no quality controls over these facilities worthy of the name; the weak inspection and licensing system that did exist was ineffective.

The Texas House of Representatives' Committee on Health and Welfare held hearings and reported: "Testimony indicated that Artesia Hall had an unbroken record of objectionable and questionable conduct, and that several

Department of Public Welfare employees had adamantly opposed the issuance of the license." But Artesia was not the only place that was troublesome. "This investigation quickly proved that there were many irregularities in the private, child-caring facilities and services in Texas. Also brought into question were the activities of the DPW and other state agencies legally responsible for regulating private child-caring institutions."

There was "growing concern" within the legislature over the operations of state institutions by the Texas Department of Mental Health and Mental Retardation (TDMHMR) and the Texas Youth Council. At the time, the TYC was in the midst of the *Morales* v. *Turman* suit over conditions in the kid prisons, and there were reports coming out of the state hospitals that patient deaths may have been caused by "strangulation with restraints used to tie residents to their beds" and that there had been "imprudent and excessive use of tranquilizing drugs." Investigations had been held, but, according to the committee report, no evidence of wrongdoing had been found. Coincidental with these reports and the investigations into the Artesia Hall incident, there was a scandal brewing in Illinois over the placement of children in Texas — triggered by Pat Murphy's legal actions on behalf of the girl who had been given a hysterectomy. In addition, Bill Rittenberg was working on the *Gary W.* case.

The critical issue in all of this was and still is the lack of accountability. The primary quality control mechanism in all community-care systems provided by purchase-of-service contracts with private vendors is a strong licensing and certification effort by government. Yet neither the Texas licensing staff nor placement workers from other states exercised any control over the dozens of facilities later found to be mistreating kids. Ultimately, when pressured by the politics of media exposés, the Texas attorney general found community-care standards "unacceptably low," and a private consultant hired by the legislature reported that the state had "one of the worst child-care licensing laws in the nation." As a result, the attorney general's investigation revealed that there was a "highly organized, profit-seeking child-care establishment" operating throughout the state. The Texas legislature reacted by drafting new, tougher laws, which were in place in 1975, but the lawmakers failed to provide the needed funds to beef up the license investigation and enforcement staffing.

Time and again, in state after state, the patterns were repeated. Licensing and certification divisions or departments were the stepchildren of government. The drafting of regulations was subjected to heavy political pressures from the nursing homes, from the private kid business establishment, from welfare conservatives in and out of politics who are more concerned about saving tax dollars than funding quality control in child care. Even in states like Massachusetts, where there is a concerted effort to make deinstitutionalization work, the problems in licensing were gross. The Office for Children had been created by the Massachusetts legislature to act as a children's advocate and to coordinate services for children. An important part of the OFC's task is the licensing of day care, foster care, and group homes. In 1978, the OFC was overseeing four thousand public and private facilities that were providing care and treatment for seventy thousand children; approximately one third of these children were in some kind of twenty-four-hour foster care or in institutions. On paper, the OFC looked good and, as Joyce Strom, then the OFC director, described what was supposed to be happening, the design of the OFC sounded good. However, because of budget constraints and bureaucratic structuring, the monitoring and licensing functions were never carried out properly. Strom had only seven licensing specialists for the entire state, and their case loads were impossibly heavy. As a result, Strom said, the OFC had to rely on each agency to set and maintain its own standards. The state did impose "minimum standards," she said, but added, "We're far behind [in inspections], and we're not going to put kids in the street and the programs out of business just because the license expires [every two years] . . . so we have licenses that are beyond expiration dates, we have as many as a hundred group homes that are a year beyond expiration."

Put another way, Strom was saying that a hundred group homes had not been inspected or monitored for three years. And she failed to mention that many of the licensed facilities were only "provisionally" licensed because they had failed to meet standards. In addition to operators with expired licenses and provisional licenses, there were operators who had no license at all, according to Steve Bing of the Massachusetts Advocacy Center. Bing said "Mass. Advocates" had checked and found that 24 percent of the providers of children's services were operating openly without licenses: "The private providers control their own intake and their own programs . . . The problem is, there are a whole lot of independent contracts and little [governmental] capacity to monitor these programs or evaluate them. Neither the Department of Youth Services or the Office for Children monitor as they are supposed to. The DYS is resisting the OFC's efforts to take over monitoring and evaluation."

Despite such reports, the state did little to upgrade its licensing systems, or to resolve the conflicts between the agencies. In the spring of 1981, one top state official who had an overview of the licensing situation, when asked about the conditions Strom and Bing had described three years earlier, said, "Oh, yeah. That's still a problem. There are a lot of group homes that aren't licensed or monitored. And we don't have a good system for auditing these programs."

In Illinois, the federal Department of Health, Education,

and Welfare audits of foster-care programs revealed that that state's Department of Children and Family Service (DCFS) was placing as many as 10 percent of its children in facilities that were either unlicensed or overcrowded or both. The General Accounting Office investigation of foster-care institutions in five states found: "Licensing and placing agencies did not regularly inspect institutions and enforce licensing standards. As a result many institutions had serious deficiencies." The GAO selected these five states because they handle two thirds of the children who are placed in foster-care institutions. Two major problems were brought out in the 1977 report. First, the federal government has never set national standards for community care, so each state regulates foster homes, group homes, and child-care institutions pretty much on its own. The second problem noted was the general failure of state legislatures to provide sufficient funds to staff the licensing and regulatory enforcement actions that are required to ensure quality control.

This shortage of funds was reflected in the performances of the various licensing departments. The GAO noted that in Georgia, licensing renewals had not been issued for most of the institutions for several years and that "one New York licensing agency did not visit half of the facilities" it was relicensing. Ironically, the GAO singled out California as the only state among the five that "had fully complied" with the annual inspection requirement set by Congress. Clearly, Congress wanted the states to operate a licensing inspection program and, technically, California's computerized license renewal system — which had relicensed Oak Creek Ranch automatically — met federal regulations. California did have problems, however. The GAO investigators noted that the state's Licensing and Certification Division was so understaffed that it could not pursue the lengthy procedures required to revoke the licenses of offensive facilities.

First Reagan and then Jerry Brown had cut the budgets
of the Licensing and Certification Division and increased
the workloads. One licensing evaluator told me that he had
153 group homes and institutions in his case load. "That's
just too much, man." This fellow has a master's degree
in social work. He is a tough investigator who cares deeply
about children and who was outraged by much of what he
saw going on in community care, but he told me:

Look, if I try to close a place down, where will the kids go?
Back on the street? Back in the state hospital? My God, do
you know how bad things are in there? But say I make the
decision to go after the license of a really bad place: it takes
months to get enough evidence to convince my bosses that
we ought to act. They want to cover their asses, so they will
buck it upstairs and they'll waffle it around Sacramento, come
back with requests for more information, or they may order
a special study, anything to avoid action, because they know
how long a hearing takes and if the lawyers appeal a revocation
decision, how long the thing is tied up in court. In fairness
to the brass, they know such a case will tie me up *for years*,
man. The system is fucked, but you work with it, try to force
a place to clean up its act, coax them, threaten them, anything
that will help make it better for the kids, because you always
get back to that original question: If you close the place down,
where do the kids go? There are never enough places for the
kids to go. You ought to hear the placement workers argue
with us to leave some of those places open. If a place is really
bad, when the kids are being hassled or even hurt, if we close
it down, we get blamed for causing problems. *We get blamed!*

In the late 1970s, the Licensing and Certification Division
was a $24 million-a-year, five-hundred-employee operation
with headquarters in the new Department of Health headquarters building constructed during the Reagan years.
From the top floors of the twin towers of glass and steel,
the DOH Licensing and Certification Division executives
could look over the tree-lined streets of downtown Sacramento, see the gleaming gold dome of the capitol and

beyond to the snowcapped Sierra Nevada. A year after Dr. Jerome Lackner had taken over the DOH, he named Charlene Harrington to head the division. Harrington, a bright, young registered nurse who held a doctorate in public health administration, had worked with the Little Hoover Commission on the investigation of DOH problems and she had written the scathing thirty-seven-page section on licensing and certification that laid the bureaucratic structures bare, exposing the featherbedding and ineptitude.

In the Little Hoover report, Harrington had started from the beginning, in 1973, when the division was called Health Quality System, and followed it through a series of crises that finally resulted in the changing of the name to Quality Review System. She pointed out that shuffling people around and changing the name didn't solve problems. At the time of the review, the new title, Licensing and Certification Division, had been in place only a short while; but, even so, the problems were once more building within the division. Harrington singled out the Facilities Licensing Section, one of five sections in the division, for special comment. She pointed out that within the Facilities Licensing Section,

> there is an extra layer of administrative bureaucracy which does not seem to serve a useful purpose. District administrators report to the supervisor for District Operations, who in turn reports to the chief of the Licensing Section, who reports to the manager of Licensing and Certification. A licensing surveyor reports to a licensing supervisor in the district offices, who reports to the district administrator. This makes a total of six layers of administration between the clients and the division manager . . District administrators do not have access to the division manager, but rather report through the hierarchy of administrators within the division . . . District administrators of licensing sections do not have the authority to make decisions on revocation, temporary suspension, or nonrenewal of certifications but rather must prepare requests which travel a complicated, slow path. A request for legal or

administrative action must go to the legal coordinator within Licensing, to the Licensing Section chief, and the legal counsel of the director of the Department of Health. If it is approved, the request is sent on to the state attorney general's office where the case is assigned to an attorney who proceeds . . . Actual licensure revocation process takes about nine to twelve months, and a nonrenewal action takes over six months.

Result: In 1975, the division staff had filed more than two thousand complaints at the field level, but these resulted in only thirty license denials or license-revocation procedures being initiated. Harrington reported, "The Licensing and Certification Division has been weak in the enforcement of the laws."

The Little Hoover Commission report was released in January 1976, but it made few headlines. The report was so massive and so complex that it did not fit into daily journalism's format; there was *too much* wrong. So newspapers singled out bits and pieces, and television simply warned that a "scandal was brewing" in the DOH. Harrington, who had been temporarily assigned by Lackner to help the Little Hoover Commission in 1975, returned to her regular job as one of his administrative assistants. Six months later, she was appointed director of Licensing and Certification. She told me:

I had no inkling Lackner was going to do that, but I wouldn't say I objected too much. What had happened was that between January and August they had stalled on doing anything about the Hoover Commission report. Then the commission announced it was starting hearings, beginning in September, and we knew they meant to call in everyone they could to uncover what was happening in the hospitals. After Lackner was informed about that, he decided to move. To get the heat off of him, he decided to put me in there. He didn't care whether I survived or not, after the hearings were over. He didn't have any commitment [from the governor] to back me up . . . but I thought, "Give me two weeks to get at those guys [Licensing's top bureaucrats] and I'll enjoy it. I'll do what I can."

Well, I had done the study on licensing and I'd made the recommendations to the commission and I felt very strongly they were screwing people over, that there was no enforcement going on, that they didn't give a damn about people. Theirs was a bureaucratic process. They had the view they were working in partnership with providers; they saw *the providers* as the clients, as opposed to the people who were in the facilities and who were totally disregarded . . . a view I felt was outrageous. You need to have a commitment to people and a commitment to enforcement . . . You take your existing resources and you can do a hell of a lot more than they were doing . . . So I felt it was exciting and I could try to bring about some changes.

Within the first two weeks, Harrington removed, fired, or transferred twenty-five people; she cut the staffing levels in the Sacramento headquarters and put more people in the field; she ordered the various licensing sections to start enforcing laws, and created a special review team to tackle the state hospitals *from an enforcement point of view*. For the first time, licensing became a regulatory function, under her rule; scandalously operated community-care facilities were being shut down. She should have become the heroine in the Brown — or even the Jarvis — scheme of things; she was "trimming fat" from the bureaucracy, forcing it to act aggressively, efficiently, to protect children, the elderly, the sick, and the lame, and, at the same time, she was ensuring that tax monies were not being ripped off by free-enterprising pirates. But, from the outset, Harrington was in trouble. Neither Lackner nor Harrington had any political constituency of his or her own; both served at Brown's pleasure, and his attention was elsewhere. While children and old folks have never had any political power, the nursing home industry does, and it uses its power quickly. The industry liked the Licensing Division the way it was. The shock of Harrington's actions and word of Lackner's unwillingness — or inability — to contain her reached the governor's office.

Getting Brown's undivided attention was extremely difficult. He was not really interested in the problems of the DOH; if he had any policies or philosophical views "emerging" on the subject, they had never been communicated. Rather than deal directly with the problem, he dispatched Ray Procunier to the Health Department to contain Harrington and to take over the administrative duties from Lackner, all behind the scenes. Procunier was one of several administrators and lawyers Brown kept in reserve; like firefighters, they were periodically dispatched to extinguish controversy that could flare up into a politically embarrassing situation. Procunier was called "Pro," not so much as a nickname but as a description; he had , started out in state government as a prison guard and had worked his way up through the ranks, earning a reputation as a tough administrator who got things done. Reagan had appointed him director of prisons. Brown kept him on as a bureaucratic trouble-shooter. Pro didn't like reporters, and he didn't grant interviews readily. Twice he missed appointments with me, his secretary explaining he'd been called away on urgent business. The second time this happened, I was told he was "across town" in an important meeting, yet a few minutes later I found myself riding down in an elevator with a dapper little man who was introduced to me as Ray Procunier. He was as surprised and embarrassed as I was angered. He denied he was avoiding me or was afraid to answer my questions. By the time I finally pinned him down for an interview, Harrington had already *unlicensed* four state hospitals, and she was threatening to unlicense the remaining seven if they didn't come up to acceptable standards. She had also cracked down on community-care facilities that were brutalizing clients and ripping off the system.

The whole mess was brought to a climax by a series of explosive news stories revealing that the Ventura and Napa County district attorneys and the state attorney general were investigating nineteen deaths in Camarillo State Hospital and forty-seven deaths in Napa State Hospital. Throughout 1976, bits and pieces of controversy over these hospitals were becoming known, primarily through the Little Hoover hearings and the unrest created by the parents of children in the state hospitals. Budget-cutting had turned the once-exemplary program for autistic children in Camarillo into a nightmare. Parents complained to Lackner that they found their children heavily drugged, only partially clothed, unwashed, and given nothing to do. The number of teachers had been cut from sixteen to just three; the staff of social workers had been cut in half. The reports got into the local press and the *Los Angeles Times*, but the Brown administration managed to weather such attacks until news got out that people were dying under strange circumstances in several state hospitals. That news forced Brown to act or, rather, react.

Procunier was ordered to snuff out the various DOH controversies, starting with the hospital deaths. Procunier is a short, silver-haired James Cagney of a man who bounces as he moves, jaunty rather than cocky. He still talks like a prison guard. He doesn't discuss a situation; he "runs it down for ya." Pro explained that he had been sent in to the DOH to do a survey.

> I was there about three or four days and everybody was tellin' me what was wrong, see? I didn't want to listen to any more of that, 'cause I'd heard enough. I went to Lackner and I said, "You don't need my survey. The survey's over. You need somebody to run this place." Well, he decided he would like me to be his chief deputy director and take the program and get it shaped up. Everybody over there was supposed to be bad people, but they wasn't. They were really good, capable people. They just needed somebody to speak for them, get some money for them, argue for them when they needed . . . So I took the job . . .

Procunier talks rapidly, frequently getting ahead of himself.

One of the first things I had to deal with was the death of a [nineteen-year-old] boy in Metro [the boy had been killed when a Metropolitan State Hospital attendant had subdued him by striking him over the head with a flashlight], so I looked into that and it wasn't one death. It was three. It started with the [Ventura County] district attorney down at Camarillo. He'd accused a bunch of people of bad things that didn't turn out to be that bad. But it was a big thing. Then we found out about the boy at Metro.

Procunier hired ten investigators and teamed them with ten nurses and ordered a full-scale investigation of every death in the state hospital system.

We came up with twelve hundred deaths and some were categorized A-okay, some were B-questionable or C-definitely questionable. Then we worked the B's and moved some of them into C's and worked the C's over until we had 157 that were seriously questionable. We took a look at them, then turned them over to the local district attorneys. They went through them to see if any were prosecutable, and I don't think anybody got prosecuted . . . As it turned out there was no intention on anybody's part to cover things up. It [the death of twelve hundred people] was just sort of carelessly handled.

Harrington and Procunier didn't get along. She told me:

Pro totally sabotaged me. He didn't give a shit whether we got any enforcement done, he couldn't have cared less if we implemented the Hoover Commission recommendations. He didn't care if we straightened out the regulations. Nothing. His whole thing was to keep things quiet, to look good in the press, and don't spend money . . . I didn't kow-tow to Pro. If I disagreed with him I told him so, and if I thought he was wrong, I told him so. He doesn't like uppity women in his little club. I didn't follow him around and kiss his ass like all those guys do.

From the beginning, when she had started cracking down on the nursing homes, she had warned Lackner and then Procunier that the state hospitals were in such bad shape

that she, as director of Licensing and Certification, would
not renew their licenses unless radical changes were made.
If the state hospitals were unlicensed, that would mean
they were "decertified" by the U.S. Department of Health,
Education, and Welfare and that, in turn, would mean
California would no longer receive $40 million in federal
funds. Harrington told me:

> I think Pro was really disgusted about the whole thing, but
> he had a job to do. And he thought he had gotten me to sign
> off on [approve] the hospital certifications, and he had made
> a lot of promises [to the governor]. He didn't expect me to
> follow through on my threats to decertify those places. I kept
> telling him the hospitals were not in compliance, and he kept
> telling me not to worry about it, that he'd take care of it, so
> then I went ahead. When we had to decertify them, it just
> blew his cover; that showed he had not done the kinds of
> things he was responsible for . . . So I think that problem,
> even more than [cracking down on] the nursing homes resulted
> in my firing.

Harrington was not fired directly; instead, she was removed from her job and put back on Lackner's staff as
an assistant within his office. By this time Lackner had
virtually no remaining authority, no power. Harrington said
she was informed that if she kept her mouth shut she could
keep her present salary level as an exempt employee working directly for Lackner. She didn't keep her mouth shut,
and within a short time she was out of work.

Procunier, the tough-minded administrator, understood
the structures of government, and he could follow orders.
Given a job, he did it, even though he was sometimes
cynical about the process: "I want you to understand,
when they did all of this great stuff, moving people out
into the communities, the plan was not there and the
facilities were not there and adequate funding was not
there, so that is why we got the chaos we got right
now . . . Everybody got into the business too fast with

too little preparation, and concurrently with that the hospitals were just neglected."

I asked Dr. Lackner if he had any idea just how bad the hospital system had been when he took over. Lackner — a slight, average-looking man except for the great walrus mustache that dominates his face — gave a surprisingly bureaucratic answer for an antibureaucrat: "The hospitals are not as bad as comparable entities elsewhere. When you compare California state hospitals to hospitals in other states . . . our state hospitals are probably not much different. But as far as I am concerned, they are not adequate until they meet the same standards we require of private institutions."

He was in complete agreement with Harrington's actions in the unlicensing of the state hospitals, "Frankly, I don't see any other way we can bring about changes without dramatic actions, even though it jeopardized federal funds . . . I may want to take you off the record on this, but the fact is that for — let's go off the record."

Then, with the understanding that I could use the material once he left office — he was fired by Jerry Brown a few months later — the director of the DOH told me, "The ordinary things that would have kept the hospitals in compliance with regulations went out the window through the budgetary process." Of the $10 million Lackner had requested in his first budget for upgrading the hospitals, $4 million was blue-penciled out by the Department of Finance. "The governor was making political hay out of being frugal, out of accumulating surpluses and not raising taxes," Lackner explained.

When his budget was again cut the following year, Lackner was thoroughly discouraged.

When they do that to you twice, you say, "What the hell's the use?" I tried to get the governor to do the right thing, in the regular process, but there were a lot of voices between him and me, and they told him he did not have to worry about the state hospitals . . . So my position is "Am I going to be in charge of a system in which I think people are dying because of therapeutic misadventure, or not getting well, or, or, or going backwards in terms of their wellness, their normalness, or whatever?" And the answer was that I'm not, not when we've got an *obscene $3 billion surplus*. The state has the opportunity to do what it is supposed to do. The state should obey the law. If it doesn't obey the law, it shouldn't get the federal money. The pathetic thing about it is I tried to get [Brown] to do the right thing first. I tried to get him to do the moral, ethical, responsible thing, and I couldn't do it, except by this other way, this terrible bind, by boxing him in by unlicensing the state hospitals.

On April 21, 1978, not long after he was fired by Brown, Dr. Lackner released the embargo on the above tape-recorded interview, adding, "I realized that in order to get a substantive change in the quality of care . . . the only way that I could do it was to take advantage of the fact that I had the responsibility not only for the mental health of the patients, but the licensing and certification process . . . By decertifying certain of the state hospital units, I put the system in jeopardy, which, in turn, created leverage on the governor."

Harrington confirmed Lackner's version of what had happened. I wanted to explore the budgetary processes further, with the governor, to learn his point of view. However, several attempts to set up interviews with Brown failed.

It was obvious, as the months passed, that Lackner had underestimated the consequences of allowing Harrington to begin unlicensing the state hospitals, because, once begun, the decertification processes began to gather a momentum of their own. Over the period of almost a year, and despite the best efforts of Procunier and his subordinates to put out the fires she was starting, Harrington pursued her task all too well. Even after she was dismissed, the processes continued until every state hospital was affected in some way. The state lost $40 million a year in federal funding. Brown tried to patch together a remedy. He asked the state legislature for $24 million in emergency funding. Months later he was granted $19 million, and DOH officials rushed out with fiscal Band-Aids. But it was a case of too little, too late. The downward spiral had picked up so much momentum that only very strong leadership on the part of the governor and his top aides could have reversed the trend, and then only by pouring far more money into the process. That kind of leadership and money was not forthcoming.

Lackner was fired. And Brown ordered the DOH superagency be broken up into five separate newly named departments, each with its own separate administrative functions, its own licensing and certification processes. The order to disband provided the needed confusion and sense of motion to obscure once more the underlying problems. Bureaucrats began the scramble for positions; the teams of regulation writers trying desperately to catch up to the 1973 mandates for uniform community-care guidelines once more had to throw their work out and, in five separate fiefdoms, began proliferating five new sets of rules and regulations.

Brown's reactions to the state hospital crisis, his refusal to deal with the problems of community care, and his leadership in the implementation of Proposition 13 spending cutbacks caused a serious situation to become worse, especially for children. Brian Cahill, executive director of the California Association of Children's Residential Centers, said, "Brown has had more negative impact than Reagan . . . There is a low priority on children's services. There's not even one full-time person yet in the Department of Health Social Services Branch that deals with residential group care . . . No one really knows what is happening."

The CACRC is an association of sixty-five nonprofit corporations that provide thirty-five hundred spaces for children in 130 different facilities. In all, it is a small part of the thirteen hundred private group homes and institutions licensed by the state, but, because its membership is made up of the largest, most respected charitable institutions in the state, CACRC is an influential organization. For several years the association has been lobbying for stronger, tougher licensing efforts by the state. One member, Eric Gill, director of the Sacramento Children's Home, a nondenominational Protestant orphanage started in 1867, stated:

> I am a believer in the fact you need a hell of a lot of policemen in this field. Under the old Department of Social Welfare we were studied thoroughly every year by a team of experts that spent at least one day, and frequently two days going through. In the past four or five years, I think we've had maybe two or three visits; they [the Licensing Division] say we are well known, they know our structure, so they don't have to look at us closely . . . Licensing is only looking at the places where they've been told there are problems. There is no system to safeguard kids now . . . Society is placing kids in a lot of places where they don't know who is running them; they don't know what is being done with the kids. Every once in a while, we get a horror story, and I'll tell you right now, in my opinion there are a hundred horror stories that never get attention for every one we hear about. The system is so poorly designed, it does bad, bad things to kids. I know how bad things can get, even with the best of intentions and the best of staff. There are a lot of people in this field that have very strange ideas . . . There are also a lot of places that are doing first-class work. And I object to the fact that we all get smeared with the same brush when something bad happens . . . There should be a first-class policing system to protect the kids in California. That's the state's obligation, it's the counties' obligation, it is the cities' obligation.

## 8

## The Kate School

THE CHANGING PUBLIC MOOD in California, the political evolution from Brown to Reagan to Brown, with the resulting fiscal and administrative changes in the various foster-care and child-welfare programs, was having a devastating impact on the lives of children. But no one was paying much attention. The problems were hidden from public view, tucked away — out of sight, out of mind. In California — as in the nation — we had delegated foster-care and child-welfare responsibilities to various federal, state, and local bureaus; we had authorized the expenditure of billions of dollars. Then, satisfied that we'd collectively provided the best and the most advanced care and welfare possible, we went about the hectic pace of our individual lives, grumbling about the high cost of welfare, and passing Jarvis' antitax measures.

We were only vaguely aware that there was trouble out there in the system somewhere. The evening news flashed bits and pieces of troublesome reports about state hospitals or the mistreatment of children in foster care, but the dispatches were brief and too quickly inundated by following news blips: Inflation. Recession. Oil Crisis. We didn't have time to react. For the parents of handicapped kids, for journalists or children's rights' advocates or legislators interested in children's issues, this rush of complex situations made it difficult to get and hold anyone's attention long enough to describe the underlying socioeconomic and political problems, much less discuss possible solutions. What was needed, I felt, was a book that would provide a large enough format to set out the problems and suggest some solutions. As I worked on this book, it was soon obvious to me that the size and the scope of the problems could become overwhelming if I didn't narrow the focus, pulling it down from the nation, focusing on California, then narrowing it still further until I focused on just one facility, a place called the Kay-Tee School. The name was spelled *Kate* School.

The Kate School was a private, nonprofit residential center, licensed to care for and treat forty-eight emotionally disturbed children. The school, located in the heart of the San Joaquin Valley, advertised that it specialized in treating autistic children, at a 1975 cost of $1271 a month. Children from as far away as Los Angeles and the San Francisco Bay Area had been placed in the school by county welfare departments, probation departments, by regional centers, and by parents receiving funds from the state Department of Health.

Because the staff used a radical form of behavior modification in its therapy programs, relying heavily on painful, punishing "aversive" techniques, the school was the focus of a long-standing controversy. Not only had that controversy been my introduction to the subject of out-of-home placement of children; the school and the controversy had become for me a symbol of the way foster care works.

Norman and Martha Wilson had started the Kate School in 1970. At the time, they had little more to work with than their strong determination to help autistic children, those severely disturbed youngsters who acted out in bizarre ways, who were withdrawn, often beyond the reach of any form of communication. These were children who reacted violently, screaming and hurting themselves and others, smashing the world around them; or they sat for hours twiddling their fingers or flapping their hands or twirling a plate, oblivious of everything else.

The Wilsons were a middle-aged couple. He was a heavy-set fellow, gray-bearded and brusque, a hard-of-hearing, strong-willed man who seemed to provoke controversy. She was a pleasant-looking person, milder mannered, not quite shy, a credentialed teacher who had designed many of the educational and therapeutic techniques used in the school. Norman Wilson, an ex-construction worker, dominated the scene and carried on the school's controversial approach to behavior modification in open defiance of anyone who questioned what the couple was doing.

The Wilsons believed they had a special calling for this work, for this particular type of troubled child. To prepare for that calling, they worked and studied hard. She had a master's degree in special education; he had given up his work in construction and enrolled in a state college, earning a bachelor's degree in psychology. In 1970, they had moved to Fresno, bought a house, applied to the Department of Mental Hygiene for the appropriate licenses, and opened the Kate School in the family room of their home. To outsiders coming into the school for the first time, the couple were impressive. Their zeal was obvious, their enthusiasm was catching, their motives seemed unquestionable. Mrs. Wilson once told a reporter, "We've started the whole thing on faith. We let the Lord direct our lives. We want to help these children, and other emotionally handicapped children, and we're letting the Lord show us the way."

The school was begun modestly. The Wilsons took in two or three youngsters at a time, working with them on a daily basis. If in their judgment a child needed to remain in their home for a few days or weeks, that was arranged with the parents and the placement agency. In 1971, a local reporter wrote: "A 'typical' day begins at the breakfast table. It is here the children learn appropriate table manners and the correct use of utensils. They are corrected at even the slightest deviation. The Wilsons take the children on field trips to the park, shopping centers and to dinner." From the outset, the emphasis was on controlled social behavior.

The Wilsons met with early success. They had opened the school at a time when there was a perpetual shortage of "beds" in community care throughout the state. Placement agencies were always calling, offering more children than the Wilsons had room for, so they expanded the school. A nonprofit corporation was formed, and the Wilsons took two of the three seats on the board of directors. Under this corporate structure they purchased a four-acre "ranch" in the horsy suburbs of Clovis, northeast of Fresno, a ranch that had a large, comfortable house, a swimming pool, and room to build an education building. By 1975, they had developed the school site, and the corporation had been granted three Department of Health licenses, one for the day school, one for a "small family group home" run by the Wilsons, and one for a "group home" run by a couple hired as house parents. Applications were pending for five more group-home licenses to cover nearby suburban residential structures purchased by the corporation and put in use as "satellite" homes for the school.

In 1975, the Kate School had thirty-one children in residence. Internal Revenue Service records show the gross 1974–75 income was $395,000, assets totaled $521,000, and liabilities were up to $360,000. The latter figure included the note against a 203-acre cattle ranch the Wilsons planned to turn into the Kate-Bar-None Boys Ranch for delinquents. The Wilsons never appeared to be in the kid business for their own profit. There were no indications of lease-back schemes; their salaries as "director" and "education coordinator" were quite modest. The Kate School Corporation did provide them with food, housing, and transportation, just as it supplied those goods and services for the other house parents. The corporation had been set up to provide them a tax-free means for building a school to match their dreams, their calling. And it was doing just that. Their horizons were almost unrestricted; the school was accepted by placement workers from the various county and state agencies; no one seemed to question the school's approach to behavior modification. Each caseworker signed a release acknowledging that aversive, painful methods of therapy were used by the Wilsons and their staff.

The Wilsons called their treatment techniques "Confrontation Therapy: A realistic and humanistic approach to the treatment of autistic children." Though their programs relied heavily on forms of behavior modification considered unusual by clinical psychologists trained as behaviorists, neither Martha nor Norman Wilson was a clinically trained psychologist. He had a bachelor's degree in psychology from a state college, she a master's degree in special education. Nor did they employ any psychologists or psychiatrists to work with the children either in preadmission diagnostic testing or in the routine of the therapy programs. They were lay persons with a mission; they had developed the system on their own, based on their own knowledge and beliefs. Wilson explained that the system relied on "the principles of confrontation, expectation, and consistency." Once a child had been accepted into the Kate School, the Wilsons assumed that the child was "of average or above average intelligence, able to perform and behave and therefore expected to do so in an appropriate manner." The determination of "appropriate" was the prerogative of the Wilsons and, through them, the staff of the school.

Once the child was "confronted" with a task, the Wilsons "expected" appropriate behavior, and if their expectations were not met, they applied "negative reinforcement" or "aversive techniques" to force the issue. Although the Wilsons used the two behavior-modification terms interchangeably, they had no training in clinical psychology and little understanding of how either negative reinforcement or aversive techniques worked or should be used in a therapeutic setting. What the Wilsons — and the staff of the school — were doing was punishing children, using pain to control behavior. Public records show that between 1972 and 1975 the Kate School staff:

— Slapped children on the hands, about the head, on the back, chest, legs, and buttocks;

— Pulled children's hair, ears, pinched them and poked them, sometimes with a closed fist;

— Finger-flicked them about the face, squeezed or pinched various parts of their bodies;

— Spanked them with "various small, hard instruments," like paddles, rulers, and fly swatters;

— Administered cool- or cold-water showers when children wet their beds or soiled their pants;

— Forced one child to eat regurgitated food by holding his mouth and nose closed; force-fed other children or deprived them of food;

— Electrically shocked children with a cattle prod, until the state ordered the practice stopped in 1972.

The Kate School's classroom staff and the house parents in the satellite group homes were the primary therapists; their therapeutic tools were those techniques developed by the Wilsons. The "teachers" and house parents were hired off the street, at a minimum wage, no experience required. They were trained by the Wilsons. For years, Mrs. Wilson was the only credentialed teacher in the school. She was the teacher, instructing the staff of paraprofessionals how to reward a child positively with a word of praise, a hug, a pat on the head, if the child performed as expected. If the expectations were not met, the negative stimulus started with a sharp word, a command, and quickly escalated to a point where the child "experienced a physical sensation that is more unpleasant" than not performing the expected task.

During the Kate School's first two years, there was little indication of trouble. Then, in 1972, a Fresno State College psychology student, Mildred (Cricket) Roberts, asked the Wilsons if she could work part time in the classroom, as part of a Psych 119 class project. The Wilsons were short-staffed and readily agreed. Cricket Roberts was a shy, quiet person, not a troublemaker. At the time she went to work in the Kate School, there were fourteen students enrolled, most of them in residential care. Roberts worked with five children, ages three to eleven, and she recorded everything she did and saw in a diary, changing only the names of the children. One entry read:

> Timmy is one of the younger boys whose main occupation at this time in life is to get something in his hands and then sit for hours rolling it from one hand to another. Such behavior is forbidden. He also gets into fits of uncontrollable laughter when he gets frustrated and that is when they use the electric-shock cattle prod.

Roberts noted that Norman Wilson was the one who used the cattle prod. The diary lists other episodes that Roberts found shocking, day after day, until, on April 18, she wrote:

> Today was it, as far as I'm concerned. I refuse to go back. This is the second time I've been sick because of what is happening. While I was with Ricky today he was very quiet, his head bent over his work at all times. I noticed between his fingers there were red rash-like welts and scratches that looked like poison oak or something. So I casually leaned over to [the teacher] and asked about the marks. She answered, "Oh, I did that. He wouldn't follow through and didn't respond to the palm slap so I jabbed him with a pencil. They're really tender in that area. As you can see, it worked." I could not

see what other responses one expects except hostility or withdrawal when such methods are used. What else can they ex-
pect but hostility from a child who is slapped so hard on the
back of the head his forehead is thrown forward onto the
table, all because he was taking too big a bite out of his sandwich . . .

Cricket Roberts turned her Psych 119 report in to Professor Allan Button. Alarmed by what he read, Button
made a copy of the report and mailed it to the Department
of Mental Hygiene on May 23, 1972. The student report,
Button's letter, and the department's response were the
first indications of trouble in the Kate School licensing
files.

Alger Gillespie, a community program analyst with the
Department of Mental Hygiene, investigated, confronting
the Wilsons with the report and the letter. A memo in the
files shows that Gillespie shortly after informed the Wilsons
that since they had admitted the use of the cattle prod and
agreed not to use it anymore, and since no additional support was found for other complaints, the incident would
be resolved as soon as the Wilsons furnished the department with a new program statement, describing treatment
procedures and goals and including specific details on how
disciplinary actions and behavior problems were handled.
"Upon satisfactory resolution of the above we will be most
happy to assist you in your expansion plans."

The Wilsons felt stung by the criticisms. They countered
by enlisting the aid of people like Dr. Charles Davis. Dr.
Davis, a psychiatrist employed by Kings View, a nonprofit
mental health conglomerate that operated the mandated
mental health programs for a half-dozen San Joaquin Valley
counties, wrote a letter in August 1972 supporting the
Wilsons: "I have been familiar with the Kate School since
it opened in 1970 and I consider our Central San Joaquin
Valley area fortunate in having such a resource." The letter
noted how successful the Wilsons had been in treating the

case of a "very disturbed" boy from Madera County who had been unmanageable in foster care. (Madera County contracted with Kings View for its mental health services.) At the time, Dr. Davis was under contract to the Kate School as a consultant, although there is nothing in the records to indicate that he was regularly involved in the school's therapy programs or did anything more than refer patients for placement.

Another letter commended their services for mentally retarded children, and still a third praised their treatment of autistic, schizophrenic, and multiply handicapped children. The three letters from different sources were revealing because they demonstrated the wide range of behavioral problems the Kate School was attempting to treat. This was not just a school for autistic children; it was a facility that took in virtually any child offered for placement. Some were autistic; some were emotionally disturbed; a few were retarded. Some of the children in the Kate School had been placed there simply because they were hard to handle and had not fit easily into foster homes. Jonathan was one such child. In 1975 he was five, a ward of the Kern County Juvenile Court, in Bakersfield, California. Jonathan's case is significant because it demonstrates how haphazardly children in need of a nurturing home are moved about and misplaced by those bureaucratic structures that place children.

Jonathan had never known his father. His mother drifted in and out of his life periodically. He lived with his maternal grandparents for much of his young life. As an infant, the boy had fussed and thrown screaming tantrums with increasing frequency. One doctor suggested that he was hyperactive and had prescribed tranquilizers; another said that the child needed more structured controls in his life and suggested that a behavior-modification approach — with time-out periods in a locked room — might help. Clearly, Jonathan was a troubled child, and the grandparents wanted help. They were dissatisfied with the medical advice they had from the pediatricians and general practitioners who had seen the boy only briefly. But they could not afford to take him to a psychiatrist or a psychologist. They turned for help to the Kern County Welfare Department. They were told yes, the department could help, but to get the necessary funds, Jonathan would have to be made a ward of the Kern County Juvenile Court. The grandparents agreed. Once he became a ward of the court, Jonathan was eligible for help. He was examined by a clinical psychologist from the University of California at Los Angeles and found to be of normal intelligence. He functioned one year below his 3.5 year chronological age, and he lacked proper limits and controls. The trauma of his mother drifting in and out of his life, and the unstructured home provided by his grandparents, had created emotional problems: Jonathan was destructive, aggressive, noncommunicative. When he did speak, he was difficult to understand, and the psychologist recommended "extensive inpatient evaluation" to work up a full diagnosis and treatment plan. The recommendation was not followed.

Jonathan continued to live with his grandparents, and he was placed in a church-operated day school that offered a tightly structured environment for preschool-aged children. The grandparents took the advice of the UCLA psychologist and worked to set limits and controls for the boy. Within a few short months the Kern County social worker was reporting that the grandparents were "providing superior physical and emotional care" for the boy. Then Jonathan's mother returned and, with the social worker's permission, took Jonathan back and tried to make a home for him and her other widely scattered children. It didn't work out, and Jonathan was back with his grandparents, more uncontrollable and "wildly destructive," according to the Welfare Department files. A child-guidance clinic suggested twenty-four-hour residential treatment. The boy's caseworker convinced the grandparents that Jonathan was a seriously disturbed child who needed to be placed in such a facility.

Up to this time the case had been treated symptomatically by a social worker who had to deal with a wide variety of children in a case load that was far too heavy for one person. There was no time to work with the boy's mother or the grandparents, other than on an emergency basis, and then only in brief, often quarrelsome and emotionally draining quick bursts of effort. But even if there had been time, there were no resources available to assist the mother or the grandparents in any effort to stabilize the home and family environment. It was much easier to accept the child-guidance clinic recommendation and place Jonathan in residential care. In 1975, Kern County had 114 children in out-of-home placement, nearly all of them in foster care and group homes in other counties. Nothing was available in Kern County. Jonathan's caseworker phoned his way through lists of out-of-county facilities and found that every listed facility was full. Then he remembered that one of his colleagues had found a "new" place a few weeks earlier for an emotionally disturbed twelve-year-old girl, a pretty freckle-faced little redhead: Mary.

Mary — who was later placed in the Napa State Hospital because of Proposition 13 funding freezes — and Jonathan and a third Kern County youngster were all placed in the Kate School, a hundred miles north of Bakersfield. All three were emotionally disturbed; they did need help, sometimes desperately. They had been deprived of love and a warm, nurturing family environment in which to grow and learn. However, none of these three children really belonged in a twenty-four-hour residential treatment center. All three ultimately were placed in strong foster homes, and there their lives began to stabilize.

Jonathan was admitted to the Kate School on May 5, 1975. The Wilsons reported that he was a verbal manipulator who threw temper tantrums, that he knew no structure or limits. They took him into their own home and placed him with the preschool-aged youngsters in the Kate School classroom. Through June, July, and August, the reports contended, the boy was making amazing progress. Not long after, his Kern County social worker noted in the files that Jonathan might not be as seriously disturbed as was first thought. What was interesting was that Jonathan's needs were relatively simple, when compared to those, say, of an autistic child; his attitudes and behavior patterns were far more controllable. While the Kate School by its advertised design was treating autistic children, it was reporting remarkable success with youngsters like Jonathan. For Jonathan, for Mary, and the third Kern County youngster, the Wilsons were providing little more than a foster home, albeit an expensive one. (Where they charged $1271 a month — on the basis that they were operating a residential treatment center — the foster-care program in Kern County paid foster parents only $160 a month). These three youngsters were living with the Wilsons or in Kate School group homes, and they were soon enrolled in nearby public school classes. As Jonathan's behavior improved, Mrs. Wilson asked the Kern County Welfare Department if the Kate School could place the boy in a foster home; the proposed foster parents were both teachers in a neighboring public school, and they had become acquainted with Jonathan when he had been enrolled in regular kindergarten classes. The plan was approved, over the grandparents' objection. On October 1, 1975, Jonathan was placed in an unlicensed foster home. He attended kindergarten in the mornings, came to the Kate School in the afternoons, and, after his foster parents finished work, they picked him up and took him to their home. The Wilsons paid the foster parents $350 a month, according to the records.

On the surface it looked as if the school and the social worker from Kern County had arranged a good home for the boy. But the situation was not that simple, not for Harry Morris, a career bureaucrat in the DOH Licensing and Certification Division, Facilities Licensing Section regional office, in Fresno. For Morris the primary problems were (1) the Kate School was not licensed as a placement agency, and (2) the foster home in which Jonathan had been placed by the Wilsons was not licensed. Morris asked his superiors in DOH Licensing what he should do, and Leroy Burton, chief of Policy and Support Services, wrote back:

> Mr. Wilson, administrator of the Kate School, or any other licensee is not permitted to admit a resident to a licensed facility and then, in turn, relocate such a resident in an unlicensed facility . . . the Welfare Department of Kern County, it appears, is a party to the fact in that they are aware that Jonathan, a dependent child, is placed in an unlicensed home . . . There is a question of propriety raised in this situation whereby Mr. Wilson received approximately $1100 per month for the care of Jonathan and in fact "farms" him out to another home, whether licensed or not, for $350 per month, for a gross profit of $750.

Why had Kern County approved this arrangement? When I asked Kern County Welfare Department Director O. C. Sills and his subordinates for an opportunity to interview Jonathan's social worker, I was told the man was ill; then — weeks later — that he was on vacation. The boy's case file was transferred to another caseworker. The juvenile court judge who had acted in *parens patriae*, approving Jonathan's placement in the Kate School, refused to talk about the case. He would say only that the responsibility was *not his*; he had acted on the recommendations of the social worker, the one who was missing.

After several attempts, I finally located a midlevel welfare bureaucrat who would agree to be interviewed, but he waffled his answers, was vague and reluctant. The rules of confidentiality, he said, prevented him from discussing the case.

QUESTION: How or why were the Wilsons allowed to subcontract any child out to a foster home, licensed or unlicensed?

BUREAUCRAT: We assumed . . . the home was one of their satellite operations, ah, we trusted this was a special home . . . We assumed it was licensed.

QUESTION: How had the department chosen the Kate School? What criteria or standards had been used?

BUREAUCRAT: That's a difficult question. I'm not certain.

QUESTION: What kind of treatment procedures were used?

BUREAUCRAT: A variation of behavior modification, but we don't know much more than that . . . Our kids aren't autistic, and I'm told they were not involved in the aversive techniques. It's a family setting, an academic training, ahh . . .

[His voice trailed off, then he shrugged.] I guess I'm at a loss for details.

[At the time of the interview, Kern County was in the process of returning the three wards of the juvenile court to foster care in the county. I asked him why.]

BUREAUCRAT: Because of the controversy. We feel this is not a proper placement. What if something happens?

"The controversy" was the one touched off by my original December 28, 1975, Kate School story in the *Fresno Bee* that detailed how Confrontation Therapy worked. The heart of the controversy was the treatment approach. The Wilsons took the children as they were handed them by placement agencies, complete with whatever records and diagnostic work-ups had been done previously. They lacked professional diagnostic services of their own, so they started with what they were given and applied their Confrontation Therapy. If a youngster conformed and performed as expected, he or she was reported to be making "progress," and some of the children, like Jonathan and Mary, did "progress." However, children who had far more serious problems were not so simply treated. If a child resisted the attempts to establish basic, controlled behavior patterns, that resistance was quickly met with increasingly more painful aversive techniques. Evidence showed that the same basic therapy techniques were used on all children. One problem with this, of course, was that the school was taking in so many different kinds of problem children: some were autistic; some who were thought to be of average or above average intelligence were actually retarded; two of the boys in the school who were treated as hearing children were, in fact, deaf.

In the fall of 1972, the first of two widely separated events took place that would ultimately have a major influence on the future of the Kate School. An eight-year-old boy named Pete was placed in the school by the Alameda County Juvenile Court, working through the Welfare Department, with the consent and cooperation of the parents. Pete was an extremely difficult child to cope with, a deaf boy who had serious emotional problems that were manifested in bizarre, autisticlike behavior patterns. At night he would sit on his bed screaming and rocking back and forth, refusing to allow anyone near him. Doctors at the University of California Medical School in San Francisco examined Pete when he was a year old and said they thought the boy was deaf. As he grew older and his behavior became wilder and harder to cope with, his parents searched for treatment and for other clues to his behavior patterns. One doctor suggested that Pete might be autistic. A note was made on his charts to that effect, and forgotten. As Pete approached his eighth birthday, that note became a key factor in his life.

His mother said, "We didn't want to send him away. We wanted to keep him home and educate him through the public schools, but he was almost unmanageable, and he had so many special needs. We didn't want to send him away. He was so little."

But there were no other choices. The parents explored residential-care possibilities, and they were shocked. So little was available, and the cost was high, $1000 or more a month. Like so many others before them, they turned to welfare and the juvenile court to qualify their son for help. On September 21, 1972, Pete was declared a dependent ward of the court, and the Alameda County Welfare Department began the search for a residential placement. The welfare caseworker assigned to Pete's case saw the notation about autism. He knew of the Kate School, so he called, and Pete was enrolled. His parents admitted they understood at the time that the school used aversive techniques like hand-slapping and cold-water showers. "We were uneasy about it, but yes, we knew about it," his mother said. "We were uneasy too because the Kate School was two hundred miles away and our access to Pete was restricted. Even on the days we were allowed to visit, they restricted us."

From the boy's first days there, the Wilsons ordered their staff to treat Pete as if he were a hearing child. But the eight-year-old boy could not hear the commands he was given, nor could he understand why he was slapped or yanked about by the hair by teachers who seemed to be angry with him. For two years, this kind of confusing, hurtful treatment continued; then the second of the two events that changed the course of Kate School took place. A woman named Lorraine Foster answered a job advertisement in the *Fresno Bee*. The Kate School needed teachers' aides, and Mrs. Foster thought such a job would be interesting. She was a graduate of the University of Chicago, had a master's degree in English from Yale, and was then taking postgraduate work in both education and psychology at Fresno State College, where her husband was teaching philosophy. Haig and Lorrie Foster have four children; they live in an upper-middle-class neighborhood. Lorrie Foster is a humanist, a gentle person of great determination and stubbornness. Mrs. Foster explained that once her children were all in school, she had enrolled in the psychology department master's program. The job at the Kate School, she said, seemed like a chance to gain experience.

At the Kate School, teachers' aides were paid $275 a month, no experience required. The aides were trained by the Wilsons and were told that in time they would become "teachers" and even "master teachers," receiving an additional $50 or $75 a month. Lorrie Foster reported for the two-day prehiring indoctrination period on October 21, 1974. After a briefing by Mrs. Wilson, Lorrie Foster and four other prospective employees were taken into the big, open-space classroom to observe the school in operation. The big room contained clusters of desks and tables, arranged in "stations." Teaching aides were working in close contact with the children, one aide for each two youngsters. Teachers and master teachers roamed the room, assisting aides where needed, supervising, making suggestions. In one section of the room, the preschool-aged children were individually boxed in wooden cubicles that were closed on three sides and the top. Only one side was open. The boxes each contained a seat and a folding desktop that acted as a gate across the open front. When the desktop was in place, the child could neither stand nor get out of the box. The children were let out of the boxes only for recess and lunch.

Mrs. Foster said that as she moved about the room, watching the instruction, she saw that the routine was essentially the same: command, demand, punishment for avoidance or failure. She said the punishment "progressed from hand-slapping to grabbing a handful of hair and turning the child's head to the desired position, to repeated pulling on the hair at the nape of the neck every time a child uttered an 'inappropriate' sound." For a day and a half, Lorrie Foster watched the workings of the Kate

School classroom. One of the incidents that stuck in her mind involved a small, crippled child who required an arm brace to assist his muscular control. The brace was taken away and he was forced to try to write the letter *D* without the brace. The youngster, speaking with great difficulty, pleaded for the brace. The aide ordered him to write the letter. The boy asked for his brace. "The request seemed to infuriate the aide, who hit him harder and harder until finally the boy himself clenched his fist and, while remaining seated at his desk, attempted, relatively weakly, to strike at the hands of the aide who was striking him."

The final incident that convinced Mrs. Foster the Kate School should be shut down involved the deaf boy, Pete. "I noticed a young male aide somewhat impatiently ordering Pete to get up from his chair. Pete responded with only a slight motion, if any, going limp, and remained seated very quietly with his hands on the desk. At this, the aide became slightly more irritated and repeated the order to get up. A [woman] master teacher happened to be passing through the middle aisle . . . She immediately went behind Pete's chair, grabbed his hair at the back of his head, yanked him by the hair out of his chair, and forcefully pulled him by the hair down into one [chair] which was right beside it. While doing this she said loudly, 'If Pete does not obey at once, Pete is pulled by the hair and set right down again.' "

The master teacher remained at the station, slapping Pete's hands down as the boy tried to protect himself. She forced the deaf boy to pick up chips that had been knocked about by the ruckus. Then she ordered him back into the original chair, and immediately began giving him a math lesson. When the boy attempted to use his fingers to add numbers, Mrs. Foster said the master teacher became angry and "yanked him out of his chair and proceeded to take him the full length of the room to the very back, where there was a partitioned small space." Though she could no longer see what was happening, Mrs. Foster could hear that the confrontation was becoming more intense. When she walked back to the partitioned space, she saw that two adults — a man and a woman — had Pete seated and were standing over him, one holding the boy, the other shouting commands. When the boy failed to respond to each command, he was slapped full in the face. "As I entered, the man was on the left of Pete and I saw him smacking the child across the left side of his face while the woman was holding him. To my amazement, my stepping into the cubicle did not result in any change in their behavior."

Outraged, Mrs. Foster ordered them to stop and to explain what they were doing. The male teacher quickly escorted Mrs. Foster out of the classroom and took her to the Wilsons. There, she was accused of interfering with school discipline and teaching techniques, and by mutual agreement she left immediately. Mrs. Foster reported the incident to the Fresno County district attorney and the state Licensing and Certification regional office. In this report, she explained:

> I have decided to record these observations and to file official complaints . . . because of my deep feeling of outrage at the existence of so heartless an atmosphere under the guise of a therapy program. My decision was also strengthened by the realization that these children have no one else to speak for them. They are, for the most part, not in the care of their own parents or relatives. I am not speaking out in order to assign blame. It is possible that the intentions of all other adults involved are as good as my own. However, some may be acting out of other motives than the welfare of the children. In either event, intentions are not the issue. Especially in the case of these children who cannot speak for themselves, advocacy on their behalf seems to be an absolute necessity.

Lorrie Foster is a convincing witness, but after a brief investigation, the district attorney notified the state that his office planned no action. There were no bloody bodies, no children appeared beaten or injured; there were too few witnesses willing to testify, and no experts in behavior modification were immediately available to say that the Wilsons' techniques were criminal. If the district attorney had taken action, a great sigh of relief would have gone up in the DOH Licensing and Certification Division, Facilities Licensing Section regional office in Fresno. The responsibility for qualifying and regulating what was happening in the Kate School rested squarely on this regional office and the entire licensing bureaucratic superstructure. The failure of the district attorney to take action meant that state officials once again had to face the Kate School issue, a painful task they had been avoiding for years. Dennis D. Dunne, chief of the Facilities Licensing Section, ordered an investigation of Mrs. Foster's complaint: "We will then evaluate whether or not a revocation action is called for. Mr. Wilson defends his use of harsh discipline as a treatment approach to working with autistic children. In order to evaluate his contention, we will probably ask Treatment Systems for assistance."

Tracing what happened within the bureaucracy is intriguing and quite complicated. The paper trail of memos that fluttered up and down through the superstructure of the Department of Health shows how the engines of government worked in the Kate School case. To understand better what happened, it is useful to have some picture of how the Facilities Licensing Section was structured. Dunne, the section chief, and his assistant, Gil Wilmer, were headquartered in Sacramento. They transmitted their orders and decisions down to the section's Fresno office, to district administrator Bill Smith, a jowly, soft-spoken bureaucrat. Smith reviewed and interpreted the Dunne-Wilmer memos and passed the appropriate orders or directions to a subordinate field supervisor, Harry Morris. Morris was a cautious, suspicious fellow who not infrequently asked his superiors for clarification. He liked to have responsibilities for actions clearly defined. Below Morris, at the bottom of the chain of command, were the licensing evaluators, David Feinberg at first, then David Guinan. The evaluators did the actual inspections, made the personal contacts with the Wilsons, issued the directives to the school. However, neither Feinberg nor Guinan could take direct action on his own. When an evaluator discovered some problem or infraction, he only recommended action to Morris, who could reject the recommendation, ask for more information, or approve the recommendation and pass it to Smith. Smith had the same options. If he approved the recommendations or substituted some of his own, they had to be approved by Wilmer and then Dunne.

If such radical action as a license revocation was recommended, even Dunne could not make any final decision, nor could he submit the issue to the Department of Health lawyers, or to the director of the Licensing and Certification Division, without going through the office of the legal coordinator, Tom Richards. Richards was not an attorney, but he screened each case and decided if it was ready to be submitted to the DOH lawyers for review. If, in his opinion, the case was not ready, he could ask for more information, create task forces to study the issues, or simply file the issue. In the scheme of things, as the DOH operated in 1975, Licensing Division bureaucrats worked on the premise that license revocation was the ultimate step, one that was not to be taken until the field offices had "worked with" facilities like the Kate School in an attempt to correct whatever was wrong. Facilities Licensing officials did not view themselves as regulators; they were not policemen enforcing laws. So when Dunne, the section chief, ordered the investigation but also said "we will probably ask Treatment Systems for assistance," he was *really* saying to everyone concerned, "Hold up all action; don't make any moves until qualified behavior experts from the DOH state hospital system can be called in to evaluate the Wilsons' Confrontation Therapy approach.''

The ever-cautious Morris got the Dunne orders, and he drafted a memo through Smith to Wilmer, saying that, with their approval, the Kate School operators would be notified that the Wilsons' pending applications for five new group home licenses would be held in abeyance until ''the Department's investigation of the use of corporal punishment is concluded. We feel it cannot be completed until the treatment plan at the facility is evaluated by experts in the field of authism.'' The word *autism* was misspelled. Smith bucked the memo up to Wilmer, and Wilmer agreed. He notified Morris that Tom Richards, the legal coordinator, was appointing a team of experts to evaluate the Kate School. Wilmer asked Morris to let Wilson know that ''we will complete this evaluation as quickly as possible.''

At this time no one on the Department of Health legal staff had even heard of the Kate School case. Quin Denvir, chief counsel of the DOH, told me nearly a year later that neither Lorrie Foster's accusations nor information on any of the lower-level bureaucratic responses to those accusations was communicated to his office. Denvir was the one who had the ultimate responsibility for reviewing the accusations and the evidence gathered in any investigation and for making the final recommendation to Charlene Harrington, the director of Licensing and Certification, and to Lackner.

Richards appointed Dr. Samuel E. Paul, a staff psychiatrist at Camarillo State Hospital, to head the Kate School evaluation team, which also included Dr. Lincoln W. Shumate, staff psychiatrist at both Metropolitan and Fairview State hospitals, and an outsider, Bernice S. Zahm, a psychologist who was then chairman of the Division of School and Educational Psychologists for the California Psychological Association

The team visited the Kate School in February 1975 and reported a month later that, though the school had a good physical plant and an adequate paraprofessional staff–pupil ratio, it didn't have the kind of credentialed teachers or licensed professional mental health staff needed either for education or therapeutic treatment of severely disturbed children; the school didn't involve psychologists or psychiatrists or psychiatric social workers in the day-to-day program or in diagnostic intake work; the treatment program not only didn't meet the needs of the children, but it potentially was harmful, both physically and emotionally; staff training was inadequate and was based on the Wilsons' Confrontation Therapy. The team wrote:

> In reviewing Mr. Wilson's Confrontation Therapy paper, we believe he reveals marked distortions in many areas. This paper reconfirms our observations of the school and our impressions that the program is basically punitive . . . under this program the child has become an impersonal robot . . . Under the guise of applying "avoidance principle" and "physical experience" [words used by Wilson in his paper on Confrontation Therapy], corporal punishment was observed . . . Training children by means of inducing pain and fear is, in and of itself, inhumane and intolerable. Our opinion is that to sanction this mode of behavior modification, particularly on a vulnerable, powerless and inarticulate population, is to make way for potential sadism under the guise of "treatment."

The evaluation team's findings were clear. Its recommendations were precise. The state should immediately order the Kate School to halt all forms of "painful physical contact." No matter what the school operators called such treatment, it was, in fact, corporal punishment. The report listed other deficiencies in the school operations and recommended corrections. The report was filed with Facilities Licensing Division community-care evaluator David Feinberg. In April, Feinberg drew up a tentative list of deficiencies in a memo recommending that the division order the school to discontinue "corporal punishment" of any type and that the state require that all behavior-modification techniques used in the school be reviewed and approved by a psychologist or psychiatrist expert in the field of behavior modification. Feinberg also recommended that the school be forced to contract with psychiatrists, psychologists, and social workers to conduct "on-going program evaluation and staff training."

In the meantime, a copy of the evaluation team report had been sent to the Wilsons and to their attorney, James M. Bell, who responded with a twelve-page, point-by-point refutation that denied all of the allegations and argued that, while the school staff admittedly slapped pupils' hands, this could not be considered corporal punishment. Bell accused the evaluation team of sophistry and prejudice and invited the three experts to provide him with a definition of corporal punishment. He contended, "No definition is found in Title 9, or any applicable provision of the California Welfare and Institutions Code and/or the Regulations promulgated by the Department of Mental Hygiene [now the Department of Public Health.]" Bell concluded, "In short, the entire Report is full of inaccuracies, misplaced innuendos and conclusions that are not based upon evidence or legal principles . . . because of the numerous shortcomings of the Report, it must be rejected in total."

That was for the record, a point from which to begin negotiations. Bell set up a meeting for his clients with Facilities Licensing officials on May 9, 1975, nearly seven months after Lorrie Foster had filed her complaints. The Wilsons, forewarned by Feinberg's proposed findings and recommendations, knew that they had to come up with the services of a supervising psychiatrist, one who would at least appear to approve of their program and their techniques. They contracted with Dr. Ralph Victor, head of the Fresno Community Hospital's psychiatric unit, to act as the Kate School's professional consultant. In addition to consultation, Dr. Victor was to provide the services of a psychologist and a social worker twice a month to assist the Wilsons in staff training. The Wilsons and Bell went into the May 9 meeting ready to negotiate.

The meeting was called an "informal conference," and was as a way of bringing pressure on a facility without formally filing accusations. Facilities Licensing Section district administrator Bill Smith presided. During the meeting it was agreed that the Wilsons would get Dr. Victor to review all of the aversive techniques then being used and determine if any of them fell within the category of corporal punishment. Further, Dr. Victor was to approve all behavior-modification techniques that were retained for use, and the Wilsons were to spell out in detail how these techniques were to be used and when.

The letters and memos between the Wilsons, the Facilities Licensing district office, and the Sacramento headquarters continued through the summer. During this time, Feinberg was transferred to Sacramento, and his case load, including the Kate School, was assigned to David Guinan. The change proved to be significant. Guinan inspected the Kate School in late September and reviewed the Wilsons' efforts to comply with the agreements reached the previous spring. The school still did not have a second credentialed teacher as ordered, but other than that, it seemed that the Wilsons were moving along well. However, there was one troublesome point: while Dr. Victor had observed the classroom operations and reported that the techniques he saw used "cannot be remotely considered abusive," there was nothing in the file to indicate that Dr. Victor had actually reviewed the whole of the Wilsons' negative treatment procedures. Guinan ended his report by explaining that when Dr. Victor had reviewed and approved Confrontation Therapy in its entirety and another credentialed teacher was hired, the school would be in compliance with DOH regulations.

Dave Guinan had taken over the Kate School file only a month before I was alerted to the controversy by a Fresno State psychology professor, who had given me a packet of material containing, among other things, Lorrie Foster's eighteen-page report and Cricket Roberts' Psych 119 term paper. In the packet were recent memos showing that Guinan had taken over the case. I called Guinan, and we had lunch. After some preliminary sparring over hamburgers and iced tea, he told me confidentially that he was concerned, he felt that some children were being mistreated and he was worried that some of them might be injured in the process. He was certain that, sooner or later, the Wilsons and their staff were going to make a serious mistake and that enough evidence could then be gathered so that his section could "go for their license." But gathering evidence in such cases was very difficult, especially when the *Kate School was just one of 169 facilities in his case load*. I asked him to repeat what he had said, certain I hadn't heard him right. "I've got *169* cases to take care of, and that doesn't count the thirty-one new applications that have to be taken care of on a priority basis. There's no way I can get to every place once a year, like I'm supposed to. The only thing I can do is try to keep up with the new apps and work the squeaky wheels. And a case like this one takes a lot more time than I've got, unless . . ."

The public licensing file on the Kate School was thick and useful. It contained episodes, caseworker field reports, inspections reports, correspondence between the school and the state, memos from Gillespie, Feinberg, Morris, and Guinan sent up through the chain of command and the responses coming back down, with copies to everyone concerned. I was struck again by how often the name Tom Richard or Tom Richards — it was spelled both ways — appeared. It seemed that almost every piece of information crossed his desk in one form or another.

In a telephone interview, Richards explained that the agreements reached in the May 9 "informal conference" had halted all uses of "corporal punishment." Once the Wilsons and Dr. Victor had agreed on an acceptable method of operations, then Richards said he would appoint a second investigating team of experts to go back in and re-evaluate the Kate School operations. Richards' comments began to bring the situation into focus for me. Licensing bureaucrats did not want to get trapped in a fight over what constituted corporal punishment. All Richards would say was that he could find no grounds to revoke the Kate School licenses, adding, "We never seem to get the abuse documented . . . Legally we must reissue the license until we take legal steps because these places have a vested interest in that license."

It was clear, now, that the evaluation report had served its bureaucratic purpose: it had never been intended as a definitive evaluation; rather, it was supposed to trigger more bureaucratic inaction. The key person then became Dr. Victor, the one expert who could validate or invalidate Confrontation Therapy. I needed to talk to Dr. Victor, but first I had to have more background on the school and on behavior modification as a therapeutic tool, especially on the negative aspects of behavior modification.

In an interview, Wilson himself recommended a UCLA psychologist, Ivor Lovaas, saying that Lovaas was familiar with the Kate School, and he, Wilson, was familiar with Lovaas' work. Lovaas is a controversial clinical psychologist who believes aversive techniques are a small but essential part of a broad spectrum of behavior modifiers needed in the treatment of severely disturbed children. Lovaas has experimented with the use of electric shock stimulus as a way of intervening in the self-destructive behavior patterns of autistic children.

Lovaas told me that, though he had heard of the Kate School through the parents of an autistic child who had

been in the UCLA program for autistic children, he knew
nothing of the school's operations, other than what the
parents had told him. They were quite impressed, he said.
I asked Lovaas under what conditions he used electric
shock intervention. He explained that the use of *any* painful
aversive technique needed consultation, strict supervision,
and accountability. "To use these techniques you must
have at least a clinical psychologist's training and knowledge of the clinical work and background of the technique," Lovaas said. He explained that aversive techniques are considered punishment because they are painful,
and great caution must be exercised in their use.

To get another outside opinion, I contacted Anthony
Davids, director of the department of psychology of Brown
University, who has worked with aversive techniques and
written extensively on the subject. He also had experimented with electric shock intervention, he said, but only
in extreme cases, where the child was self-destructive and
in danger of serious injury or death, and then only under
the watchful eye of a full research committee. First, he
said, he got the consent of the parents and their lawyer;
then every application was closely monitored. Davids explained that normally, in the university's hospital, the regulation of clinical work with autistic children *does not allow
the use of any physical negative stimuli* because such treatment is too hard to control. The clinic does use positive
techniques, including the offering of small candies, foods,
cookies, hugs, praises, and smiles as rewards.

Before talking with Dr. Victor, I spent an hour in the
classroom with Norman Wilson. What I saw closely par-
alleled what Lorrie Foster had reported, and it was unsettling. It appeared to me that children were being treated
harshly.

It was time to talk to Dr. Victor, to discuss with a trained
psychiatrist, who had observed the classroom, what he had
seen and felt. Dr. Victor had been in the classroom several

times, and he had written the Licensing Division to report that, while he had seen the staff slapping hands, "I did not observe, nor did any member of my staff observe, anything that could remotely be considered abuse."

The letter appeared to answer the state's questions. I asked Dr. Victor if he had, in fact, approved Confrontation Therapy. The question puzzled him. He had seen nothing more than hand-slapping, mildly administered in an "attention-getting" way. He did not see, nor did he approve of, the use of cold-water showers, food deprivation, force-feeding, hair-pulling, or anything similar. My questions prompted Dr. Victor to write another letter to Licensing Division officials to explain that he was "*not*" validating Confrontation Therapy. The letter came as a surprise.

On December 23, 1975, Guinan wrote to the legal coordinator, Tom Richards, to inform him that the school *was not* in compliance with the May agreement: the Wilsons had no psychiatrist to approve and supervise the school treatment program. Guinan wanted to go after the school's licenses. His bosses, Morris and Smith, were not supportive. And Richards wanted to form another task force to restudy the matter. Exasperated, I called the Department of Health's public affairs director, Bob Nance, and asked him what the hell was going on. Why wouldn't the department make a decision, some decision, one way or the other? Either tell Guinan to back off or help him go after the license? Nance suggested I talk to Quin Denvir, the department's chief counsel.

Denvir was one of those young, quietly aggressive lawyers who, on graduation from law school, had gone into legal services and had earned a reputation as a poverty-fighting lawyer with the California Rural Legal Assistance. As a CRLA attorney, he had spent much of his time jousting the windmills of government. Now, as the chief DOH counsel, he was helping defend one of the government's largest windmills. I called him to see why he hadn't gone

after the Kate School license. Denvir had never even heard
of the school. But he said he would brief himself and call
me back. And he did. He took the matter out of Richards'
hands, and on March 29, 1976, wrote to the Wilsons' attorney to inform him that a review of the Kate School file
revealed "a continuing pattern of violations of the ban
against the use of corporal punishment and physical abuse
. . . in light of this and other difficulties the Department
has decided that it must institute administrative action to
revoke existing licenses for the Kate School and to deny
pending applications for new licenses . . ." The issues
were finally joined.

Quin Denvir's decision to revoke the Kate School existing licenses and to deny the pending applications was
approved by Charlene Harrington, director of Licensing
and Certification. She quickly issued the revocation no-
tices. As expected, the Wilsons contested the revocation,
forcing the proceedings into formal hearings before an administrative law judge. The California attorney general's
office assigned Elizabeth C. Brandt to prosecute the Department of Health complaints. James Bell represented the
school and the Wilsons, and a third lawyer, Gerald W.
Palmer, intervened on behalf of a small group of parents
who had children in the Kate School and who supported
the Wilsons' approach to treatment.

The Kate School license-revocation hearing began on
November 1, 1976, and lasted fourteen days. Brandt called
thirty-one witnesses, including former employees who testified in detail how they had used physically painful aversive techniques, but only when the regular staff was present. They explained that if visitors, placement workers, or
state inspectors came into the classroom, the staff, as instructed, did not use any technique more painful than a
mild hand-slap, and that only sparingly. Brandt put Lorraine Foster and Cricket Roberts on the stand, then three
parents — including the mother of the deaf boy, Pete —

to explain how their children had been placed and mistreated. Pete's mother reported the agony undergone by the parents in deciding to place their child in residential care and then finding out he was mistreated, and she highlighted the uneven ways in which the various bureaucracies approach such child care. In 1975 Pete's parents had moved from Alameda County to a rural area in Northern California, and the boy's case file was transferred to the Alta California Regional Center. His new caseworker ordered a full diagnostic work-up. This established once and for all that Pete was deaf and that he had been inappropriately placed. Using a different combination of funding programs, the regional center transferred the boy to the state school for the deaf in Berkeley. His mother reported that she immediately began to see some improvement in his behavior as expert teachers and therapists worked to help him to develop communication skills. He was able to come home periodically during the late 1970s. By 1980 Pete had been discharged and was living at home with his parents and attending a special class in the public schools.

Deputy Attorney General Brandt, with her factual case established, turned to expert witnesses to describe behavior modification and how aversive techniques fitted into that form of treatment. Chief among these expert witnesses was Laura Schreibman, a clinical psychologist, with a doctorate, who was an associate professor of psychology at Claremont Men's College. Schreibman, who taught behavior-modification courses and conducted advanced research with autistic children, had studied under Lovaas at UCLA and had participated with him in federally funded research projects. Her work was widely published.

On the stand, Schreibman first gave a primary lesson in behavior-modification techniques, explaining that to decrease an undesired behavior, therapists first try to use positive reinforcement in a competing behavior to reduce the frequency of the inappropriate behavior. She said, "If that failed, then we would try to identify what stimulus in the environment was maintaining that [unwanted] behavior, what kind of pay-off was the child getting. That is called extinction modification. That's how it should start. Then, if that failed, I would start another procedure, such as punishment.''

The word *punishment* startled Jim Bell, the Wilsons' attorney. Throughout the hearing, Bell had been contending that the Wilsons were not punishing children; they were treating them. Bell asked Schreibman to repeat her testimony.

Schreibman repeated the word: *punishment*. Aversive techniques were ''punishers.'' She made it clear that if punishment was selected as a therapeutic tool — and it was only one of several tools to choose from — it was always the *last* choice, and then it was used with great care and control. Once the decision had been made to try the use of punishment, the *least* aversive technique, such as a shouted ''no'' or a slap on a tabletop, were used first. Only if these failed would Schreibman and her colleagues slap a child on the leg or on the arm.

BRANDT: Do you use things that are more painful on a child than a slap on the leg or a slap on the arm?

SCHREIBMAN: No. If that doesn't work, then I have to find something else.

BRANDT: Do you ever strike a child anywhere other than the arm or the leg?

SCHREIBMAN: The rear end.

BRANDT: Have you ever used striking on the face?

SCHREIBMAN: No . . . it's too easy to cause damage, especially [to] a small child; you risk damaging the eyes, damaging the ears, or breaking a nose or something like that. It's a very sensitive area.

During the course of the questioning, Schreibman was asked if punishment ''worked.'' She explained, ''If it is used correctly, yes . . . punishment suppresses behavior;

it suppresses the behavior that it follows . . . If punishment is punishment, and if punishment is going to work, then behavior drops right away."

But there are serious problems with punishment as a treatment technique, Schreibman warned:

Number one, you are exposing the child to pain . . . Number two, punishment only has a temporary suppressing effect. Just the use of punishment alone does not teach the child anything. [More important], we don't use it unless we have to because it has the property of being too easy to use, and being too easy for the staff to use, and since it does produce an immediate change, it is quite rewarding for a therapist to use those kinds of techniques because it is easy for them . . . If somebody does kind of get into that thing where they find the use of punishment is rapid and causes immediate change . . . they would be more inclined to use an aversive as a first resort rather than exploring other more effective and positive means of changing behavior.

As an expert, Schreibman was asked her reaction to the Wilsons' Confrontation Therapy concepts. She replied, "It was negative because my impression is that the first treatment of choice is aversive; that is, in every instance in the Wilsons' Confrontation Therapy paper where they identify a particular behavior and they describe or prescribe what the treatment should be, it is always aversive."

Brandt asked if Confrontation Therapy could be effective, expecting a "no" answer. Schreibman surprised her.

"Would it work?" Schreibman repeated the question, thinking, then responded, "Yes. It might work, it just might work."

BRANDT (somewhat taken aback): Is it a method you would use?

SCHREIBMAN: No.

BRANDT: Can you give us some reasons why you wouldn't use it?

SCHREIBMAN: Sure. You could stop a child from flapping

his hands by slapping his hands. You could also do it by cutting off his hands. That doesn't mean that because it works that it is a method I would use. I would disagree with [Confrontation Therapy] because I think it is overly punitive. It is unnecessarily punitive.

The prosecution case was damning, yet neither Bell nor Palmer called Lovaas or similar witnesses to counter Schreibman's testimony. Attorneys for the defense and the intervenors failed to discredit or impeach the testimony of Lorraine Foster, Cricket Roberts, or the former Kate employees. Their primary expert witness was Dr. Raymond E. Reedy, a child psychiatrist who had come out of retirement to work as a part-time medical director for the nearby Madera County Mental Health Services, a subsidiary unit of Kings View. After Dr. Victor had backed away from validating Confrontation Therapy, the Wilsons had contracted with Reedy for consultation and validation. Reedy said he had spent a considerable amount of time in the Kate School, and that the staff appeared to be dedicated to its task, lovingly so. He testified that from 90 to 99 percent of the behavior-modification techniques he saw used were positive: a hug, a stroke, mussing of hair, a kind word. The only negative stimulus he had witnessed was an occasional mild hand-slapping. Under cross-examination, Reedy was asked if he considered himself an expert on behavior modification, and he replied, "Absolutely not."

The Wilsons and their staff denied slapping children's faces, spanking, or pinching them. No one had authorized the use of wooden spoons or fly swatters on children. Hand-slapping was used only sparingly. Yet, on cross-examination, Deputy Attorney General Brandt had Norman Wilson examine school records and acknowledge that some youngsters were routinely slapped as often as every half-hour, day after day, month after month. She established, through testimony and the records, that cool- or cold-water showers were administered daily by some house parents, week after week, with no effect on the bed-wetting or feces-smearing conduct. Bell asked Wilson to describe the Kate School and he responded:

> The Kate School is an educational center for children whose behavioral and/or emotional problems prevent them from functioning in other private or nonprofit [he paused, then corrected himself] private or public programs . . . The philosophy of Kate School is based upon three premises: expectancy, consistency, and the confrontation. To us, expectancy means to verbalize to the child our expectancy, whether it be to speak, tie his shoe, take a shower, whatever, and continually confront the individual with these expectancies. Consistency is an [pause] — well, it's a word that's been around a long time. We believe that one of the major difficulties with emotion that the disturbed child has is the lack of stability within his environment. Therefore, consistency is of prime importance, and it also must include a twenty-four-hour situation, in which the school, home, and community, and everything is brought into play with the same expectancies verbalized to the child from every side within his environment. Confrontation means confronting the child with adults, with new and unique situations, confronting him both positively and negatively with a positive experience of life and also with a negative aspect of his behavior. Many of our children come to us that have never experienced anything such as a normal situation in the way of community living. Therefore, we believe that the child should be confronted with these normal situations and also he should be confronted with his abnormal behavior, socially unacceptable behavior.

Wilson talked at length about the school, demonstrating "negative reinforcement" hand-slaps that were gentle and not at all like those described by prosecution witnesses. Wilson denied he had pinched youngsters on the shoulder; he denied he had slapped children anywhere but on the hand. He did not approve of cold-water showers, nor did he approve of staff members banging children's heads on desks as a form of intervening therapy to stop self-destructive head-banging by such children.

Under cross-examination by Brandt, Wilson was asked if he had ever forced a child to eat his own vomit, as some testimony indicated.

WILSON: I remember once an incident which might be termed by some people as "force-feeding," but not with me . . . We had one child that was very [pause] — he regurgitated at will . . . So one lunch period I went in and worked with the boy and what he would do is he would take a bite of sandwich and chew it up and make an attempt to swallow it and then regurgitate it. The food came out on the table in solid, but chewed-up form. And so I told him when he did spit up this one time it was about a bite-size and so I told him to pick it up and put it back in his mouth and eat it and I told him very firmly which he started to do and then when he did put it in his mouth I placed my hand lightly on his mouth and so that he wouldn't spit it up and he indeed went ahead and ate it and I continued with this.

Wilson vigorously denied he ever held the child's nose to force him to swallow, stating, "No, sir, that's dangerous."

After fourteen days of testimony, the case was submitted to Administrative Law Judge Robert Coffman for a decision. On February 28, 1977, almost a year after Quin Denvir began the licensing-revocation proceedings, some twenty-eight months after Lorraine Foster complained to officials that children were being abused at Kate School, and fifty-six months after Dr. Button had first reported Wilson's use of the electric cattle prod, Coffman issued his decision and his "findings of fact." The state's case *was* supported by the weight of the evidence. Coffman wrote: "Most of the acts described [during the hearing] are not recognized or valid forms of care, treatment or education of autistic or emotionally disordered children. Nor were said acts approved by a psychiatrist, psychologist or physician. Some such acts were often administered in such a manner as to constitute conduct inimical to the health, morals, welfare or safety of the children of the Kate School."

Coffman recommended that the school's licenses be revoked; the pending applications denied. Charlene Harrington followed the recommendations on March 16, 1977, and Dr. Lackner supported her decision. The Wilsons appealed the decision to the Fresno County Superior Court. During the course of the appeal hearings, lawyers for the defense argued that the state laws and regulations governing the conduct of private, community-care treatment centers were so vague and so poorly drawn that the Wilsons — a dedicated couple who had developed a successful treatment regimen for troubled children — could not have known what was and was not allowable under these laws and regulations. Judge Hollis B. Best heard the oral arguments and then took the case under submission.

Judge Best agreed that the evidence proved the children were routinely slapped about the body, spanked, poked, and pinched. He found Norman Wilson had spanked the deaf boy, Pete, "hitting him on the buttocks with sufficient force to cause bruises to appear." Best recognized that Pete was "profoundly deaf . . . unable to respond to verbal commands," yet the boy had been slapped, his ears and hair pulled, because he had failed to respond to oral commands. Judge Best found as fact that one autistic child had been slapped on the mouth, and when the child wouldn't keep his mouth closed, it was taped shut. On two occasions the Wilsons' chief assistant, Rowan Settles, "lifted a child . . . off the floor by holding the child's head between his hands." Another staff person threw a boy to the floor, sat on him, and then "struck the minor's chest and shoulders with his closed hands." That same staff person kicked the same boy in the buttocks, long after the Department of Health had put the school on notice that its licensing would be revoked. Best ruled, "It is true . . . some children who engaged in self-destructive behavior were dealt with in a manner that involved infliction of similar abuse on the child. Such was done by an employee of the Kate School with the knowledge of Norman Wilson and Martha Wilson."

This last finding referred to testimony indicating that it was school policy to force a child painfully to repeat unacceptable self-destructive behavior. One former employee explained, "Whatever [named child] did, you did it, only more so . . . If she banged her head on the desk, then we were instructed to grasp her head and bang it into the desk and make sure it hurt."

Despite such evidence, Judge Best found the defense reasonable. He ruled that the acts set out in the findings of fact occurred "without evil motive" and that "no acts occurred which were clearly proscribed by law or regulation." The conclusion reached by Judge Best was that the Wilsons had never been provided with clear guidelines "having the force of law" to indicate that acts which occurred were specifically forbidden. The various laws and regulations were so "vague," he ruled, that the school was "without prior notice" of what conduct was proscribed, and he found that "*it is in the best interest of the children at Kate School and the parents of such children that the Kate School continue in operation*" (emphasis added).

The decision, as rendered, meant California's laws could not prevent *child abuse* or *corporal punishment* because those terms were not sufficiently defined when they were applied to an educational or therapeutic setting. Deputy Attorney General Brandt wanted to appeal the decision immediately. To do this, she had to have the consent of her client, the DOH Licensing and Certification Division. There was a problem. Charlene Harrington had been fired, and her replacement, Don Hauptman, was stalling because he was under pressure to negotiate some kind of settlement. The pressure was coming from the small group of parents who had approved of the Kate School and had stood by the Wilsons through the long fight. One of these parents had solid political connections.

Dr. Lackner, as the DOH director, was directly responsible to Mario G. Obledo, secretary of the Health and Welfare Agency, a cabinet-level position in the Brown administration. Someone from the parents' group set up a meeting with Obledo, a command performance attended by all the principals, to see if some kind of compromise could be worked out that would allow the school to continue to operate. The meeting produced no results.

A week after the February 1, 1978, meeting with Obledo, I learned that Evelle Younger, then the attorney general, had been approached directly by a parent at a social gathering, and that Younger had ordered any decision on the appeal to be held up until he reviewed the case. I called one of Younger's assistants to ask him to confirm or deny the report. He acknowledged that the attorney general's office was trying to work out some kind of settlement with the school in an attempt to avoid a long appeals battle, arguing that corporal punishment might not be corporal punishment if it was carried out in the name of therapy. At the end of our conversation, the assistant attorney general pointed out that the decision to appeal was really up to Dr. Lackner, not to the attorney general.

Lackner told me, "I've never before seen the ambivalence I saw in this case on the part of the attorney general. There was a lot of pressure on him, and on me, not to appeal." Lackner didn't like the pressure, and he reacted by sending the attorney general a one-sentence letter: "This is to formally request that your office file a notice of appeal in the above-titled case."

The appeal was filed in the spring of 1978, and almost a year later the Fifth District Court of Appeals overturned Judge Best's decision, ordering the matter returned to the Department of Health. The decision came down after Lackner had been fired and after the DOH had been broken up into its component parts (in a typically political maneuver, Brown had torn the DOH apart and scattered it across the bureaucratic landscape as a way of defusing the growing health-care and state hospital problems), and the case was turned over to the legal staff of the newly formed Department of Social Services.

The Kate School lawyers still had one appeal left, but when the California Supreme Court refused to hear the case, the Kate School legal issue was finally resolved. The school's licenses were revoked. The school was closed. But the basic issues still remained. There still was no agency in charge of treatment or program quality control in state-licensed community-care facilities. Department of Social Services director Marion Woods "solved" the problems raised in the Kate School controversy by instructing all of the DSS licensing evaluators to stick to the basic health and safety regulation inspections. Licensing evaluators would no longer judge whether or not a treatment technique was valid; they would no longer be asked to decide if a facility was physically or emotionally harming a child; there would be no more attempts to qualify a behavior-modification program.

Woods explained that this was really the job of placement workers, anyway. Placement workers, he explained, were supposed to visit their clients at least once a month. Licensing evaluators made only yearly inspections. When pressed, Woods acknowledged that a Kate School–like episode could happen again, if individual placement workers failed to monitor the quality and type of program, or if placement workers who see such a program simply pulled out their own youngsters and didn't try to force the issue.

QUESTION: In other words, no one is in charge, no agency is responsible for overall quality and kind in any state-licensed community-care program?

WOODS: It is true, no one agency has accountability. We need to elevate the public debate on accountability.

# 9

# A Better Way

"WE NEED TO ELEVATE the public debate on accountability." The words were intriguing, coming at a time when Marion Woods had just divorced his Department of Social Services from any accountability. For years, state licensing agents had been trying unsuccessfully to deal with their mandate to evaluate and police the quality of treatment and care, ensuring that children in foster-care institutions were not being mistreated or abused. The task *was* difficult, fraught with politics and the ever-changing opinions of behavior experts. Woods solved the long-standing problem by a simple administrative decision: licensing evaluators would no longer be accountable for the kind or quality of treatment and care in the community-care facilities they licensed.

It is remarkable that in the 1980s, no legislator, no bureaucrat, no agency of government, wants to be held accountable, not in foster care, not in the child-welfare system, not in Washington, D.C., not in California, or in any other state. The Congress and the great bureaus of the federal government contend that accountability is a state's right and responsibility. State governments insist that local agencies have the prerogative and the obligation. Local bureaucrats and politicians complain that they are bound by tangles of federal red tape and more tangles of state red tape, and therefore have no alternatives. They are not responsible, not accountable.

The resulting vacuum creates an environment in which a Kate School can flourish. In that case, no government agency had invited the Wilsons into a very difficult area of child care  no placement worker had required that they qualify themselves or questioned their Confrontation Therapy before they undertook such demanding work. The only responses from government came after (1) it was obvious something had gone wrong in the school, and (2) the public was made aware of the problems in a way that proved embarrassing to both the licensing and placement agencies. Despite all of the regulations qualifying how funds are to be spent and children placed, despite all the regulatory inspections and memos pointing out the controversies in the Kate School, no bureau of government held itself accountable for the way children were being treated. Had it not been for one outraged citizen named Lorraine Foster, who became an impromptu children's advocate with the stubborn good sense to persevere, the issues would not have been joined, the school would probably still be operating and still be embroiled in the paper-shuffling controversy over what was and was not corporal punishment. Mrs. Foster, after a frustrating year of attempts to get some agency of government to act, turned over her accumulated information to a friend, a psychology professor at Fresno State, who suggested that the only recourse was to expose publicly not just the Kate School but the government as well. Because I was a reporter who worked on controversial subjects and had written a book on the exploitation of child labor, the Kate School material was brought to me. The initial story in the *Fresno Bee* in December 1975 set in motion the processes that ultimately unlicensed the Kate School.

Those processes took five years, and, though they resulted in the closing of the school, they solved none of the basic issues, Marion Woods's abdication of accountability notwithstanding. This individual controversy was treated as just that, an individual case. Time and again across the nation I ran into similar horror stories, similar exposés, where the actions of one individual or group gained the attention of the media or legal-aid attorneys or of an advocacy group like the Children's Defense Fund or the California Children's Lobby, and public exposure of the problems brought some government response. Bureaucrats found it was time to "elevate the public debate," create a task force, make up a list of deficiencies and recommendations and a plan of action and a list of excuses: there were budget shortages, a lack of staffing, a lack of jurisdiction. But change was possible, the bureaucrats promised, and new bureaus were formed, agencies were merged one into another, names were changed, and the individual controversies always subsided.

The process was and is endless, mindless. There is change, but nothing changes. There is no commitment to children. And through it all there is the maddening realization that it doesn't have to be so. All of the bits and pieces of a good, sound national children's program are there: the money, the knowledge, the expertise. But as a nation we've never put it all together. We spend and we spend and we spend, buying more Band-Aids to patch up the system, never getting down to treating the basic flaws, the traumatic problems that have caused the wounds and keep them festering.

The basic flaws are two: *lack of a national children's policy* and *a strong bias against those families caught up in the child-welfare and foster-care systems*. The first flaw is obvious, and I feel it is the inevitable consequence of the second flaw. The bias against the family is seen in the public attitude toward welfare of any kind; it is seen in the government regulations that provide natural parents little or no help to care for children in need while establishing foster care that encourages the separation of parent and child. Foster parents providing a surrogate family environment are expected to donate their time and subsidize the cost of care for foster children; group homes and institutions are paid by government through systems that encourage long-term custodial care with a minimum of services and treatment for the children involved. To qualify for federal funding, children must be made wards of the juvenile court in a procedure that requires the judge to find the parents unwilling or incapable of caring for their children. Social workers, because of the cant and bias built in the regulations to protect the public dollars, find it easier to take the children from their homes and place them in some form of foster care or institutional care.

In theory, there is a clear federal commitment to support the family unit so that children will have a place to grow and mature. But that commitment is built on fantasy. We imagine that families still live on Waltons' Mountain, where grandpa and grandma and a sense of community are a natural part of growing up. We want to see the little house on the prairie, the strong man and woman raising children in a self-sustaining environment. But the average American family lives in the city, far away from traditions of the family farm and small towns; many children do not have two parents. And in the inner cities they are lucky if they have a single loving mother or father who can cope with the bitter frustrations of life in the low-rent projects, sustained by a welfare system designed to prevent unqualified people from receiving public assistance. We say that if a child is homeless we will provide a surrogate home. But that's not the way the system works. The Children's Defense Fund, in a survey of 140 counties in five states, found that within the foster-care system "overt and covert practices discourage parents from keeping children in their own homes and from maintaining contact with the children who are out of their homes." The CDF reported that juvenile courts and welfare and probation departments are quick to remove children from their homes, because, once removed, they become eligible for various forms of federal and state aid that are not available if the children stay at home. Example: Children who are physically or mentally handicapped, but who could be cared for at home, are not eligible for Supplemental Security Income payments if their parents are in the middle-income brackets. Yet the cost of care and treatment is so expensive that the parents cannot afford to keep the child home. Once these children are removed from their homes, by court order, they become eligible for SSI and for Medicaid or, in California, Medi-Cal.

While the courts are quick to remove children, there is a strong reluctance on the part of child-welfare agencies and the courts to sever completely the child-parent bonds, even when it is shown the parents are abusive and the child's life is in danger. Thus, foster children are caught in limbo: seldom released for adoption, they are moved through a foster-care system that is frequently recognized as harmful to their best interests.

These facts are all clearly recognized at the highest levels of government. Arabella Martinez, the former HEW Assistant Secretary for Human Development Services, explained in an interview that the two major child-welfare programs — AFDC Foster Care and Title IV-B Child Welfare provisions of the Social Security Act — are "perverse incentive systems which . . . have led to practices which are clearly not family supportive and in many cases are grossly negative for children . . . No one intended that foster care be as uncaring as it unfortunately is . . . Society has been too busy with other priorities to notice that no one is responsible for guiding each child through until the child is rapidly united with the strengthened family, or is placed in a welcoming adoptive home."

Martinez got up from the conference table in her outer office and walked to a blackboard. Taking up chalk and eraser, she began to discuss the other basic flaw in our system, the lack of a national children's policy. "There has never been any policy development in this office; I have to tell you that." She drew circles and squares and cross-connecting lines on the blackboard, explaining the multiplicity of services, mapping each one, showing overlaps and gaps through which "children fall through the floorboards." Martinez, the pedagogue — expert in the language of the bureaucrat — was educating a journalist. Often using the word *fragmented,* she worked through the system:

> The problem is technological, as well as political. Let me speak to the issue of fragmentation. When you think of fragmentation, you think of a whole that has chipped into fragments. You don't think of pieces unrelated to the whole . . . I am beginning to realize that we never had a whole system; there never was a rational system out there; nobody ever thought about that. What they did was respond to the critical needs that they saw and they wanted to do something about, and they wanted to take care of those children who were being abused . . . You see it now on the Hill, in all of the legislation that is going on. None of that is related to each other; it is all very singular in focus; it is developed in a policy vacuum.

And she was right. Neither the administration nor the Congress has ever established clearly, simply, and forcefully what should and must be done for children at risk of losing their home life; we as a nation have never committed ourselves to forging a national foster-care or child-welfare policy. At the time I interviewed Martinez, she was lobbying for the passage of HR-7200, the Miller bill, which would have strengthened the foster-care system. Congressman Miller had been working for years to push the foster-care reforms through the Congress, building a constituency, pulling together more and more support as he publicized the issues and tried to educate the key people who could influence the legislative processes.

One of Miller's allies was the California Children's Lobby, the nonprofit agency that had been promoting similar reforms in California. Children's Lobby President Sue Brock tried to bring the process into perspective during an interview in 1980:

In California we finally got SB-30 passed even if Jerry Brown did cut it to a two-county demonstration. We have a law that makes it clear that preserving the family is our first priority . . . Look, there is never going to be enough money to meet the needs of every kid . . . Kids are not considered worth the cost, in our public view. Kids are not a political constituency: they don't vote; they don't pay taxes; they don't speak for themselves; and the groups that advocate on their behalf, like the Children's Lobby, are nickel-and-dime operations in terms of financing . . . But little by little we are making progress. We do get demonstration projects, and wherever people put such efforts to work, whether it's in California or Oregon, they get results. My concern is that over the next thirty years we [have to] change the framework in which we look at families and kids . . . Unless we are willing to deal with prevention and not remediation, we are always going to be treading water. If we think we can save a couple of hundred million bucks in the next two years by skimping on a program that is going to help children remain in their homes, we are whistling "Dixie," because we are going to pay that bill fifteen years from now. *We are going to pay that bill*; we are paying it now. We are paying for the shitty programs in the jails and juvenile halls . . . After you screw a kid up for ten or fifteen years in foster care, you are going to have a lot of trouble trying to turn that kid's personality around . . . but if you work with the family with a baby, or better still, a high school mother with a baby, or better still, provide sex education and family-life education early in school, if you provide child care for young families that are trying to make it, if you provide support for those families . . . the families can make it.

Her words were almost an echo of what Sister Mary Paul had said when she testified four years earlier in support of HR-7200. At the time, she was the director of the Family Reception Center founded in Brooklyn's Park Slope neighborhood in 1972 by the Sisters of the Good Shepherd. The reception center over the years has developed a fully integrated, multiservice approach to helping families stay together and cope with their problems. Aided at the start by the Edwin Gould Foundation, the Sisters rented a four-story building in Park Slope, a racially mixed neighborhood of 120,000 people where juvenile crime was unusually high. There were an estimated forty-three thousand children under twenty-one years of age in the area. With the help of local judges, law enforcement agencies, civic leaders, and the New York City Board of Education, the Sisters developed a crisis-oriented counseling service for individuals and family groups. They created family-life education programs, family and group therapy clinics, peer group therapy, psychiatric consultation, legal advocacy, educational advocacy, a crash pad for those needing brief residential care, and a special-education "minischool" for youngsters who had been kicked out of regular classes. The Edwin Gould Children's Services operated foster homes and a group home for those few children who had to be taken away from their own homes. The center's Children and Youth Development Services program set up afterschool and evening recreation, an odd-jobs market service, a Safe Homes Project that provided services for battered women and their families, including a hot line, counseling, shelter, and community education.

Adrienne Lawler, program director of the Family Reception Center, in 1980 reported that the center annually had about three hundred families within its active case load. The goal is for the twenty-five to thirty staff people to work with existing governmental and private agencies providing various services, bringing these services and the center's own skills into focus on the family problems. Only 10 percent of the children involved are removed from their homes, according to Lawler. In the beginning (1972), the Catholic order and the Gould Foundation funded much of the program but, by the end of the decade, the Family Reception Center was operating on a $475,000-a-year budget funded by the Department of Public Social Services. There were 110 youngsters enrolled in the several mini-schools operated jointly by the Sisters and the Board of Education.

Children's rights' advocates like the Children's Defense Fund and the Child Welfare League of America have given the Park Slope Family Reception Center high marks. The CWLA, in an evaluation made in 1974, reported, "The indomitability of the leadership appears to have infused the staff with the courage and the optimism that flavors the whole program. The prevailing attitude is that anything can be coped with. If you don't have a needed service, find one. If it doesn't exist, find resources to develop it." As a result, the CWLA said, the reception center was successfully keeping families together and improving children's lives.

The "leadership" referred to was in great part provided by Sister Mary Paul, who, as the decade of the seventies came to a close, had moved out of the Park Slope center and had started another center in nearby Sunset Park. When Sister Mary Paul testified before Congress in support of HR-7200, she suggested that the nation needed a total reversal of its priorities in the field of foster care and child welfare. She said that the "pittances" now provided for family-oriented services were so small and the amounts spent on out-of-home placement were so exorbitant that they caused an imbalance serious enough to destroy families. "My most urgent recommendation . . . is for the immediate strengthening of family-centered services in a holistic design for which either a specific agency or group of agencies in a community take responsibility."

Nearly four years after Sister Mary Paul testified, Miller's bill (reintroduced in the Ninety-sixth Congress as HR-3434) was passed, and it was signed into law on June 17, 1980. The Adoptions Assistance and Child Welfare Act of 1980 amended the foster-care provisions of the Social Security Act, placing more emphasis on social services to troubled families, foster parents, and foster children. The total appropriation package for foster-care Social Services came to $161 million, three times what had been spent in 1979. The adoptions subsidy portions of the bill were funded, for the first time guaranteeing adoptive parents of handicapped children a wide range of services. The new law, cast in the legislative pattern set during the New Deal, was designed to entice the various states into passing their own versions of the federal law. States did not have to participate, but if they were to qualify for funds under the new act, they had to meet the federal guidelines.

J.F. terHorst, a syndicated columnist, wrote: "The federal government has agreed to share in the local costs of moving these children with special needs from institutions and temporary foster homes and placing them with families eager to adopt them."

Maybe. Certainly that was the intent of the law. But that was before Ronald Reagan moved into the White House and began his campaign not only to cut $45 billion from the federal budget but to radically alter the way federal funds were to be passed along to the states. In addition to proposing deep cuts in the "big ticket" federal aid programs, like AFDC, the Reaganomics planners were proposing "block grants" to states and local governments, in lieu of categorical aid. Each block grant would lump together a dozen or so categorical aid programs, total the costs, and subtract 25 percent. What was left would go to the states, or local agencies, no strings attached. According to the Reagan arguments, the federal funding processes had grown so cumbersome they were not only intrusive, but grossly inefficient as well; from now on, the states, not the "feds," would decide how the money was to be spent

The Reagan plan was being sold primarily on the basis of the supposed "efficiency" of state and local government. However, there was another, perhaps less obvious motive for the block grant approach. Over the past half-century the federal government — as an expression of our national will — had been coaxing, threatening and legally challenging the various states trying to get them to accept certain minimum standards of human welfare. In the process, the federal government had underwritten much of the cost of programs like AFDC–Foster Care on the theory that children and their families living in any part of the nation had certain basic needs and those needs had to be met. Along with the basic aid programs came laws like the Wagner Act that gave workers the right to organize, and child-labor laws and a federal minimum wage. But such federal aid programs and the laws setting minimum-wage and working-condition standards disrupted local social and economic patterns, and that was unsettling. Local politicians, especially in the South, argued that such programs and laws were a violation of states' rights. Then, in 1981, the Reagan administration promised that block grants would return spending controls to the states, and in the process, the size and power of the federal government would be reduced.

Certainly Public Law 96-272 — the Adoptions Assistance and Child Welfare Act of 1980 — was in the New Deal tradition. Like the Juvenile Justice and Delinquency Prevention Act of 1974 and PL 94-142, which promised all eight million handicapped children a free education, no matter what their handicaps, the new law held great promise, if the states went along. Such laws sounded good and offered a certain amount of help. However, the Reagan block grants aside, these laws did not and could not bring about the kind of national change that is required if this country is ever to meet its obligation to *every* child. While Miller's PL 96-272 was to provide children in foster care with permanent homes, it must be remembered that the existing law in 1975, as Miller began the long reform process, also required that all foster-care programs funded by the federal government had to either reunite children with their families or find them adoptive homes. The then-existing law was not accomplishing its purpose, so we spent another five years patching together a new version to accomplish the same end. But this new law did nothing to change the basic Rube Goldberg processes used to build the house of mirrors. Given that fact, plus the increasingly conservative mood of the country in the early 1980s, it was difficult not to be pessimistic.

The Reagan administration was obviously bent on a laissez-faire course. And, given the history of states like Louisiana, Alabama, Texas, and Illinois, and, yes, even California and New York, the future did not look promising for child-welfare programs of any kind. But it didn't have to be this way. It was and is possible for a nation to reorder its priorities to make way for a more humanitarian child-welfare system. Sweden did it. Over the past thirty years, the Swedes, acting through their elected representatives, have forged a model system that puts health, education, housing, and employment needs of the people ahead of industrial production and corporate profits. The Swedish government serves the needs of people, not industry; it guarantees every child born the kind of opportunity only the children of the middle class and the rich enjoy in the United States. Such a model should be an attractive point for starting a discussion of what ought to be done in the United States. Yet whenever and wherever I began such a discussion, citing one or another of the various parts of the Swedish system, I was quickly reminded that such comparisons were not valid because Sweden is a small country (8 million population) that has a homogeneous population and has a socialist form of government.

The responses were disconcerting. Actually, Sweden is not a socialist country; production there is controlled by corporate enterprise. In Sweden, corporations thrive on profits earned from the sale of their products; they compete in world markets, selling steel, 350,000–ton supertankers, Volvo autos, exquisite crystal, and many, many other products. The fact that the Swedish economy is based on industrialized capitalism, like our own, combined with the fact that governmental services in Sweden are financed through a system of taxation not unlike our own, should make the Swedish example quite worthy of study. Sweden's small size and its ethnic homogeneity should be rated as a plus by those social scientists, economists, and health experts comparing child-care services because the model is less complex, structurally more open to observation, comparison, and evaluation.

Comparisons can and have been made. Dr. Albert P. Scheiner, a pediatrician who worked for seven years as the director of the New York State Hospital for the mentally retarded in Monroe County, and who in 1980 was teaching early-childhood development at the University of Massachusetts Medical School, reported:

> The inadequacies and shortcomings of the mental retardation system in New York State could easily be rationalized on the basis of our heterogeneous, large population and the absence of a socialistic form of government. This oversimplification would overlook our lack of emphasis on appropriate staff training, our lack of county control and the presence of large control agencies such as Civil Service and the Bureau of the Budget . . . Sweden does have half the population of New York State, but their deep concern for their fellow man has resulted in the obliteration of poverty, *the lowest infant mortality rate in the world and an incidence of mental retardation that is one-third that of the United States* [emphasis added] . . . they are a healthy, industrial nation differing only in that their morality and ethics compete with Volvo and Saab for their major national products. They are reaping the harvest of a labor force of efficient middle-class people. Their moral integrity, as manifested by their willingness to give to the

handicapped, and their functional equality between men and women has enabled them to create a place to live where a person is first a person, and secondly retarded; where the philosophy of service is primary and the financial and political consequences are secondary.

The Swedes have nationalized medicine and health care, a fact that sends shivers up the *collective* spine of the American Medical Association. The AMA has long opposed "socialized medicine," arguing that under the fee-for-service system the American public gets the best medicine possible. That simply is not true, not if the infant mortality rates are used as a measure. The Swedish infant mortality rate was 10.8 per one thousand live births through the late 1970s. The rate in the United States was nearly double that, and in inner-city areas like Watts, in Los Angeles, the rate reaches thirty per one thousand births.

In Sweden every pregnant mother, regardless of her income or marital status, has a right to extensive prenatal care, childbirth, and postnatal care. All Swedish children receive medical exams at specific times in their lives as part of a health-care system that stresses preventive medicine. The results of such programs can be seen in indicators such as the lower rate of mental retardation in Sweden. In the United States no one has the *right* to health care. Those who are poor and qualify for aid must rely upon welfare and health-care services provided by local government and private charity. The level of such services, while federally subsidized, is uneven and can change with the political climate. For example, in 1981 Reagan's budget director, David A. Stockman, proposed to cut $330 million from the program that provided nutritional supplements to 2.2 million pregnant women, nursing mothers, and infants.

It is not health care alone that sets the Swedes apart. In Sweden every family has the right to decent housing. If the cost of housing is beyond the economic means of the family, rent subsidies are available. In the late 1970s, more than two thirds of the women who had children were employed. Local governments provided child-care centers, preschool programs, leisure-time schools, child care, and sick-leave pay. In Sweden, when a child is born, *either* the father or the mother can take a seven-month child-care leave at 90 percent pay. Every child receives a small national allowance. Child-care facilities are available from infancy through age six. Preschool programs are mandatory and are separate from the nine-year compulsory education programs.

The national government sets policy and mandates these programs; it provides leadership and some funding. But the primary governmental structures operating health care, social services, and education are local. The county governments and municipalities have the responsibility to raise the necessary funds and to operate these programs, under the guidance of local boards of directors and public committees. By national policy, every child born in Sweden has a right to these services and funds, regardless of his or her economic or social status. Handicapped children are considered a normal part of the Swedish society, and it is recognized that society *benefits* from the presence of these handicapped persons — child or adult. Everywhere you go in Stockholm and in the smaller towns and villages, there are constant reminders that the handicapped are part of society. They are there, riding the subways, walking the streets, coming in and out of apartment buildings. By national design, the Swedish people have required their government to provide the handicapped with the kinds of special programs and services that will help them lead normal lives. But it was not always that way.

A background paper entitled "Children's Policy in Sweden," published by the Swedish Institute, reported, "As recently as the first decades of this century large sections of the community were in need. Children were starving.

Mortality was high, especially in the lower socioeconomic groups. Supervision of the children was scarce. Both parents were compelled to work hard. Children were often left on their own or looked after by elder brothers and sisters."

Early on, sociologist Gunnar Myrdal warned the Swedish people that the Industrial Revolution had brought about very significant and very damaging changes in what had once been an agrarian society. Myrdal wrote: "The fault lies in society's organization of production and distribution which cannot keep pace with technical development. Small adjustments in economic distribution . . . give only a short-term illusion of improvement. If we want to achieve something more, it will probably be necessary to reform the whole of society more or less from top to bottom."

Radical change was required, but radical change never comes quickly in a democratic process. In 1930, the Swedes outlawed child labor in certain dangerous jobs; they created maternity insurance for the uninsured the following year; and in 1936 they created a seven-year compulsory school system. Special allowances were authorized for invalids, orphans, and children of widows. By 1937, the Parliament created preventive health care for mothers and children by establishing child-care clinics. By the 1940s, the government was administering state-subsidized day nurseries, play schools, and afterschool centers. Free school meals were instituted for all children. Then in 1947 the Swedes demanded and got children's allowances and family housing allowances. Step by step, under the leadership of the Social Democrats, the Swedish people rebuilt their society and in the process forged a new national attitude toward children. They have created a national children's policy. Children were recognized as important, individual human beings.

One of the most startling facets of this radical change was the evolution of people's attitude toward handicapped children. Originally, institutionalization was thought best and the government made major improvements in the established, institutionalized system, developing bigger and more sophisticated hospitals and prisons. But there was a growing realization that the handicapped were a part of the society and that isolating them was not the best form of therapy or rehabilitation. It was decided that everything possible had to be done to help families keep their children at home, all of their children, no matter what their problems. By the late 1970s, a third of the mentally retarded people in Sweden were living with their parents. These were children, for the most part. As they grew older, the government assisted them in moving out, into group care or independent-living situations, encouraging them to learn skills, to work in sheltered workshops, to live as independently as possible, giving housekeepers and homemaking assistance where needed. Only 4 percent of the mentally retarded people in Sweden are hospitalized.

Dr. Karl Grunewald, director of the National Board of Health and Welfare's Department for the Care of Mentally Retarded, explained, "We do not try to make the mentally retarded person normal, but we fight for the right of the mentally retarded person to be a part of our society."

Those youngsters who still must be institutionalized are placed in small facilities, like the twenty-four-bed Rosenhill Residential Treatment Center in the community of Huddinge, just outside Stockholm. At first glance, Rosenhill looks like a large, contemporary house, long and low, set against a hill, surrounded by grass and play areas. The wing on the left contains classrooms, special therapy areas, a dining room and kitchen in the rear. A large basement recreation room doubles as the parents' meeting hall. To the right of the bright, cheerful entryway are the children's rooms. There are three wards, with four rooms to a ward, two beds to a room. The rooms are large and well lighted. Large windows let in lots of sunlight and create a feeling of open space. Each child has his or her half of a room individually furnished and decorated by parents or by the staff. Each aide is assigned to work as a surrogate mother for two children. The child's idiosyncrasies, preferred foods, favorite toys, most comfortable sleeping positions are all currently noted.

The director of Rosenhill, Dr. Zoe Walsh, is a pediatrician and cardiologist. In the late 1970s, she was spending twelve hours a week in the center and teaching in the Karolinsky Institute, a prestigious medical school in Stockholm. Also on the Rosenhill staff were one full-time registered nurse, two half-time nurses, a matron, assistant matron, and from ten to twelve aides. In addition, Rosenhill had its own school, staffed by three specially trained teachers who work with the twelve severely retarded children in the specially equipped classrooms. The twelve youngsters who are ambulatory and moderately retarded attend the nearby public schools and are involved in other community activities outside Rosenhill.

Dr. Walsh explained, "Our attitudes here are that, while many of the twelve most severely retarded children will never learn to count or to say the alphabet, they can achieve through teaching by feeling. We work on feelings. The children are sensitive to feelings, so we work to improve their emotional lives through close human contact."

Most of these twelve children were unable to stand, or even to sit up without aid of some sort; some are blind or deaf or both; most have very little motor control of any kind. These are the most severely retarded children in Sweden. As Dr. Walsh talked, we watched a teacher working with a little girl who was seated in a slinglike chair that supported her weak spine and muscles while she painted a picture with her fingers and a small brush that was suspended from the top of the easel. Nearby, an aide was lying on a soft floormat beside another child, holding him, touching, working slowly with some blocks. Walking into the next classroom, Dr. Walsh was explaining, "Only a third of these children in here still have contact with their families. For years, Sweden discouraged family contact with the severely retarded [as did doctors in the United States] . . . but now we are trying to re-create the family ties if we can. We want the families to participate in this program. We have set up room for parents and children to be here, alone, together, and we have special programs for the parents."

In the fall of 1977, there was a controversy being debated. Some of the experts on Dr. Grunewald's staff wanted more of Rosenhill's youngsters integrated into the public school system. This meant transporting some of the nonambulatory students into the Huddinge schools. Dr. Walsh was opposed: "It is a good experience for the moderate and mildly retarded, but for the severely retarded, I'm not sure. I feel they need the security, the closeness and consistency we offer here. That daily trip to public school would be very disruptive."

Rosenhill was at the very core of the Swedish system for caring for and treating those mentally retarded children who were not living at home. The goal was to move the children outward from such centers, through education, training, and therapy, into group homes and, eventually, into independent-living situations, if possible. The independent-living services are provided by county government. For example, in the Göteborg region, an area about the size of New York's Monroe County, Dr. Scheiner reported that there were ninety rented flats or hostels for the mildly retarded adults, 225 private residential homes or hostels for the severely or moderately retarded children, and twenty special foster homes staffed by both house parents and a housekeeper.

Göteborg also had three vocational training centers, each training 150 to 200 individuals. Approximately 25 percent of those in training were retarded persons. Dr. Scheiner said:

The remarkable characteristic of these training centers was that they could not be distinguished from an industrial plant. Here I saw persons with Down's syndrome working with power machines, welding equipment, and other heavy industrial machinery. They had the appearance of capability well beyond their traditional known levels of intellectual function . . . I visited several flats where five persons lived together. The staffing of these flats was minimal . . . An aide visited each morning to assist with breakfast and each evening to help with supper and cleaning. The only skill necessary for the client to be head person of a flat is the use of a phone and the ability to cook breakfast and to call when an appropriate need arises. The flats are located in traditional apartment projects. Several people were living as man and wife.

The responsibility for providing these services falls on the local community, but there is a "strong central Department of Mental Retardation committed to the concept of normalization, a strong parent advocacy group, a national commitment to education and training of staff, and a visible commitment to handicapped persons within the communities," Scheiner noted. He pointed out that the bureaucratic structures at the national level in the Swedish government were very small, and that there was no police-auditor mentality that required large agencies devoted to the prevention of cheating and fraud. Result: "A large part of the mental retardation dollar is channeled to direct services." And, Dr. Scheiner found, the per capita costs in Sweden were less than in New York. He concluded, "Sweden is far more successful in providing quality human services to the retarded . . . because of a cultural morality which demands that all people lead a quality, dignified life."

The absence of costly, top-heavy bureaucracy was quite obvious the morning I went to Dr. Grunewald's office in Stockholm. There was no opulent wood paneling, no rich carpeting. As soon as the secretary rang, Dr. Grunewald came out, greeting me in an open, friendly way. I commented on the absence of large numbers of busy people that seemed so vital to the American bureaucracy. There seemed to be no more than a dozen people working for him. He laughed and explained that the relationship of the national government to the counties did not require more people than that. The counties and the municipalities had the basic administrative and fiscal responsibilities; the national government provided the leadership and coordination. For example, in Sweden there were twenty-five thousand children in foster care for various reasons; six hundred of them were retarded. The individual counties licensed foster-care homes, using nationally set standards: two children to a home. The county paid the cost of foster care, provided foster parents with one day a week off, one week of vacation a year. The county provided preschools and public schools for all children, health care, and leisure-time centers. Like all children, those in foster care received a national children's allowance.

Foster parents receive no special training, but they are provided the same full range of children's services as those available to natural parents. Almost daily, foster children are in contact with schoolteachers, health-care workers, mental health workers, and social workers. Group homes in Sweden are staffed by a social worker, a nurse who is specially trained to work with the retarded, house parents, and aides. Each group home has a teacher for each seven students, and access to a psychologist as needed. The orientation is homelike rather than medical; only the house parents stay in the home overnight. Dr. Grunewald and an architect on his staff approve each group home. He explained, "We are trying to get away from the twenty-person homes; we want to establish that eight children is an ideal unit, with twelve as a maximum . . . We want a heterogeneous mixing . . . but the staff always wants a homogeneous grouping because it is easier to handle."

I asked Dr. Grunewald what happens in Sweden if a

child is found to be autistic. First, he explained, the diagnosis would probably be made much earlier in Sweden than it is in the United States because the nationalized health-care services in Sweden provide for full diagnostic and treatment services for the child from birth. Once the diagnosis had been made, the entire family would become involved in the processes of care and treatment.

"We pay the parents to keep the child at home," Dr. Grunewald explained. "The national and county funds are allowed up to the full cost of what institutional care would have been, which allows the parents enough money to bring in the kind of help they need. There is no practical limit on how much the cost will run. We don't even discuss maximum payments."

What kind of controls are exercised by the national or county government to ensure that the money is properly spent? None. Dr. Grunewald explained, "We don't exercise control over the money. We work with the parents and the children, not only those children affected, but with the siblings as well."

Through the government-operated clinics, through the preschool and public school programs and the social-welfare services, the family gets all the help that is needed. If a handicapped child is confined to a wheelchair, for example, the government will provide the funds to modify the home structurally so that child can move about more readily. And what was available for families with retarded or autistic children was available for families with physically handicapped or emotionally disturbed children. Each county has clinics for the emotionally disturbed; there are psychological and psychiatric services and counseling available for children and for their families. The national government operates three twenty-bed hospitals for seriously disturbed children.

Like most industrialized nations, Sweden is reporting disturbing increases in juvenile-crime rates. Two thirds of the people seized for serious crimes like robbery and grand theft are under twenty years of age. And the Swedish judicial system is faced with a familiar dilemma: children fifteen or under are not considered "responsible" for criminal actions and are handled separately from the adult criminals, yet increasing numbers of fourteen- and fifteen-year-olds are being picked up for criminal conduct. The one major difference between Sweden and the United States is in the incidence of violent crime. Sweden has not undergone an increase in the kinds of murderous street crime we are experiencing in this country.

If a boy or girl under fifteen is suspected of committing a crime, the police report that fact to the Child Welfare Committee, which functions under the Central Board of Social Welfare in each county. A social worker is assigned the case, makes house calls, talks to teachers, neighbors, and witnesses, and makes a recommendation to the Child Welfare Committee. The committee can recommend supervised probation, medical or mental health casework with the child and his or her family; the committee can put the child in foster care or a group home or a remand house. The latter is a small, closed, or locked facility that provides intensive rehabilitation services. A juvenile between fifteen and twenty years old can be treated as either a juvenile or an adult. Juveniles under eighteen who are tried as adults and convicted seldom go to prison; rather, they are placed in remand houses.

The Swedish system is not perfect, and Swedes are quite open when discussing the problems and criticisms. In 1973, because of a concern over reports of increased child abuse, the Parliament designated the international organization Radda Barnen (Save the Children) to act as a children's ombudsman. In 1977, the Radda Barnen persons who officially acted on behalf of the children were Rigmor Von Euler and her assistant, Christina Fenno. Fenno explained, "We are social workers, and we work closely with BRIS

[Children's Rights in Society, a volunteer organization with chapters in every community]. Our expertise is in working with the various agencies. We know how to deal with them. The most problems come from divorced couples, when the family is under stress and there are economic problems."

While Von Euler and Fenno work primarily on a national level, lobbying children's causes, pushing and coaxing legislators and bureaucrats, each BRIS chapter operates a telephone hot line. Children, parents, neighbors, teachers, anyone, can call BRIS to report a problem. BRIS volunteers will investigate and, if there is a problem, work with the child and the family, contacting appropriate agencies, arranging for whatever help or services may be needed. Von Euler was not satisfied with the system as it was working in 1977. She wanted to see the Swedish government recognize the need for an independent, government-financed and -operated children's ombudsman agency that would be fully equipped to act as children's advocates. For example, children caught up in divorce proceedings need attorneys to represent their interests, "as long as society puts more emphasis on solving the economic aspects of a divorce than the emotional ones," she said; then she added, "As long as a child can be placed in foster care through a political decision by a committee of laymen without professional knowledge, there is a need for somebody who does not take part in the decision procedure and who looks after how the law phrase 'to protect the interest of the child' is interpreted. As long as children are used as therapy for adults, as long as beating is considered appropriate for an educational purpose, as long as children under the age of fifteen can be kept in jail while waiting placement in correctional schools, foster homes, there is a need for a children's ombudsman."

Von Euler concluded, "The laws say society is to do the best for the child, but the point is meaningless unless the child is truly considered a person with rights."

Von Euler and Fenno had provided me with a brief look into some of the problems in Sweden. To get some sense of comparison or measure, I described the Kate School to them, and the controversy attendant on the license-revocation procedures. They looked at me incredulously: "In Sweden it would not be possible to have a Kate School. If there are four children or more, there would be a medical doctor — a psychiatrist — and a staff of trained people available. There would be too many trained professional people involved and they would not allow such things to happen."

It was said matter-of-factly, with certainty. Although private individuals do operate foster homes and some group homes, these individuals and their houses are carefully selected. The group homes for the retarded are inspected by experts like Dr. Grunewald. They are professionally staffed. And, as Dr. Grunewald explained, "there are constant contacts, daily, with outsiders, so any child abuse is quickly picked up."

As Dr. Grunewald described the Swedish system, I began to realize that the primary difference between what was happening there and what was happening in the United States was caused by an attitude. The Swedish people had forged a national will that was expressed in a concern for people's well-being, and out of this care and this concern for people had come a national children's progràm, a program that focuses on the family and the full range of social, economic, and health-care problems that beset parents and children in the postindustrial society. It was an uncompromising, humane attitude that had brought about radical changes in the socioeconomic fabric of the nation.

And it was the realization that the people in Sweden had reordered their national priorities that brought the whole picture into focus for me. Without the comparison, it was difficult to understand why our system worked against children. At first glance, the Swedish emphasis on local government control seemed not unlike the insistence on the rights of states and counties within the United States to control public welfare and foster-care programs. However, there is a startling difference between the two systems. In Sweden, there is a national mandate, a national policy. The people of Sweden have decided local governments *will* provide health care, preschool programs, rent subsidies, social and rehabilitative services for children and their families. In the United States, the local governments decide whether or not they will provide public assistance in any form, and, if so, how much. And, with the Reagan block grant system in place, the prerogatives of the states will be strengthened.

In Sweden, the government functions primarily to serve people, not the conservative voice of corporate interests, and the Swedish people have set a high priority on children, all children. In the United States, the reverse is true: the corporate interests, large and small, dominate the political and governmental functions of our society.

In America there is an on-going tug of war between the collective power of the people and the forces of the free-enterprising capitalists. The goal: control of local, state, and federal government. The organized pull of the corporate interests is heavy and incessant, while the energy of the people comes in spurts of angry reaction and outrage. The public force is erratic and most often uncoordinated. The effect of this long, long struggle has been a steady pull to the right, interrupted by violent heaves and tugs to the left. While neither side has won the match, there has been a steadily increasing shift to the right. Government favors the corporate interest, as the Kate School controversy demonstrates. It took the State of California forty-seven months to revoke the school's licenses because, legally, the nonprofit Kate School Corporation had a vested interest in continued operation, an interest that prevailed over the public interest in the way children were treated. Government at all levels protected the school's vested interest and failed to protect the public's dual interest in the children's well-being and in the wise and useful expenditure of tax dollars. No matter that the Kate School Corporation was a nonprofit venture or that it was a mere flyspeck on the corporate landscape; the controlling mechanisms of government were and still are weighted in favor of that vested corporate interest. It is this kind of corporate bias that makes government unworkable as the protector of the public interest. Watching the government as it reacts to a Kate School controversy or the crisis caused by the oil shortage gives one the feeling that government is clumsy and inefficient. That feeling is fostered and promoted by conservatives like Ronald Reagan who see in it a chance to further erode the power of government. When our movie-actor president speaks his lines, we nod in agreement: big government is cumbersome and wasteful and cutting it down to size is a good idea. We seem to cling to the idea that *we* are not involved, that it is the government's fault, whatever it is that's wrong. We forget that *we are the government* and that whatever is done in the name of government is an expression of our collective will. The house of mirrors is of our own construction. We didn't plan it. We didn't want children hurt. But we are hurting them. Thousands upon thousands of children caught up in the foster-care system are not growing up in a permanent home; they have been cast adrift in a system that is as apt to harm them as help them. We are the child abusers.

We must recognize that *we are the government,* Exxon and Dow Chemical notwithstanding, and that we are living in a highly advanced postindustrial society that is fast becoming a technocracy. Our families are no longer growing up on farms and in small towns. There are no extended families to care for and assist individual members in times of stress. Our sense of community has been completely lost in cities like Los Angeles. We are living insular lives, caught up in the too-rapid pace of an urban existence that is hard to understand, that has leaped the bounds of family and community and comprehension itself. In 1981, it seems that government does not benefit people so much as it provides the mechanisms to guarantee corporate existence, if not profit.

Slowly at first, then with more frightening speed, our political system is being pulled away from our grasp; we are losing the tug of war. The American political system is being corrupted. There are the surface corruptions typified by congressmen stuffing their pockets with money and presidential candidates seriously arguing that bribery is an accepted business practice. But there are the more serious, more subtle forms of corruption, as evidenced by the failure of the political system to present any range of political thought or alternative philosophies. As much as the old politics of smoke-filled rooms and brokered political conventions was criticized, candidates in and out of office had to build constituencies, had to develop a power base that held them accountable. But during the past decade, politicians — and their corporate backers — have slipped the bonds of tradition and, through the instant magic of television, have managed to package and sell themselves like cornflakes or sticks of underarm deodorant. Nowhere was this more obvious than in the 1980 presidential election.

All of this could be changed, of course. Change is possible. There *is* a public mood of anger and frustration in the land that can be gathered in and organized. We, the people, do have the power to bring about change. We proved that point recently in our reaction to the Vietnam War. Then the public anger and frustration eventually generated a rebellion against the power of the military-industrial complex and the deceit of corrupt politicians. For a brief period a new political mood swept in young, idealistic candidates who were attuned to the issues of Vietnam, the environment, and the problems of the cities.

But the mood did not last. There is yet another recent example of how change was dramatically brought about by harnessing the public outrage: Proposition 13, in California. The resentment against big government and high taxes was manipulated by Howard Jarvis and his free-enterprising associates into a surprisingly powerful force that brought about radical change. At first glance the Jarvis–Proposition 13 forces that swept through California were disheartening. But, on deeper reflection, I think the Jarvis–Proposition 13 episode and the subsequent defeat of Jarvis's proposed Proposition 9 cut in income taxes, two years later — proved two very positive things about our public responses. First, the Jarvis–Proposition 13 campaign did harness the public anger and turned it into a clear public message; second, we the public proved that, as angry and disenchanted as we all are, we can still reserve judgment. We can say yes and we can say no, and in the process create public policies, albeit imprecise, often confusing policies. Through the passage of Proposition 13 and the subsequent defeat of the Proposition 9 income tax–cutting measure, we expressed our anger with the big, clumsy, nonresponsive bureaus of government that wasted our resources, but we clearly pointed out that we recognized the need to continue taxing ourselves, that we recognized there are public needs that must be financed with public funds.

And, in the California legislature, we expressed a willingness to create a Family Protection Act. This was a message of the heart. We wanted to help children. But then — through Jerry Brown, the intellectual — we ruled with our heads: we cut the spending from $25 million to $2 million, demonstrating we could be "good" people, but on a scale we thought we could afford. And, in the Congress, we made it clear we wanted children to live in permanent homes and then, recognizing our hearts were in the right place, we agreed to the "practical" arguments that said the individual states knew best how to take care of such matters. Privately we knew full well the prejudices of several states would hold back the flow of promised federal dollars, and that the election of Reagan would hold back still more funds. The problem in all this, of course, is that we are penny wise and pound foolish. By saving $300 million here and $50 million there over the next two or three years, we create the need for big new institutions and intensive remedial services that can cost us billions.

The sadness in all of this is that it does not have to be. We can let go of the past. We can make changes. We are presently injuring thousands of children every year, changing their lives, causing more problems than we solve, and at a staggering cost. We are turning children into institutionalized creatures who can't function outside the walls we've built around their lives, and still we complain about the cost of those walls. It simply doesn't make sense to continue on such a course.

We can do what the people of Sweden did. We can decide that it will be different. It is silly to argue that Sweden is a disqualified model because the country is small and the population is homogeneous. The Swedes are no more or no less powerful a people in relation to their corporate structures than we in the United States. Using their elected government, the Swedish people have set priorities; they have decided it was in their national best interest to regulate the earnings of corporations, diverting excess profits to help finance such things as day-care centers, pre-school programs, and a nationalized health-care system.

In the United States, our priorities have been bent another way: while inflation eroded the consumer dollar, while government spending on social programs was restricted and reduced, we allowed the large corporations to make larger and more obscene profits. There were exceptions, of course, like Chrysler, the car company that insisted the public should have gas-consuming Imperials at a time when Honda of Japan was capturing the American car market. Yet when Chrysler's chief executives went to the administration and the Congress, hat in hand, and asked for help, they were not scorned and publicly humiliated, as the poor are when they apply for public assistance. Think about our national priorities, when a small family farmer who can't make his bank payments loses his farm; the land is taken up by corporate structures, frequently by an oil company searching for the extraordinary tax write-offs. Consider the priorities of a system that pays a family of four $6000 a year in AFDC benefits while it pays medical doctors $100,000 or $200,000 or $300,000 a year in Medicaid fees for treating the poor. Think about the priorities of a system that puts a fifteen-year-old girl in a state hospital at a cost of $3185 a month rather than pay $1800 for her care and treatment in a well-run private institution or, even more appropriately, finding her a loving, permanent home at even less cost.

It's time for change, time to reorder our national priorities. We must strip away the archaic concepts of charity that suit the needs of the givers and not the recipients, and we must forge a national policy that guarantees every child born in the United States the right to a permanent home, food, health care, an education, and, eventually, a job. This means we will have to make radical reforms, starting with a national health-care system that guarantees every pregnant woman prenatal care, that guarantees children the right to a full range of diagnostic, preventive, and treatment services. But health care for the pregnant woman and for her newborn child is obviously not enough; the entire family unit must be seen as the target of such health care. Every family ought to have the right to a home in an adequate structure, not simply a crowded apartment in the low-rent projects that turn into instant slums for lack of design, and adequate maintenance, for lack of national commitment to providing a social environment that welcomes and cherishes new life. We need to create a social environment that accepts the single-parent family, that provides infant care and preschool child care, that recognizes children as individuals, with individual rights.

To do all of this will require radical changes in our socioeconomic systems and our political thinking. It will require that corporate profits be regulated and taxed to serve the public need; it will require the creation of a national health-care delivery system designed along lines similar to those used in Sweden, and it will require a major restructuring of all governmental welfare systems. Attitudes and priorities must be changed so that the bureaus of government function to serve people, not to police those who must ask for help. While the Swedish model may not provide an exact blueprint, it certainly sketches some very desirable outlines. In Sweden, the central government is small, and the primary functions of child care and family services have been delegated to local government. The people of Sweden control these services, nationally; they set the priorities, and then they take an active part in carrying them out through their local governments.

The key to all of this, of course, is the involvement of people in the local communities. People, through their collective strength, make the system work for people. Individuals are far more powerful, in the United States or Sweden, than they seem to realize. One person, like Lorraine Foster, can bring about change, did bring about change. She, with the help of one or two others, began a process that generated its own energy. In other places, in other times, individual children's advocates, individual lawyers, individual teachers or licensing inspectors or social workers began a process that brought about some change. The mechanisms for change are out there, right now, in virtually every state and in virtually every county. New laws, new children's rights, exist because individuals took action. The thing that has been lacking thus far is the sense of "movement" that sparked the Vietnam War revolution. In that revolution there were a multitude of individual causes, a series of organizations that grew out of disparate causes, causes that had not a great deal in common until they merged into the antiwar movement.

While the cause of the children in foster care is not as dramatic as that bloody Vietnam War, nor as quickly attractive as the fight over too-high taxes, it is a vital issue. The entire foster-care system must be questioned. We need to develop a sense of purpose, a national urgency that is expressed from the local levels of government up through the political structures of this nation. Out of this questioning process must come a strongly worded expression of our national will, a national children's policy. We must set national standards and we must hold government at all levels responsible and accountable. The processes that evolve out of our national children's policy and out of these federally mandated standards must be oriented toward keeping children with their parents in a permanent home. If children are separated from their natural home — however or for whatever reason — the processes of foster care must help them find their way back into their own homes or, if that is not possible, find them permanent loving homes elsewhere. All of this must be conducted in a community environment that is open to public inspection. There must be a simple, forceful qualification process by which the government licenses foster homes, group homes, and institutions. And there needs to be both on-going governmental inspection and a public review process, one official, the other ad hoc. Citizens advisory panels and review boards should be an integral part of the process. If children are ever to be viewed as individuals, with special needs and rights of their own, we must make a place for a strong children's advocacy process that gives voice to children's interests and rights, separate from the interests and rights of parents and the public.

Given a national sense of purpose and direction, this

mixture of public and private interests and opinions will, when freely and openly debated, provide a vitality to our national concern for children. Quite obviously, we must make changes in our present system, radical changes, or we must learn to live with the fact that some children in the United States will never be free to grow up into mature, productive adults. We must change our ways, or accept the fact that many of the several hundred thousand children in foster care in 1981 will grow into adults who can never fully participate in society. Some will spend most of their lives in institutions; some will grow up as abused children who become abusing parents; some will make it, despite what happened to them as children. As I close this book it is hard to know what will happen to youngsters like Mary and Jonathan and young adults like Tyrone and Jerri. And it is sad to think their lives could have been different, should have been different, would have been different if . . . IF.

We can change. We must change. As Camus said:

> *Perhaps we cannot prevent this world*
> *from being a world in which children*
> *are tortured.*
> *But we can reduce the number of tortured*
> *children.*
> *And if you believers don't help us, who else in*
> *the world can help us do this?*

# Index